FLIGHT
OF THE
HIGHLANDERS

FLIGHT OF THE HIGHLANDERS

THE MAKING OF CANADA

Ken McGoogan

PATRICK CREAN EDITIONS
An imprint of HarperCollins*PublishersLtd*

Flight of the Highlanders
Copyright © 2019 by Ken McGoogan.
All rights reserved.

Published by Patrick Crean Editions,
an imprint of HarperCollins Publishers Ltd.

First edition

Pages 327–28 constitutes a continuation of this copyright page.

HarperCollins books may be purchased for educational, business,
or sales promotional use through our Special Markets Department.

HarperCollins Publishers Ltd
Bay Adelaide Centre, East Tower
22 Adelaide Street West, 41st Floor
Toronto, Ontario, Canada
M5H 4E3

www.harpercollins.ca

Library and Archives Canada Cataloguing in Publication
information is available upon request.

ISBN 978-1-4434-5259-5

Printed and bound in the United States
SHR 9 8 7 6 5 4 3 2 1

For Sheena
Long may we run

CONTENTS

FLIGHT
OF THE
HIGHLANDERS

Introduction

I WAS AN EYE WITNESS OF THE SCENE," THE STONEMASON
Donald Macleod wrote. Strong parties of men "commenced
setting fire to the dwellings till about three hundred houses were
in flames, the people striving to remove the sick, the helpless, before
the fire should reach them. The cries of women and children—the
roaring of cattle—the barking of dogs—the smoke of the fire—the
soldiers—it required to be seen to be believed!" Macleod was writing of a Clearance, a forced eviction of families living in a glen or a
valley in the Scottish Highlands. He was describing events of 1814,
the Year of the Burnings, as they unfolded in Strathnaver, a wide
river valley in the Highland county of Sutherland.

The man supervising the destruction, acting for the aristocratic
landlord, had already ordered his men to burn the hill-grazing areas
so there would be no food for cattle and the people would have no
choice but to leave. When this failed, he escalated the action to
the destruction and burning of villages. He had the roofs of houses
pulled down and timbers set ablaze to prevent rebuilding. In the
month of May alone, he dispossessed and rendered homeless at
least 430 people.

Those 430 farmers were among the approximately 200,000 Highlanders driven from their ancestral lands during the Clearances, with estimates varying from 170,750 to more than 300,000. To argue that the Clearances were the result of the inexorable advance of capitalism is to ignore the cultural targeting of Gaelic-speaking, Roman Catholic, clan-oriented Highlanders.

Savageries and brutalities became possible after the decimation of the Highland forces at the 1746 Battle of Culloden, when Bonnie Prince Charlie, claiming the Scottish throne, led a ragtag army of farmers against one of the most professional military forces in the world. The British government, determined after its victory to destroy centuries of Highland independence, unleashed the most violent of its shock troops on a defenceless people. Soldiers went about the business of state-sanctioned murder with gusto, shooting some people in cold blood and burning others to death.

When the killing was done, the government banned "Highland dress" and stripped clan chieftains of their traditional authority, encouraging them to sell their clan's estates to absentee landlords. The Clearances proper began when landlords realized they could dramatically increase their incomes by expelling farmers from their ancestral holdings and dedicating those lands to sheep.

Between 1760 and 1860, as this book shows, the expulsions grew increasingly violent. Most of the cleared Highlanders who relocated to Canada were fleeing persecution. People often call them settlers or colonists. But today, with an international refugee crisis providing a new context, this book suggests that, because they were forcibly evicted from the lands of their forefathers, they should rightly be recognized as refugees.

For Canada, as for other countries, refugees were not defined into official existence until 1951, when a United Nations treaty recognized them as persons forced to flee persecution (violence, war, destruction) in their home countries. To qualify, the newly arrived had to have "a well-founded fear of persecution for reasons of race, religion, nationality, membership of a particular social group, or political opinion."

Since becoming a signatory to that treaty, Canada has welcomed successive waves of refugees, among them: 37,000 Hungarians after the 1956 uprising; 11,000 Czechs after the 1968 Prague Spring; 7,000 Ugandans in 1972, after Idi Amin Dada began confiscating property; more than 7,000 Chileans in 1973–1978, after Augusto Pinochet staged a military coup; 60,000 Vietnamese in 1979–1980, following the Vietnam War; and, since November 2015, more than 40,000 Syrians fleeing devastation.

But what of those tens of thousands of farmers who were driven from lands where their ancestors had lived for hundreds of years? To argue that they were victims of the advance of capitalism is to ignore that they belonged to an identifiable minority, marginalized by language and religion. After Culloden, they were targeted. Some saw their houses burned to the ground. Others were beaten unconscious. Still others were tricked into attending meetings where they were seized, trussed up, and heaved like bundles into "coffin ships" bound for Quebec.

Were those people refugees? They arrived in what would become Canada before 1951, when that category of immigrant had yet to be identified. But looking back from the twenty-first century, we can see that, had the term "refugee" existed, those Highlanders would certainly have qualified. Indeed, because First Nations people had long since established residency, and most of the French who settled Quebec had come of their own free will, the fleeing Highlanders were Canada's first refugees.

Of course, not all immigrant Scots were refugees. Several thousand, having served as British soldiers during one war or another, received land grants of various sizes. As well, hundreds of Scottish Orcadians, having arrived in the North Country with the Hudson's Bay Company, later became settlers. Nor can we forget that eighteenth- and nineteenth-century Scotland also sent talented, high-energy figures seeking to improve their lives. I wrote about some of them in *How the Scots Invented Canada*.

In *Flight of the Highlanders*, I focus on the common people. I trace the challenges and fates of those forgotten Scots who were betrayed by their own chieftains and ruthlessly evicted from their homes, only to find themselves battling hardship, hunger and adamant rejection in a New World wilderness. Some moved initially to Britain's southern colonies, such as New England and the Carolinas. Of those, some forty or fifty thousand remained loyal to Britain and ended up fleeing for their lives during the American Revolution.

Numerous books have explored the Clearances and many have examined Highlander arrivals in pre-Confederation Canada. But none has intertwined these two complex stories in the context of today's international refugee crisis. *Flight of the Highlanders* repudiates the notion that Canadian settlement history is, as some have suggested, "a white, hetero-male narrative of power that erases the existence of the marginalized."

Those penniless Highlanders who arrived here after being torn from their ancestral lands were themselves among the marginalized. The sad irony is that, in some locations, the persecuted refugees displaced nomadic peoples whose way of life had emerged out of the fur trade and depended on wilderness and wide-open spaces. The brave-hearted Highlanders eventually made good in

Canada, though often they needed a few generations; the trauma-tized Indigenous peoples, their prerequisites eradicated, their way of life overthrown, almost inevitably continue to struggle.

Over the past several years, while researching this book, I have travelled extensively throughout Scotland, from Orkney and Shetland in the north to the Mull of Kintyre in the south, and from Aberdeen in the east to Lewis and St. Kilda in the west. Here in Canada, I have visited most locations relevant to the arrival of the Highlander refugees—from Prince Edward Island and Pictou, Nova Scotia, to Churchill and Fort Garry in Manitoba. I have undertaken these travels—and interviewed contemporary descendants of those driven out—to bring this historical narrative into the twenty-first century. I view this as necessary because I believe, along with Booker Prize–winner Kiran Desai, that the present changes the past: "Looking back you do not find what you left behind."

Not long ago, writing in the *Walrus*, Charlotte Gray voiced a corollary perspective while predicting that we will see more group biographies: "I also expect tomorrow's biographers to increasingly insert contemporary preoccupations into their reconstructions of past lives, in order to shrink the gap between past and present." In this era of fake news and postmodernist skepticism, she anticipates "more biographers dropping the veil of omniscience and putting themselves on the page."

While the academic and the writer of biographical or historical narrative often explore the same material, the scholar leans towards summarizing, analyzing and arguing, while the storyteller evokes and dramatizes. The one writes for fellow experts or students in the field, the other for a broad general audience. Here in Canada, Pierre Berton and Peter C. Newman fought endless battles against academic historians. In Scotland, that brave and perceptive scholar

Catriona MacDonald has been driven to defend not only such popular historians as Andrew Lang and John Prebble but historical novelists like Walter Scott and Nigel Tranter.

Academic historians and history writers have been known to exchange contradictory opinions.

—Your work is fanciful! You imagine scenes and insert first-person observations. These things are simply not done.

—Your work is unreadable. You analyze and argue but you cannot tell a story.

—If you cannot produce written documentation, you cannot say what happened.

—Readers are tired of your sermonizing. Welcome to the twenty-first century.

—You must never infer, surmise or incorporate.

—No wonder history is on the ropes. Narrative requires voice, imagination, anecdote, scene.

So it goes, round and round. But with omniscience dismissed and my bias declared, we begin Part One of this book, The Gaelic World, with a glimpse of barbarities. Then, launching into rough chronology, we track the evolution of the old way of life through the Battle of Culloden and the emergence of Highland regiments.

In Part Two: Omens of Resistance, we find landowners becoming increasingly violent while evicting tenants to replace them with more profitable sheep. We visit Dunrobin Castle and discover why it is the most politically incorrect edifice in Scotland.

Part Three: Atlantic Arrivals crosses the ocean to Nova Scotia and Prince Edward Island. It tracks early Highland refugees and then some of their descendants through to the present day. Here, too, we see Highlanders engaging the American Revolution.

Part Four: Barbarous Clearances is a linchpin section that takes us back to Scotland and depicts the kind of ruthlessness and brutality that precipitated the flight of the Highlanders.

The last two parts, set in Canada, balance the first two, which focused on Scotland. In Part Five: Western Travails, we see newly arrived Highlanders suddenly plunged into a life-and-death struggle with fur traders led by other ex-Highlanders.

Part Six: Upper Canadian Pioneers shows that all new arrivals faced a challenging wilderness and some had to deal as well with exploitive clan chieftains parading around in kilts.

Through it all, the refugee Highlanders persevered. Today, almost five million Canadians claim Scottish ancestry. Because so many of them are in leadership positions, we sometimes forget that, statistically, many if not most are probably descended from those dispossessed emigrants who, having arrived with nothing but the clothes on their backs, went to work laying the foundations of a modern nation. We forget that those originally displaced Highlanders were themselves targets of prejudice and persecution. If today Canada is more welcoming to newcomers than most countries, it is at least partly because of the lingering influence of those unbreakable refugees. Together with their better-off brethren—the lawyers, educators, politicians and businessmen—those indomitable Highlanders were the making of Canada.

PART ONE

THE
GAELIC
WORLD

Scottish Highlands and Islands

■ Major Emigration area

Atlantic Ocean

Orkney
○ Stromness

Thurso ○
Bettyhill ○
Strathnaver
○ Wick

Gearrannan ■
Lewis Stornoway ○
Kildonan ○
Helmsdale ○

Loch Broom
Harris
Culrain ○
■ Dunrobin Castle

St. Kilda
Sollas ○
Kilmuir Cemetery ■
Ullapool ○
Croick Church
Dornoch ○
Tain ○

N. Uist ○
Lochmaddy ○
Dingwall ○
Cromarty ○
■ Fort George

Benbecula
Dunvegan ○
Raasay
Beauly ○
■ Culloden
Inverness

S. Uist
Skye
Portee ○
Strathglass

Lochboisdale ○
Knoydart ○
Glengarry ○

Isleornsay ○
■ Newtonmore

Barra Eriskay
Loch Hourn

○ Fort William

■ Glencoe

Coll
SCOTLAND

Tiree
Tobermory ○
Mull
Oban ○

Dundee ○

Auchindrain ■
Inverary ○

Jura
Greenock ○
Glasgow ○
○ Leith

Finlaggan ■
Edinburgh ○

Islay Gigha

Kintyre
Irvine ○

Campbeltown ○
Ayr ○

N

I

Knoydart Clearances

O N DAY FOUR OUT OF THE RESORT TOWN OF OBAN, WE awoke to find our cruise ship anchored in Isleornsay Harbour off the Isle of Skye. June 2018. We were among two hundred passengers, my wife, Sheena, and I, sailing around Scotland with Adventure Canada. I was one of several resource people hired to talk about matters of historical interest. In July 1853, during the Highland Clearances, a ship called the *Sillery* had anchored at this precise location opposite Knoydart on mainland Scotland. It had arrived to carry off farmers who lived along the north coast of a broad inlet, Loch Hourn, due east of where we lay.

The ancestors of those farmers had been among the six hundred Highlanders who, in 1746, joined the Glengarry Macdonells in fighting at the Battle of Culloden. After that catastrophe, some had emigrated to Upper Canada and others to Nova Scotia. Still, when the *Sillery* arrived just over a century later, roughly six hundred people remained in the coastal settlements.

In 1852, the greedy, tough-minded widow Josephine Macdonell had gained control of the Knoydart estate following the death of her more humane husband, who had been reluctant to act against his people. She had found a possible buyer for her lands—industrialist James Baird, a Tory member of Parliament—but only if they were not encumbered by paupers for whom he would become legally responsible. Ignoring the people's offers to pay arrears caused by the recent potato famine, the widow Macdonell issued warnings of removal. "Those who imagine they will be allowed to remain after this," she wrote, "are indulging in a vain hope as the most strident measures will be taken to effect their removal."

In April 1853, she informed her tenants that they would be going to Australia, sailing courtesy of the landlord-sponsored Highland and Island Emigration Society. In June, she amended their destination. They would travel instead to Canada, their passage paid as far as Montreal. On debarkation, they would each be given ten pounds of oatmeal. After that, they were on their own.

On August 2, 1853, with the *Sillery* anchored at Isleornsay, men with axes, crowbars and hammers rowed across the inlet and landed. They joined a gang of mainlanders and began clearing farmers from their homes. According to activist-journalist Donald Ross, the factor in charge ordered that after removing the tenants, his men were immediately to destroy "not only the houses of those who had left but also of those who had refused to go."

Burly men ripped off thatched roofs, slammed picks into walls and foundations, and chopped down any supporting trees or timbers. Eventually, Ross wrote, "roof, rafters, and walls fell with a crash. Clouds of dust rose to the skies, while men, women and children stood at a distance, completely dismayed." According to Ross, "The wail of the poor women and children as they were torn away from their homes would have melted a heart of stone."

The factor and his men proceeded methodically through one small coastal settlement after another, destroying everything but a few huts that belonged to "declared paupers," who remained protected by law. He warned these impoverished people that if they gave anyone else shelter, "for one moment by day or night," he would level their homes as well.

The marauders dragged resisters out of their houses, threw their furniture and possessions after them, then set about the work of destruction. Ross writes that a few able-bodied men could have seized the factor and his men, bound them hand and foot, and sent them out of the district. Instead they "stood aside as dumb spectators," he wrote, because they knew that any such resistance would end with them in jail and their wives and children left to fend for themselves. And so "no hand was lifted, no stone cast."

The destruction went on for a week. Then, on August 9, 1853, the *Sillery* departed for Montreal carrying 332 homeless Highlanders. In Knoydart, when the gangs departed, about 60 people emerged from the rocks and the ridges, most of them old and decrepit, but among them a few children. They set about creating what shelter they could. They were working in the wreckage when, on August 22, under the same factor, marauders returned and launched a new wave of demolition. Over the next weeks, the destroyers returned again and again.

A local priest sent out a plea for help. Donald Ross answered the call. In November, when he arrived from Glasgow bringing tents and supplies, he found sixteen families subsisting among the ruins. He told their stories in a thirty-one-page pamphlet, a howl of protest entitled *Glengarry Evictions or Scenes at Knoydart in Inverness-shire*. Ross was outraged that decent, respectable, well-behaved people were being treated worse than slaves because they refused to allow themselves to be "packed off to the colonies like so many bales of manufactured goods."

Donald Ross wrote of John Mackinnon, a forty-four-year-old cottar (farm labourer) who had a wife and six children. He led them to safety while his house was torn down. For the first night or two, he burrowed with his family among the rocks near the shore. When he thought the way clear, Mackinnon emerged, surveyed the ruins of his home, and judged salvage impossible. He brought his family into the ruins of an old chapel, where parts of some walls remained standing.

The family swept away rubbish, removed grass and nettles, shored up the walls and created a shelter of sails and blankets. They built beds of meadow hay. They kindled a fire, washed and boiled some potatoes, and ate these with a few fish—their first regular meal since the devastation. Neither of the adults was well, and two of the boys, Ronald and Archibald, lay on the hay suffering from rheumatism and colic. Their doorless abode provided no protection from the wind.

Mrs. Mackinnon, pregnant when first banished to the outdoors, gave birth prematurely. She then fell ill with consumption, from which she had no chance of recovery. Having taken refuge in the ruins of the chapel, the Mackinnons hoped to remain unmolested. But the estate manager and his men soon invaded this helpless family's shelter, even within the walls of the sanctuary. They pulled down the sticks and sails; drove father, mother and children out onto the cold shore; tossed tables, stools and chairs over the stone walls; and burnt up the hay on which the family slept. Four times the officers returned and renewed their destruction. When Ross visited, the Mackinnons had just learned that the destroyers would return again the following day.

Donald Ross wrote of Archibald MacIsaac, a sixty-six-year-old crofter with a wife twelve years younger and ten children.

Archibald's house, byre, barn and stable were levelled to the ground. The invaders threw the family's furniture down the hill. They smashed roof, fixtures, and woodwork, razed the walls to the foundation and reduced the house to a black dismal wreck.

Archibald gathered his children beside an old stone fence. Nothing like this had ever happened, he said. They needed to seek guidance from above. His wife and children wept, but the old man said, "Neither weeping nor reflection will now avail; we must prepare some shelter." The children collected timbers and turf, and in the space between two ditches, the old man constructed a rude shelter for the night. Next day the family examined the ruins, collected some broken pieces of furniture and dishes, and added to their shelter.

They carried on for a week. Then the men came again. After unleashing much verbal abuse, they destroyed the shelter and put old Archie and his people back out on the empty hill. Donald Ross found the family still at Knoydart in a shelter beside the old ditch. He had never seen any dwelling place more wretched or melancholy. A peat or turf erection, about three feet high, four feet broad, and five feet long, lay at the end of the shelter, and this formed the sleeping place of the mother and her five daughters. They crept in and out on their knees and their bed was a layer of hay on the cold earth of the ditch.

Donald Ross wrote of Elizabeth Gillies, a sixty-year-old widow. Her home—a traditional blackhouse with a peat firepit, a thatched roof, and a byre for animals at one end—sat on a hill near a stream that formed the boundary between Knoydart and a large sheep farm.

The poor widow, who took care of her little granddaughter, had hoped for mercy. She was sitting inside her house when the factor and his men arrived. They ordered her to remove herself and her effects instantly, as they were going to pull down the house. She asked where she would go. The factor gave no answer but kept insisting that she leave.

Because it has two doors, this blackhouse at the Highland Folk Museum at Newtonmore is grander than was the single-door house of Elizabeth Gillies.

When at last the widow flatly refused, two men seized her arms and tried to pull her out by force. She resisted furiously. A third man extinguished the fire in the hearth and then joined the other two in dragging the old woman out of the house. She seized every post within her reach, but the men struck her fingers, forcing her to let go. Then all she could do was to cry out, "Murder!" She was thrown out the door and, with her granddaughter wailing beside her, crawled away on her hands and knees, weeping, exhausted and panting.

The men began their work of destruction, heaving out stools, chairs, tables, cupboard, spinning wheel, bed, blankets, straw, dishes, pots and chest. They broke down partitions, removed the crook from over the fireplace, destroyed the hen roosts, and then chased the hens outside through a vent in the roof of the house. This done, they went at the stone walls with picks and iron levers. They pulled down the thatch and removed supports until the roof fell in with a crash.

As the shades of night closed in, Ross wrote, "here was the poor helpless widow sitting like a pelican, alone and cheerless." When he reached Knoydart, he found the old woman at work in the wreckage of her home. She said that her predecessors had lived, from time immemorial, on the Glengarry estates. Many of them had died in defence of, or fighting for, the old chieftains. Ross asked why she refused to go to Canada. "For a very good reason," she said. "I am now old, and not able to clear a way in the forests of Canada; and, besides, I am unfit for service; and, further, I am averse to leave my native country, and rather than leave it, I would much prefer that my grave was opened beside my dear [dead] daughter, although I should be buried alive!"

Donald Ross multiplied examples. On the *Ocean Endeavour*, gazing over the water in 2018, I could only shake my head at what had transpired on the shores that I could see. Within six months of the original devastation, the widow Macdonell had her factor remove almost all of those she had allowed to remain "for motives of charity," she said, through the winter. Before long, protected by a provision in his lease that prohibited him from sheltering any of those evicted, industrialist James Baird installed sheep in the surrounding hills. In 1857, with all the people dispersed, Baird completed the purchase of the Knoydart estate. There he built a mansion, which he occasionally used as a country retreat.

2

—

View from Finlaggan

THE GREAT HALL AT LOCH FINLAGGAN IS TODAY A stone ruin. The edifice was never especially impressive, as any visitor can see. But back in the twelfth century, it gave rise to a definitive Scottish moment. That explains my excitement as—for only the third time in my life—I hiked towards it along a board-walk from the nearby visitors' centre. This was on Islay, one of the most beautiful of Scotland's west-coast islands (which are also considered part of the Highlands).

On day two of our circumnavigation of Scotland, having sailed overnight from Oban to Islay, we had piled into Zodiacs and roared into the town of Bowmore. Not far from the whisky distillery of that name, we boarded buses for a fifteen-minute ride to Finlaggan. The Great Hall is now little more than two triangular end walls made of stone, sitting at the edge of a tiny lake.

But for almost three centuries, this hall served as the command centre of the Lords of the Isles, early champions of Scotland's Gaelic culture and distinctive clan system. Before the emergence of the Lords, in the twelfth century, Loch Finlaggan had provided a base for Somerled, the most powerful sea lord of the western isles. From here at Finlaggan, in 1164, the ambitious Somerled had organized an invasion of the Scottish mainland.

The ruins fail to impress, but in the Great Hall at Loch Finlaggan, the peerless Somerled organized his ill-fated invasion of the Scottish mainland.

Standing in the Great Hall, now just a ruin, I remembered the words of Pulitzer Prize–winner Katherine Anne Porter: "The past is never where you think you left it." For the past decade I had been sifting through Scottish history seeking Scotland's earliest defining moment. I had considered the Clearances, the Battle of Culloden, the battles of Stirling Bridge and Bannockburn, and several other risings and rebellions. But now Somerled's invasion of the mainland emerged for me as the signal turning point, the earliest definitive clash between two rival cultures—Norse-Gaelic and Anglo-Norman. My own background—paternal DNA of Scandinavian origin, clan alliances with MacNeills and MacDonalds—has undoubtedly biased me in favour of Somerled and his descendants, the Lords of the

Isles. But few things are more boring than a narrative that lacks a point of view.

My predilections made me keen to investigate. Loch Finlaggan takes its name from the Irish saint Findlugan, who helped St. Columba bring monastic Christianity to Scotland in the sixth century. Over the next couple of centuries, Columba's disciples proved hugely successful in creating monasteries and filling them with precious relics. These became centres around which the common folk, Gaelic-speaking Christians, could build rough huts, grow crops and trade goods. This bucolic existence came to an end in the early 800s, when Scandinavian sailors discovered the rich, undefended monasteries and saw them as ideal targets. They had developed graceful, speedy longships that enabled young men to "go a Viking" or plundering every summer, and to wreak unprecedented havoc.

At first, these "Vikings"—Norse, Danish, Swedish—ransacked their targets and sailed home. But soon enough, with land in short supply, they began settling and integrating, giving rise to a Norse-Gaelic culture. In Ireland, they founded Dublin. In England, the Danish king Canute and his descendants ruled from 1016 to 1042. By late in the eleventh century, the Islay-raised Godred Crovan ruled a sea-based kingdom from the Isle of Man, which is equidistant from Ireland, Scotland and England. His domain extended from Dublin in the south to the Isle of Lewis and Orkney in the north.

One of Crovan's descendants, Godred IV, ruled with too heavy a hand. The people of Loch Finlaggan—now a flourishing farming community protected by its hard-to-reach location and possibly a timber palisade—sought the intervention of the most powerful sea lord in the western isles. Either that or Somerled decided on his own to seize control of Islay and so expand his domain.

In 1153, in a major sea battle off the coast of the island—just a few miles north of Finlaggan—Somerled routed Godred IV and drove him off to Norway. As a result, he became known as the Hammer of the Norse—even though his own ancestry was Norse and Irish. Over the next few years, while fending off competing demands for obeisance from both Norway and Scotland, Somerled consolidated his independent, sea-based kingdom.

And in 1164, he organized his invasion of mainland Scotland. Working at Finlaggan from the Great Hall and nearby Council Island, Somerled raised a massive fleet. He drew warriors from as far away as Dublin, Lewis and the Isle of Man. Historical novelist Nigel Tranter writes of 160 longships and galleys carrying nearly twenty thousand fighters—though probably he exaggerates.

Historian John Marsden estimates that the total was more likely ten or fifteen thousand—for that era, still an enormous fighting force—and adds that Dublin probably supplied sixty of the longships. Yet Tranter is the one who, in his novel *Lord of the Isles*, brings the scene vividly to life, evoking the clanging gongs and flashing oars, and working the same magic with Somerled as he did with many another historical figure.

The sea lord led the way into the Firth of Clyde and up the river to Renfrew, which was headquarters to Walter Fitz-Alan, the first high steward of Scotland and the progenitor of the House of Stewart. Somerled camped near the town and, though he brought an overwhelming force, that is where he lost his life. In the most dramatic version of events, he was betrayed by a kinsman or a servant. But this is unlikely. The earliest accounts indicate that a force hastily assembled by the bishop of Glasgow killed Somerled. In the *Carmen de Morte Sumerledi*, an eyewitness clergyman wrote that Somerled was "wounded by a [thrown] spear and cut down by the sword." Such were the times that the priest then severed his head and brought it to the bishop. Having lost their leader, the invaders retreated in disarray and sailed away home.

What else is certain? As Marsden writes, Somerled was "the one historical figure who reflects in his every aspect the same fusion of Norse and Gael which binds the deeper cultural roots of modern Gaelic Scotland." History would have taken a very different course, he adds, "had Somerled's great host of west Highlanders, Islemen and Dublin Norse not failed in the venture of 1164."

At Loch Finlaggan, in the ruins of the Great Hall, I stood imagining how a Somerled victory would have transformed the story of Scotland. With Somerled in control of the Scottish mainland from the west coast to Glasgow, Edinburgh and Inverness, as well as the western isles, then together with his Irish allies he could have created a powerful new political entity—a Roman Catholic, Gaelic-speaking kingdom encompassing all the lands west and north of England. Imagine how differently history would have unfolded. As it happened, Somerled made his mark by establishing a vibrant and distinctive culture. His direct descendants, the Lords of the Isles, did much to engender and foster the clan system— that sense of kinship and collective identity—which would forever characterize and distinguish Gaelic Scotland.

By the time Somerled died during his ill-fated invasion, the mainland kings of Scotland had adopted the European feudal system. That line of kings started with Kenneth MacAlpin in 848 and continued through King David (1124–1153), Malcolm IV (1153–1165) and on through the houses of Balliol and Bruce. Under the feudal system, the king controlled all lands and could grant charters in return for money and/or military service.

In *Highland Folk Ways*, I.F. Grant discusses how, against this feudal background, the Highland clans emerged, noting that "pride of place belongs to the clans descended from Somerled." After his death, the sea lord's sons Dougal and Reginald founded their clans, or kinships groups. Reginald gained control of Islay, Kintyre and parts of Arran and Mull. Reginald's son Donald gave his name to Clan Donald and is the progenitor of all the MacDonalds. In 1336, one of his descendants, John of Islay or John MacDonald, styled himself Lord of the Isles. He was the son of Angus Og of Islay, who in 1314 had fought alongside Robert the Bruce at Bannockburn. By 1346, thanks partly to the alliance with the Bruces, he controlled the Hebrides (except Skye) and much of the western seaboard.

This most powerful clan had numerous branches, all of them descended from Somerled. These included various MacDonalds— of Glencoe, Kintyre, Loch Alsh and Sleat—and "cadet clans" descended through younger sons, among them MacIains, MacAlisters, and Macdonells. In this world, ancestral lineage was paramount. Smaller families allied with a powerful chieftain became "septs," or divisions, of his clan. For the record, the McGugans/McGougans/ McGoogans are a sept of both the MacDonalds and the MacNeills.

As Grant explains, whatever their ancient lineage, most clans entered history when one prominent member received a land grant. Smaller families lived on lands controlled by more powerful chiefs— the MacColls, for example, on lands owned by the Stewarts. The MacRaes, Mathesons and MacLennans lived on MacKenzie lands.

The Highland clans varied in size and makeup. They arose between the late 1100s and the 1400s and reached their most powerful point early in the eighteenth century, before the Jacobite Rising of 1715. The clans multiplied quickly. Consider the Frasers: five branches in 1650 became thirty by 1745. The Grants, Campbells and MacKenzies manifested similar growth. The idea of "kinship" became malleable as chieftains grew their clans—and so increased their power—by encouraging and even bribing tenant farmers to adopt their surnames.

The MacDonalds, one of whom succeeded to the earldom of Ross, eventually controlled not only the Hebrides but lands stretching across the north of Scotland. Four Lords of the Isles in succession claimed to be more than subjects of any king. From Islay, they frequently controlled parts of the Scottish mainland and for years occupied Inverness. Eventually, in 1493, King James IV of Scotland forced the Lords into submission.

Here again we discover a clash of cultures. James IV was well-educated and spoke Gaelic as one of several languages. He would be the last king able to do so. The Lords of the Isles had been the great champions of Gaelic culture and nobody took their place as patrons of Gaelic literature and music. Five times, various Lords of the Isles tried and failed to restore their mainland dominion. Only the clan pride survived. The scholarly Grant quotes a bemused eighteenth-century visitor to the Highlands: "The poorest and most despicable creature of the name of MacDonald looks upon himself as a gentleman of far superior quality than a man in England of one-thousand-pounds a year."

The Campbells and MacKenzies gained control of much of the MacDonald territory. But as Grant explains, they did not even try to replace the Lords of the Isles as patrons of Gaelic arts: "By the seventeenth century, the learned classes of Gaeldom were disappearing and Highlanders were getting their education at Lowland universities. The degradation of the old Gaelic civilization to a folk culture was beginning." In a footnote, she observes: "Contemporary Scots history was written by Lowlanders who say as little as they can about the Gaelic Lordship."

3

The Old Way of Life

I N THE CELTIC TRADITION, "THIN PLACES" ARE SITES where the natural and spiritual worlds meet and intermingle, separated by the merest veil. The ancient Celts would visit these sacred sites, among them Stonehenge in England and the Ring of Brodgar in Orkney, to experience the presence of their gods. For secular types like me, the concept works better historically. I think of the reconstructed Gaelic village in the Highland Folk Museum seventy kilometres south of Inverness, where you can wander in and out of blackhouses and see people at work in the clothing and spirit of another time. The same goes for Auchindrain Township, ten kilometres south of Inverary. It is the only stone-built settlement to survive essentially unaltered from among hundreds that existed before the Highland Clearances. And what of the Gearrannan Blackhouse Village at a beautiful waterside location on the Isle of Lewis?

All three sites provide a sense of how most Highlanders lived in the decades before and after the mid-1700s, when the Battle of Culloden marked the beginning of the end for the Old Order. Political and military historians of the Middle Ages focus on kings and aristocrats and the battles they fought, won or lost. But most Highlanders were farmers who stayed home in small townships made up of extended families.

They lived in "blackhouses," so-designated because they were dark, windowless, and blackened by peat-fire smoke. The term distinguishes them from the "white houses" which came later and introduced such amenities as windows and toilets. In *Thatched Houses: A Contribution to the Social History of the Old Highlands*, author Colin Sinclair identifies three types of blackhouses according to their roof styles. The Hebridean has four walls of the same height and a ledge running around the edge of the roof. The Skye has four similar walls but no ledge: the thatch runs over the edge. And the Dalriadic has a Skye-style roof but pointed walls at two opposite ends providing for a pitched roof.

At the Gearrannan Blackhouse Village on the west coast of the Isle of Lewis, we see restored blackhouses in two styles. The Hebridean (directly above) has a ledge running around the edge of the roof. The Dalriadic has pointed walls at two opposite ends.

All three styles of blackhouse had thatched roofs. The house above, at the Highland Folk Museum, is in the Skye style. It has four walls of equal size and the thatched roof runs over the edge all the way round.

The Dalriadic blackhouse, named after the ancient Gaelic sea-kingdom of Dalriada, has two pointed walls creating a pitched roof and thatch running over the edge. It has no ledge, which makes it different from the Hebridean house on the previous page.

The common features among these three types tell us more about how people lived. Besides their thatched roofs and walls made of stones or peat slabs, blackhouses were usually oblong and divided into three compartments. Shall we visit one? You enter the house through a flimsy door that opens into the byre, or cowhouse, that forms one of the two end compartments. When your eyes adjust, you see a couple of small black cows reclining on a bed of straw. The place stinks of cow dung and chicken droppings, so why tarry? You turn right and, through an opening or pass door, step through an internal wall into the main apartment. A third compartment is straight ahead, divided from this room by a wooden partition containing another pass door covered with a blanket.

You can't help but notice the smoke, which gets thicker higher up, and you crouch to avoid the worst of it. The smoke curls upwards from a peat fire, which sits on a stone slab in the middle of this dirt-floor apartment. It drifts eventually through a hole in the thatch located off-centre so that heavy rains do not douse the flames. A three-legged iron pot hangs over the fire from a chain attached to a beam in the roof. You sit down on a bench that occupies a side wall and notice a dresser neatly displaying rows of plates. Beneath it sits a washtub and beside that, a wooden bucket.

Welcome to the house of the Gael in the Old Highlands. It allows for conversation and conviviality around the peat fire, but mainly it provides shelter from the storm—though the roof is not watertight. In rainy weather, heavy drops of inky black water make their way through the thatch. This happens often enough that people have a name for those falling droplets: *snighe.*

When weather permits, not surprisingly, the common folk spend most of their time outdoors. They tend their crops and their cattle. When James Boswell passed this way with Dr. Samuel

Johnson in 1773, he wrote, "We had not rooms that we could command, for the good people here had no notion that a man could have any occasion but a mere sleeping place."

We have entered a blackhouse. Behind us is the byre for the animals. Directly ahead is the main apartment. Over the peat fire, now extinguished, hangs a chain with a hook for an iron pot. Beyond we see a blanket covering the sleeping compartment.

LIKE IRELAND, but unlike England and the Lowlands, the Scottish Highlands successfully resisted the invasion of the Romans and never formed part of Roman Britain (AD 43 to 410). The Gaelic-speaking Highlanders on the islands and along the mainland coast belonged to a sea-faring world—one without roads until the eighteenth century. No coach system reached Inverness until 1811.

And yet, for generations, people survived in this rugged landscape, enduring sporadic famines. What gave them the strength and ability to do so? Historians are well-nigh unanimous: the clan system—all for one and one for all. Many clansmen were not related to the clan chief by blood, but took his name to show solidarity, to obtain basic protection or to acquire foods. Loyalty to the clan was paramount.

Highlanders are often thought of as "crofters" who owned and farmed a plot of land. But that crofting organization did not emerge until the mid-nineteenth century. Before that, under a collective "runrig" system of land tenure, farmers lived in their blackhouses in townships that comprised between six and twenty dwellings adjacent to an "infield" of arable land and an "outfield" more suitable to rough grazing. They divided the infield into strips or "rigs" which were reassigned every two or three years so that everyone had a turn working the best land.

Collective ownership and cooperative activity don't come easily. In the Highlands, the clan system made them work. That system highlights kinship and shared membership in a welcoming social entity. Clan members share a common ancestor, or at least subscribe to the notion that they do. You are all brothers and sisters and cousins.

The clan chieftains, whose ancestors acquired estates from the crown, grant long-term mortgages on large holdings, or "tacks," to faithful kinsmen. The "tacksman" serves as a military officer when required, and rents sections of his large tack to subtenants. He keeps the best section for himself. While the chief lives in a castle some distance away, the tacksman resides among the people, albeit in the best house in the township.

The relative status of the chieftains depends on the number of fighting men they can bring to a battle. They recognize that they have reciprocal responsibilities and obligations to members of their clan. During periods of famine and hardship, they are known to remit rents and distribute grain. Clan members, while clearly interdependent, belong to one of three main classes. The chiefs are supreme leaders. Next come the gentlemen of the clan, the tacksmen who take care to educate their sons, who can then enter the professions or the military. The third class comprises subtenants and cottars or servants, who live in the humblest dwellings and do the hardest work of farming.

The tacksman lives in a traditional blackhouse, but his place might be set apart from the others and larger than usual, with one or two extensions and perhaps a separate byre for cows, sheep, goats and chickens. Instead of hard-packed earth, his floor might be built of flagstones.

Most Highlanders are subsistence farmers who eat what they grow—turnips, corn, potatoes. They keep a few small black cows and chickens, sometimes a goat, and use workhorses to till often rocky parcels of land. Everyone in the township is a jack of all trades and women are full partners in the collective enterprise. Except during winter, everyone works round the clock, doing whatever has to be done.

The men build the houses and continually renew and repair thatched roofs. They also make and mend furniture, dig the land, sow the seed and do jobs that require heavy lifting. The women handle the cows, make wicker baskets, and transport water and manure in buckets and baskets. They tend the corn and potatoes, and they also do the cooking. Generally, breakfast, lunch and supper vary the same elements: porridge, bread, milk, potatoes, sometimes eggs and possibly fish. Bread would be bannocks of oat or barley meal. In some areas, the grain is exhausted by the end of spring and people live on milk and fish until the potatoes are ready.

As April ends, the township turns to cutting and drying the peats needed throughout the year for cooking and heating. An average family burns fifteen thousand peats per year. Several families usually combine their efforts as cutting peats requires two men, one to cut rectangular pieces (roughly twelve inches by twenty-four) out of the ground and the other to lift them onto the bank. This tough, heavy work demands that the two frequently change places. A good team can cut a thousand peats a day.

An average Highland family would burn fifteen thousand peats a year for cooking and heating. Here a farmer in Shetland cuts one long peat in two. His work partner (not pictured) stacks them in rows for drying.

The women spread and stack the peats to dry, often with the help of older children. If the weather cooperates, the peats dry in two weeks. People carry them home in special wooden wheelbarrows called "peat barrows" and pile them near their houses. If they are lucky, they might be able to saddle up a "pack pony" to help with the carrying. This peat cutting takes place during the dry season, when men will also be working the ground and planting turnips.

The men make wooden packsaddles and collars for horses, ponies and oxen, and primitive sleds on which to drag large stones from the fields. They use fires to crack the largest stones, or else bore holes and fill them with wet wedges that crack the stone as they dry and expand. They make wooden gates to confine cattle and various kinds of rope using rushes, heather and even horsehair. For this task, they create rope-twisting devices.

In ancient times, Highlanders went barefoot. But then they took to cutting undressed hide to fit their feet, punching holes around the edges and tying what was effectively a moccasin around their ankles. By the eighteenth century people are tanning leather to make their shoes. On the west coast, where scrub abounds, the women become expert basketmakers and even make wickerwork coffins.

For townships situated on a coast, one of the hardest jobs is collecting kelp, an acidic seaweed containing iodine useful to chemical manufacturing. Once the kelp is dry, it can be burned to ash, which turns the iodine to iodide that can then be extracted by boiling and put to medical, agricultural and cosmetic uses. To collect the seaweed, men wade back and forth into the freezing water. Because they are constantly cold and wet, many suffer from acute rheumatism. Women dry and burn the seaweed into a slag-like mass for transportation.

Early in the summer, families drive their cattle to the "shielings," a term that encompasses both the grazing grounds and the nearby herdsmen's huts or shelters. Families pile carts with blankets, foodstuffs, churns and dishes, and place old women and spinning wheels on top. With cattle bawling and dogs barking, the whole community sets out along the rough track that leads to the shielings. On arrival, people unpack, share a simple feast, and say a blessing.

For a couple of months, most of the women, girls and young lads remain at the shielings to care for the cattle and make cheese and butter. Around the end of July, when the cows have cleared the grass, the women return to the township. The men are already hard at work harvesting grain, desperate to finish before autumn brings the rains.

Women do some work with textiles, but men do most of the weaving. It becomes a specialized craft and weavers are relatively numerous. Every man needs his belted plaid, after all—his woven piece of cloth roughly five feet wide and twelve to eighteen feet long, which he wraps around himself one way or another, and which, in the eighteenth century, slowly evolves into the smaller, more manageable kilt. In addition to weavers, communities need tailors and shoemakers, and every hamlet has a few smiths.

Woodworkers come into their own as fishing grows more efficient, responding to the need for boats and barrels in which to store salted herring. Boatbuilders make boats out of hollowed logs, but also draw on the Norse tradition of stretching hides over a wooden frame to make larger craft. West-coast Highlanders and Hebridean Islanders have adapted the wooden galleys introduced by the Vikings. In the sixteenth century, clan chieftains like MacNeill of Barra keep a galley and a crew of men at the ready in case a chance arises for piracy. The MacNeills produce one especially memorable clan chieftain who every evening has one of his minions poke his head out a top-floor window in Kisimul Castle. "MacNeill of Barra has dined!" the servant cries. "And now the world may dine."

The medieval Kisimul Castle is situated on the rocky islet of Castlebay just off the coast of Barra. Legend has it that from the eleventh century onwards, it was a stronghold of the Clan MacNeill.

Highlanders lived humbly, alternating between periods of hard work and leisure. But in *Highland Folk Ways*, ethnologist I.F. Grant tells us that they enjoyed a mental life "proud, vigorous and beautiful, which has existed in continuity from the days of the supremacy of the lordly Gaelic society." Grant traces that intellectual life to the Lords of the Isles, those champions of Gaelic culture and patrons of poetry and music who launched a tradition that refused to wither and die.

No description of Highland society, she writes, "can ignore the intellectual life of the people." Nearly every literate visitor was struck equally by the poverty and simplicity of the people's lives, "and by the distinction of their bearing, their beautiful manners and their courtesy to each other." In the early nineteenth century, one visitor remarked on the people's "stateliness in the midst of their poverty," while another noticed that "a vein of good breeding ran through all ranks, influencing their manners and rendering the intercourse of all most agreeable."

Again, Grant points to the Lords of the Isles, descendants of the sea-lord Somerled. Country folk even in remote districts enjoyed "a wealth of stories and traditions handed down by practised story-tellers." The "noble epics of ancient Gaeldom," she adds, "conceived and polished when Erin was a kingdom with a magnificent flowering of the arts, were the delight of the Highland society that flourished during the Lordship of the Isles." Stories from the *Feinne Cycle*, featuring Deirdre, Grainne and Cuchullin, "formed the everyday background of people's lives."

General David Stewart of Garth, writing of his youth in Perthshire during the late eighteenth century, observed: "When a stranger appeared, after the usual compliments, the first question was, 'Do you know anything of the *Feinne*?' If the answer was in the affirmative, the whole hamlet convened and midnight was usually the hour of separation." Another observer marvelled: "In every cottage there is a musician and in every hamlet a poet."

All this had ancient roots. In the 1500s, trained professional poets wrote in the elaborate, stylized metres of old Ireland. The classic *Book of the Dean of Lismore*, begun in 1512, collected the poetry of wandering bards, or "strollers," who recited lengthy pieces in the classical metres of the Old Irish that had spawned the Gaelic language.

In the 1600s, with the ancient Gaelic script slowly disappearing, Highland poets produced simpler, more tuneful works. The poets included men and women of every rank, from tacksmen, ministers and schoolmasters to cattlemen and crofters. That illustrious Lowland poet Robert Burns was not as anomalous as many people believe. Between 1645 and 1830, according to the scholar

W.J. Watson, 130 different Highland poets produced work that was "really good and some of it outstanding." Meanwhile, many people developed an ability to improvise verse, and to entertain with spontaneous rhyming couplets poking fun at those present.

Ministers of the church, while relatively few, helped keep this love of learning alive. They belonged to what might be considered a separate class. They were among the most educated Highlanders, and in the eighteenth century generally resided in a manse near the church. One of them, the Reverend Donald Sage (1789–1869), grew up in Kildonan in northeastern Scotland. He was the son of a lifelong Presbyterian minister and himself joined the church. In *Memorabilia Domestica: Or, Parish Life in the North of Scotland*, Sage adds many vivid anecdotes to our sense of Highland life before, during and after the Clearances.

Highland society was ceremonial, even ritualistic. Writing of "sacramental occasions," Sage tells us that "a distinction prevailed in the annual administration . . . which in the south was utterly unknown." By the late eighteenth century, the Lord's Supper, or Communion, would be administered in two distinct services— publicly in English when outsiders were present; and privately in Gaelic amongst local folk. For the public service, the minister would customarily "keep open table," as the services would last for hours and many parishioners lived some distance away.

In preparation, local people would bring presents of mutton, butter and cheese. Sage remembered seeing "the whole range of a large cellar so closely laid with mutton carcasses that the floor was literally paved with them," the gifts far exceeding the need. On one special occasion in Kildonan, "the congregation was assembled before the church, close by the banks of the river, and the communion table, extending to about thirty feet in length, was covered with a white cloth and surrounded by a dense multitude [from surrounding parishes] of between three and four thousand persons."

Some funerals were similarly elaborate, though most were more modest. As a boy, Sage attended the funeral of old Hugh Fraser, who had died after a long confinement. "It was in the dead of winter, a clear, hoar-frosty, short winter day." People assembled on the sloping green in front of the dead man's cottage and were served oatcakes and whisky. "When the procession moved off with the body, his wife and a female friend preceded us to the grave, 'weeping aloud as they went.'" A local man had dug the grave in the frozen ground with a mattock or pickaxe. The sod, hardened by mid-winter frost, had become a solid mass, and the middle-aged Sage writes that "the sound of the frozen earth falling in congealed fragments upon Hugh Fraser's coffin still rings in my ears."

Sage would recall that as a boy, he listened for hours at the kitchen fireside as one John Meadhonach declaimed "almost all Ossian's poems," and would "entertain his interested audience with long oral extracts from our Celtic Homer." Scholars would later judge those poems to be brilliant forgeries by the man who claimed he had found them, one James Macpherson. But to the listening boy, that did not matter.

Sage noted that Meadhonach, raconteur and antiquarian, was also a poacher, a smuggler and "a first-rate brewer of malt whisky" hired on occasion by the minister's wife to produce this liquor. Sage's father built a cowhouse of stone and turf near the burn: "There often, during the process of our whisky brews, have I sat with John, watching the process and hearing his tales."

Meadhonach's youngest daughter married and emigrated to Canada. Some years later, the man himself set out for "the Red River, in Canada, under the direction of Lord Selkirk," but then died during the voyage. "Poor John had a strong attachment to my father," Sage wrote, "and a most profound veneration for him; and though his wife and sons came to bid us farewell, he himself, after making four different attempts to come and take his last look of his minister, finally gave it up." He knew that if he came to say good-bye, he would break down.

Highlanders loved music, especially that played on the great warpipe. Even today the sound of the bagpipes, the interplay of chanter and drones, sends shivers down the spine of some listeners while causing others to flee. Historians credit the MacCrimmons, hereditary pipers to MacLeod of MacLeod, with developing classical bagpipe music, which includes laments, gatherings and salutes. After playing the air or tune, the piper presents a series of variations, elaborating according to strict conventions. In the seventeenth century, no self-respecting chief could be without a piper, and some had as many as three.

In the eighteenth century, after the Battle of Culloden, the British government sought deliberately to suppress this cultural expression. But it made a comeback so strong that, in the nineteenth century, when the Highlander George Simpson became governor of the Hudson's Bay Company, he made a point of bringing a piper into the wilds of North America, using the musician to announce his arrival by canoe at far-flung fur-trading posts. Not surprisingly, considering the training involved, and the musical expertise demanded, pipers remained an elite few.

Next to the bagpipes, Highlanders loved the fiddle. Donald Sage fondly remembered "an individual who largely contributed to our amusement." This was a Mrs. Gordon, a daughter of the Reverend Murdo Macdonald of Durness. Sage knew her when she was a widow. She inherited her father's passion for music, "played beautifully on the violin and was a periodical visitor" to countless houses in Sutherland. "Many a time and often have we tripped to her heart-and-heel-stirring reels and strathspeys in the low easter-room at the manse of Kildonan."

Music played a major role in the endless series of festivals with which Highlanders entertained themselves. They celebrated the Gaelic May Day festival known as Beltane on May 1, marking the beginning of summer and the cattle drive to the shielings. A super-stitious people, they performed rituals to protect their cows and crops, walking around bonfires or leaping over the flames or embers. They would douse their household fires and relight them from the Beltane bonfire. People would decorate doors, byres and even their cows with yellow mayflowers, and then would come the feasting.

Highlanders marked Christmas, Good Friday and Easter with churchgoing, hymn-singing and feasting. And on various islands they mounted specific festivals—for example, marking St. Barr's Day on Barra. On St. Michael's Day (September 29), Islanders held parades in which everyone rode horses, and on North Uist, young men could seize and ride somebody else's horse in a race. On Barra, the women made special bannocks from the first grinding of grain and everyone in the house was expected to eat some for luck.

On February 1, Highlanders celebrated the Feast of St. Bride, which derived from the pagan festival of the fire goddess Brid. The women of the house would make up a special bed, welcoming St. Bride by drawing covers over a sheaf of corn dressed as a woman. On that day, when the goddess warmed the sea by dipping her hand into it, the fishermen of Barra would cast lots to assign fishing grounds.

Hallowe'en (October 31) would bring the lighting of bon-fires to honour the saints and the souls of the faithful (Christian) departed. Women would attempt to foretell the future, and in some areas children in fancy dress would come around, sing a song, and expect to receive an apple or some other treat. This day is also part of Samhain, a Gaelic festival marking the end of harvest and the beginning of winter. Like Beltane, Samhain is one of four Gaelic seasonal festivals, the others being Imbolc and Lughnasa.

Hogmanay, too, has ancient roots, probably Norse. It comes on the last day of the year. On the Isle of Lewis, boys in bands, with their leader wearing a sheepskin on his back, would travel from house to house collecting bannocks. On South Uist, a man carrying a torch and wrapped in dried cowhide would lead a band of youths three times around a house. The man would pass his torch three times around the head of the woman of the house and she would give the boys three bannocks and receive one out of the sack they carried. On leaving, the boys would call out a blessing on the house—or, if unsatisfied, would build an ominous small cairn out front.

This ritual, no longer practiced, probably signals the sacrificial killing of a god. One custom that does survive is "first-footing." The first person to cross your threshold after midnight, who should arrive with a bottle of whisky and a bannock or an oatcake, establishes your luck for the rest of the year. The best luck comes when the first-footer is a tall, dark-haired man.

Ritual and superstition also marked births and christenings. People feared that the Fairies might steal the newborn and substitute a changeling. One of several strategies to protect the mother was to bang a nail into the wood of her bed or to place a smoothing iron beneath it. On Skye, midwives would carry fire in a circle morning and evening around mothers-to-be, and around unbaptized children to guard against Fairy abduction.

As for marriages, Highlanders recognized "handfasting"— clasping hands through a hole in a monolith—as legitimate, and would also accept a formal statement by a couple that they were man and wife. But as time passed, most weddings became stylized affairs. In the late 1700s, Donald Sage reports, a miller named John Ross "became the thriving wooer of the eldest daughter of Rory Bain." The father gave his consent and a hearty wedding took place in the dead of winter. After feasting for two days, "the young couple were accompanied to their own house by the greater part of their guests." At the house-warming in Kildonan, "I remember seeing John Ross, after the manner of the ancients, borne over his threshold."

Donald Sage and his siblings spent days and weeks visiting the distantly related Murray family, tenant farmers at a place called Tuaraidh. Sage vividly remembered "the scenery, as well as names of hill and dale, in that wild and sequestered spot. . . . The site of Alister Murray's house, of his barn on the brow of the hill, of his swaggering corn-rigs, of his peat-moss on the banks of the Loist, which meandered through the Lon, and the houses of his sub-tenants."

Sage remembered especially the marriages of Murray's two daughters, when he and his siblings "were amused and feasted for nearly a week, whilst our fellow-guests numbered about fifty." The younger daughter, Janet, married into the Mackay family of Ascaig, halfway between Kinbrace and Kildonan. After the Sutherland Clearances of 1819, according to a footnote, three Mackay sons and two daughters—out of a family of ten—would emigrate to Canada. In Montreal, two of the sons founded the wholesale firm Mackay Brothers and "bestowed munificent donations" on the Presbyterian Church and McGill University.

At Janet's wedding, in the late 1790s, Sage's father officiated in the church at noon. At the end of the day, the festivities over, the guests of both sexes retired to sleep in the barn. Sage and his brother lay down beside each other at the lower end of the building. "So long as the sound of the voices, after we had all lain down, rang in my ears from all corners," Sage writes, "I felt very drowsy. But when to the hum of speech a deep silence succeeded, broken only by the hard breathing of the sleepers, I became wide awake." Sage felt "an undefinable dread" creep over him, and then, in the pitchy darkness, he saw "a white figure gliding slowly down from the upper to the lower part of the building, where it disappeared." Next day, when he mentioned seeing this apparition to others, he learned that a young local woman suffering from consumption had been found dead in her bed that morning.

Another marriage taught Donald Sage that, in desperate circumstances, the formal rules and conventions could be broken. One Robert Pope, having returned from twenty years in the West Indies, rented several farms in the parish of Kildonan and so became a frequent guest at the manse. Around this time, when Sage was a small boy, his stepmother took ill and her sister, Miss Bertie, came to care for her and run the house. The children stood in awe of this young woman's "lady-like accomplishments and her rich vein of wit." Robert Pope was smitten, made no secret of it and, among the parish gentry, became the target of merciless teasing.

This was in early October, when after a long period of rain, Donald Sage as a small boy had embarked on building a house out of glorious mud. After dinner, he left the adults to their boring conversation and went outside to continue his project until he was called inside. Early next morning, he jumped out of bed to have breakfast and resume work. Going down the hall past the guest room, he was surprised to see that, outside the door, "Miss Bertie's little shoes were placed side by side with Mr. Pope's boots." He thought this very strange as Miss Bertie slept in a separate garret. One of the servant-maids, meeting him in the hall, shared in his astonishment, but with a wink added in Gaelic, "Surely they are married."

Young Donald went open-mouthed to his older sisters, "but they were already initiated in the mystery." They told him that at around twelve o'clock the previous night, Mr. Pope had insisted on getting married to Miss Bertie. Their father, "after remonstrating upon the too great privacy and precipitancy of the measure, had yielded and married them." Young Donald nodded and resumed his mud-building. Mr. and Mrs. Pope came that evening to look at his completed edifice, and he "was much gratified with their minute examination of it and with their commendations." The couple remained a few days at Kildonan, going for walks in the wooded dells, and then went on their way.

In the sixteenth century, the head of Clan Fraser of Lovat became famous for his hospitality and for keeping an open table. Each week, he went through 980 pounds of malt, the same of meal and 14 of flour. He provided visitors with slabs of beef—seventy cows per year—and poultry, mutton, venison and all kinds of game. He traded salmon for gallons of wine from France. By the 1740s, Lord Lovat's hall was often thick with visitors, the tables covered with food and drink—claret for the lords and lairds, port or whisky for the tacksmen, strong beer for the tenants, and small beer for cottars lacking shoes or bonnets. This was considered "prudent economy," as the Frasers were surrounded by MacKenzies, MacDonalds, Grants, Chisholms and MacIntoshes, not all of whom were always friendly.

Clan feuds were common and arose mainly as a result of raiders plundering horses, sheep or cattle. Stories abound. On the Isle of Lewis, one features the Dun Carloway Broch, built in the last century BC and still in use as both castle and storehouse until the Vikings arrived in the early 800s. At around the same time that Lord Lovat discovered value in largesse, a thieving band of Morrisons took refuge in that broch after getting caught raiding cattle from the local MacAulays. The Morrisons managed to block the broch entrance, which was designed for that purpose, but one Donald Cam MacAulay scrambled up the outer wall, threw burning heather down the smoke hole, and forced the would-be thieves to stumble out the door and meet their fate.

The well-preserved Dun Carloway Broch, situated on the west coast of the Isle of Lewis, was built in the first century AD. Its name points to the Norse for "Karl's Bay" and harks back to when it belonged to the Lords of the Isles.

Such raids notwithstanding, relations between clans were conducted according to traditions that had evolved over time. Any breach of those informal conventions would long be remembered. Among the Highlanders of Kildonan, as elsewhere, tradition dictated that you did not ask the name of a stranger who arrived seeking sustenance. Any breach of this rule was regarded as churlish—a grave offence against the overriding tradition of hospitality.

One oral story that survives in different versions, and is relayed by Donald Sage, tells of a clan feud that came to a head in 1511. One summer evening, when the chief of Clan Gunn was preparing to dine in his stone castle at Kinbrace, he and his clansmen heard the blowing of a bugle at the gate. The chief understood this immediately to be a demand for hospitality by a stranger. He opened the castle gate and admitted the stranger and his followers. A tall, elderly man in half-military attire presented himself to the chief, who received him with much courtesy.

At the ensuing meal, the stranger inquired about the twelve young men at the table, all of them six feet tall and well built, "Are these your sons?"

"They are," said the Gunn chieftain, "and I have no need to be ashamed to own them."

"You may well be proud of them," the guest answered. "I don't know a man in Caithness but may envy you such a goodly race—except one."

"And who is that one?"

"Myself." The guest threw back his visor. "You may know me now. I fear not your vengeance for our ancient feud as your hospitality protects me. I am Keith of Ackergill. I will brag my twelve sons to your twelve, gallant though they be, on any day you fix, in a fair field."

The challenge accepted, the two chiefs agreed to face each other with twelve men each in a spot lonely enough to preclude interference. On the appointed day, the Gunns rode out in full armour. As they approached the set location along a burn, they glimpsed their opponents through the trees. On emerging into the field, they perceived treachery. Instead of twelve men, the Keith had brought twenty-four, two men riding on each horse.

The Gunns fought bravely, wielding their two-handed swords with pitiless ferocity, but in the end numbers told. When the chief and seven sons lay dead on the field, the remaining five slowly withdrew. The Keith let them go, satisfied to carry off his dead and wounded followers. The most credible renditions of the story end there, though some find the youngest of the surviving Gunns leading two of his brothers in wreaking revenge.

The most infamous story of breaching the tradition of hospitality stems from the year 1692. A Jacobite rebellion (1689–1692) had recently been quashed. Alexander MacDonald, leader of the MacDonalds of Glencoe, had been tardy in swearing an oath of allegiance to King William III (widely known as William of Orange). But he had done so. And late in January, the Glencoe MacDonalds received a request for hospitality from more than a hundred soldiers under the leadership of Archibald Campbell, the 10th Earl of Argyll.

The MacDonalds entertained the visitors for almost two weeks. The two groups partied together. But then, on the morning of February 13, in an egregious violation of Highland tradition, the Campbells grabbed muskets and broadswords and began slaughtering their hosts. The first to die was Duncan Rankin, shot down as he tried to escape by crossing the River Coe. Nine men were shot after first being tied up. Some MacDonalds later estimated that twenty-five were slain, while certain Campbells set the number at thirty. Other sources say thirty-eight—thirty-three men, three women, two children. Those who later died of exposure totalled somewhere between forty and one hundred.

Whole books have been written about this massacre. Most of the perpetrators probably had no advance notice of the plan and only received orders to commence killing on the morning of February 13. Casualties would have been higher but some soldiers looked the other way while their intended victims escaped. By the standards of subsequent and contemporary atrocities, the numbers of the massacre at Glencoe were not great. But the story lives on at least partly because the Campbells violated the Highland code of hospitality.

For generations, thanks to the clan system and its attendant codes and traditions, Highlanders had survived in this rugged landscape, enduring sporadic famines. As the eighteenth century began, the system remained sufficiently intact that the massacre at Glencoe provoked widespread revulsion and disgust. In retrospect, Glencoe looks like a harbinger. What finally marked the beginning of the end of the clan system was the Battle of Culloden and its century-long aftermath.

4

Battle of Culloden

A T CULLODEN MOOR IN APRIL 1746, TEN KILOMETRES east of Inverness, a British government army led by the Duke of Cumberland laid waste to Jacobite forces, mostly Highlanders, who had rallied to the banner of Bonnie Prince Charlie. Twice before, during previous sojourns in Scotland, we had walked the battlefield, and Sheena Fraser McGoogan had posed for a photo beside the stone marker dedicated to those Frasers who fought here.

My own McGoogan ancestors, then subsisting on Gigha, a tiny island between Kintyre and Islay, played no role at Culloden. Yet, like many others, I found this site to be Scotland's most emotionally overwhelming. Walking the windswept moor where men fought and died is part of that. But so too is the full-circle immersion cinema, located at the tourist centre beside the battlefield, which plunges you into the heart of the thundering battle, where you see kilted warriors cut down by cannon and musket fire. Harrowing.

If in the Middle Ages the destruction of Somerled was the turning point, in modern Scottish history, certainly from a Canadian perspective, the Battle of Culloden was the most significant moment. Culloden led directly to the Highland Clearances. It threw open the floodgates. The Clearances that ensued through the next century saw more than 200,000 Highlanders vacate their ancestral homelands, most of them going to Canada. That is one profound and multidimensional human connection.

This is not the place for a book-length rehearsal of the Battle of Culloden. Historians, journalists, novelists, documentarians and feature film-makers have spent hundreds of thousands of hours and probably millions recreating that event. The wildly popular *Outlander* television series, based on novels by Diana Gabaldon, has introduced the subject to a mass audience.

But briefly, Culloden was the culmination of the "Forty-Five," shorthand for the second Jacobite Rising, or Rebellion, which began in 1745. The word "Jacobite" derives from "Jacobus," the Renaissance Latin formulation of "James." For eighteenth-century Scots, the term Jacobite referred to a follower of a royal family, the Roman Catholic Stuarts, starting with King James VII of Scotland. In the "Glorious Revolution" of 1688, he was overthrown, forced into exile, and ultimately replaced by the Protestant William of Orange.

After that initial James died in 1701, Jacobites supported his son, James Francis Edward. In England, where the kingly succession had settled on the Protestant House of Hanover, this second James was known as the Old Pretender. In 1715, when he sought to regain the Scottish throne, Jacobites used the clan system to raise an army of almost twenty thousand men. They gained control of northern Scotland except for Stirling, and only indecisive leadership allowed British government forces to regroup and rally. By January 9, 1716, when James Francis Edward Stuart arrived in Perth in central Scotland, the uprising was all but dead. Early in

February, he wrote a farewell letter to Scotland and sailed back into exile. Many Jacobites, clansmen all, were jailed, tried for treason, and executed.

This 1715 rebellion was fuelled in part by hatred of the Acts of Union of 1707, which had united two parliaments into one, fusing the separate states of Scotland and England into "one kingdom by the name of Great Britain." Many Catholic Highland chieftains rejected the amalgamation for religious reasons, but Lowland financiers wavered and were won over because they had almost bankrupted themselves in the late 1690s with the so-called Darien scheme. The failure of this would-be trading colony on the isthmus of Panama wiped out 20 percent of all the money in Scotland, rendering wealthy Lowlanders amenable to bargaining away Scottish independence.

Three decades after the first Jacobite Rising, the son of the Old Pretender decided to try again for the throne. Born in 1720 and raised in Rome, Charles Edward Stuart, better known as Bonnie Prince Charlie, fitted out two ships and landed late in July 1745 on the tiny island of Eriskay, situated in the Outer Hebrides between Barra and South Uist. He came to reclaim the Scottish throne, then held by the Hanoverian Protestant King George II.

The clan chieftains had expected the Bonnie Prince to arrive with an army. But he had lost his modest convoy at sea and reached the mainland at Arisaig with only seven men. The few MacDonalds who welcomed him expressed their dismay, but the prince showed no lack of confidence. The clansmen led the prince to Glenfinnan, near the curving viaduct made famous by Harry Potter movies, and there raised the Jacobite standard.

Many Highlanders were dubious of the plan but felt obliged to honour forebears who had fought and died for this Jacobite cause.

The chieftains spread the word through their tacksmen, who called out their kinsmen—those farmers, shepherds, weavers and other craftsmen then living peacefully with their families in their townships and blackhouses. These farmers and family men wrapped themselves in their plaids, collected what weapons they could find, and set out over the hills, hoping to receive decent muskets from their chieftains.

More MacDonalds arrived, and then came Camerons, MacFies and Macdonells, hundreds of men in their plaids, marching over the hills to the sound of bagpipes. In the end, twenty-two clans would come out for the Bonnie Prince and only eight for the government. Followed by an army of several thousand men, the clan chieftains marched on Edinburgh. Almost incredibly, that city immediately surrendered. And then, on September 21, 1745, twenty kilometres east of the city at Prestonpans, the Highlanders defeated the only British government army in Scotland.

With six thousand Highlanders, most of whom would normally be preparing their farms for winter, Charles marched south towards London. The army won another victory at Carlisle but failed to attract additional support. At Swarkestone Bridge in Derbyshire, roughly two hundred kilometres north of London, the Highlanders learned that the British government was gathering a massive army. With Prince Charles protesting, the Highlanders decided to retreat. They won yet another battle at Falkirk, fifty kilometres west of Edinburgh, but now the Duke of Cumberland, the twenty-four-year-old youngest son of King George II, was pursuing them relentlessly with an army of more than 8,000 men, among them 2,400 mounted on horseback.

On April 16, 1746, overruling the advice of his commanders, who urged a guerrilla campaign in the style of Robert the Bruce, the Bonnie Prince ordered the Highlanders to stand and fight on flat, marshy ground east of Edinburgh on Drummossie Moor at Culloden. Acting on orders, the Highlanders stood exposed to withering government artillery firepower. Many died then and there. When the order came to charge, the Highlanders attacked into the teeth of musket fire and cannon grapeshot. When in one place some of them broke through a forward line of redcoat bayonets, they were shot down by a second wave of soldiers. At last the survivors among them turned and fled.

Within two hours, while losing just 300 men, government forces killed 1,500 Highlanders. As Bonnie Prince Charlie took to his heels and fled to the Hebrides—eventually escaping, after five months, aboard a French frigate—the Duke of Cumberland launched a season of atrocities that would earn him the nickname "Butcher Cumberland."

Painter David Morier called this painting of the 1746 Battle of Culloden *An Incident in the Rebellion of 1745*. His patron was the Duke of Cumberland. For Highlanders, Culloden was a catastrophe that left them culturally vulnerable.

This 1746 print, entitled *The Highland Chace or the Pursuit of the Rebels*, celebrates the Duke of Cumberland's "glorious victory" at Culloden. Highlanders took a different view and called the English soldier "Butcher Cumberland."

On the field, Cumberland ordered his men to hunt down and slaughter any wounded Highlanders. Calvary men rode down fleeing rebels and cut their throats. The day after the battle, soldiers searched the moor, bayoneting any rebels they found alive. Cumberland himself, riding over the field with several of his officers, came upon a wounded Highlander leaning on his elbow. He asked the man, clearly an officer, to whom he belonged. Charles Fraser of Inverallochy, a lieutenant colonel to the Master of Lovat, responded, "to the Prince."

Cumberland turned to the nearest officer, who chanced to be Major James Wolfe, and ordered him to shoot "that insolent scoundrel." Wolfe, who would die in 1759 after leading a British army in taking Quebec City, flatly refused, declaring that he could never consent to become an executioner. Incensed, Cumberland tried several other officers with the same result. Finally, he ordered a private to shoot Fraser in cold blood and the man complied.

The following day, wounded men found in nearby houses were brought to the field and shot dead. Some of the wounded had crawled into a hut for sheltering sheep or goats. Government soldiers barred the door and then set fire to the hut, so burning to death between thirty and forty people, among them some beggars who had taken no part in any fighting. Robert Chambers, who compiled a book of Jacobite memoirs in 1834, wrote that after the battle, government soldiers slaughtered seventy wounded men on day one and seventy-two on day two, when they also burned to death thirty-two in the hut.

Unsupervised troops committed worse atrocities. At Inshes, just southeast of Inverness, a Mrs. Robertson returned home from that city after burying her husband, laird of the estate, who had died before the battle began. Horrified by the piles of bodies along the road, she was further shocked to find sixteen dead men at her front door. She called her servants to bury the bodies, and they were digging graves when some soldiers arrived.

In *Culloden*, John Prebble describes how these men hauled Mrs. Robertson to the back of the house to show her a rare sight. They uncovered two bodies from beneath a curtain and forced the woman up close to them. Laughing, they described how they had dragged the two wounded men outside, lit a fire "to their hinder-end," and roasted and smoked them to death. They had then taken the curtain from one of her rooms and covered the men "to keep us from seeing the nauseous sight."

So began the "pacification" of the Highlands and Islands, as the Duke of Cumberland encouraged the army in months of rape, pillage and mayhem. Soldiers killed any suspected rebels, burned "rebellious" settlements and confiscated livestock. They hanged more than a hundred Jacobites and jailed hundreds of people, including many women, aboard death-trap ships that sat offshore for months. Cumberland, bent on destroying the Highland economy, orchestrated the driving of vast herds of cattle, oxen, horses and sheep southward for auction to Lowland and English dealers. He distributed profits among his soldiers to maintain their enthusiasm.

The atrocities continued—"things shocking to human nature," as one minister wrote later—among them the torture of an old woman, blind in one eye, and the "spitting" of a baby on a hanger. On the small island of Raasay, between Skye and the mainland, a Cumberland-organized militia slaughtered 280 cows, 700 sheep and 20 horses. They destroyed 32 boats and burned 300 houses to the ground.

One of the worst marauders was John Fergusson, the Aberdeen-born captain of HMS *Furnace*, who had taken to cruising off the Hebrides, a mad dog committing mayhem while searching for the Bonnie Prince. Fergusson captured an old boatman said to have ferried the prince and flogged him until "blood gushed out at both his sides." He also captured the Irish Jacobite captain Felix O'Neil, who had assisted the Young Pretender. Fergusson "used me with all the barbarity of a pirate," O'Neil wrote later, "stripped me, and ordered me to be put into a rack and whipped by his hangman, because I would not confess where I thought the Prince was."

But now came one of a few honourable interventions. A Lieutenant McCaghan, commander of a detachment of Royal Scots Fusiliers on the *Furnace*, had seen enough. With a gentleman officer about to be whipped, he drew his sword and, as Prebble relates, told his men to present their muskets: "He dared Fergusson to continue with the flogging"—and this time, surprisingly, the mad dog backed down.

In the months after the Battle of Culloden, the British took almost 3,500 prisoners. With Cumberland advocating the transportation of entire clans, the government sent more than 930 people to North America, 866 under indenture to merchants and plantation owners.

Other Highlanders languished in the dank, filthy holds of prison ships. By September 1747, three months after convoys brought 564 prisoners to the River Thames, 157 of them had died. And worse acts were to follow—less dramatic but more consequential.

One year after Culloden, the British government passed two diabolical acts of legislation. The first was the Act of Proscription, which built on an earlier "Disarming Act" and prescribed penalties for carrying arms (even a dirk or short knife) and for wearing "the Highland Dress," which included the belted plaid, tartan and kilt. Schooling was to be conducted entirely in English, not Gaelic. Offenders would be punished with fines, with jail until payment, and with conscription into the army for late payment. Repeat offenders could become indentured servants, "liable to be transported to any of his Majesty's plantations beyond the seas, there to remain for the space of seven years."

The Hanoverian government was bent on eradicating Scottish Highland culture. The second piece of legislation was the Abolition of Heritable Jurisdictions Act, which was expressly designed to undermine and destroy the clan system. It ended the judicial and military authority of Highland chieftains. For seven hundred years, they had maintained hereditary power over their clansmen—the authority to adjudicate a dispute or an allegation of wrongdoing—while holding and administering estates on behalf of the clan. But now the government and not the chieftains would appoint sheriffs.

Highland Soldiers by Francis Grose, 1801. In the decades following the Battle of Culloden, incredibly, Highland regiments began to flourish.

Many chiefs had been killed at or shortly after the Battle of Culloden. Now, those who refused to accept English jurisdiction would lose their lands to the government, which created a Forfeited Estates Commission and took control of great swaths of land formerly held by those who, at Culloden, had supported the Jacobite cause. Those lands became recognizable, according to one critic, by "the bad condition they were in compared to other men's estates, and for the almost total neglect of their cultivation."

Some chieftains, stripped of prestige and authority, considered themselves absolved of responsibility for their clansmen. They moved to Edinburgh, London, Paris. They became absentee land-lords with no sense of duty or responsibility to anyone but them-selves. As for the common people, whose ancestors had brought language, religion and Brehon laws from Ireland, they believed still that collectively, they owned the lands on which they worked. More than that, they held to the notion of *dùthchas*—the idea that their clan leaders had a responsibility to guarantee their possession of the land in exchange for their long history of military service. They would discover to their shock and sorrow that this was no longer the case.

5

Highland Regiments

DURING THE HALF CENTURY THAT FOLLOWED CULLODEN, Highland chieftains raised twenty-two regiments to fight for the British crown. That they created any at all today seems astonishing. On the battlefield, Butcher Cumberland had ordered his soldiers to give no quarter and his men had obeyed. Wounded Highlanders? Government troops shot or bayoneted them where they lay. They burned others alive in fire pits. They took 3,470 prisoners to Inverness—men, women and children—and crammed most of them into creaky transport ships.

The victors sent 936 men to America to be sold onto cotton plantations. They banished another 222 and eventually released 1,287, while the rest either died or somehow escaped accounting. The Butcher sent 268 Highlanders to Tilbury Fort near London, a thousand kilometres to the south. They arrived on August 11, 1746, and stayed on the transport ships or prison hulks moored in the river. Conditions were such that within one month, 45 had died of typhus or some other disease.

Those who survived were selected for trial by lottery, one out of every twenty. They picked pieces of paper out of a beaver hat.

One hundred and twenty men were publicly executed on Tower Hill. Four of them, peers of the realm, were beheaded—the last being eighty-year-old Simon Fraser, Lord Lovat. The other 116 were hanged, drawn and quartered. During this period, a ferry from London ran sailings around the prison hulks, providing sightseers with handkerchiefs against the stench. Later, people could pay to view the prisoners in Tilbury Fort. The last of the unfortunates was released early in 1750.

Having banned the wearing of kilts and Highland dress and driven a wedge between the chieftains and their clans, the London government sought deliberately to "obliterate the Celtic mode of life." True, Lowlanders were also driven from their lands—but they escaped the brutality, the press gangs and the swinging truncheons that engulfed the Highlanders. Many of the chieftains, reduced in power and prestige, turned their backs on their clansmen and sold their estates to buy mansions in Glasgow and Edinburgh.

Out of this darkness, incredibly, arose the Highland regiments. The Black Watch had come into being in 1739—seven years before Culloden. English officers ruled that regiment, under orders to "watch" or police the volatile Highlands. The Black Watch had fought under Cumberland in France, impressing him at the 1745 Battle of Fontenoy in the War of the Austrian Succession. He ordered up another regiment later that year, Loudoun's Highlanders, but the Jacobite MacIntoshes routed them at Moy early in 1746 during the run-up to Culloden.

In 1754, the imperial struggle between France and Britain expanded into the French and Indian Wars of North America. The British government needed troops. Prime Minister William Pitt made the call. Lieutenant Colonel James Wolfe, having

experienced the ferocity of a Highland charge at Culloden, supported
Pitt, arguing that Highlanders would make excellent irregulars in
North America. "I should imagine that two or three independent
Highland companies might be of use," he wrote. In a phrase that
Canadian novelist Alistair MacLeod later made famous, Wolfe
added: "They are hardy, intrepid, accustomed to a rough country,
and no great mischief if they fall."

The British army went recruiting, usually offering land grants
in exchange for soldiers and lucrative commissions to chiefs and
landlords who could produce them. The army also presented a
singular opportunity. While serving with the British forces, Highlanders could wear kilts. Between 1757 and 1763, the army raised
and disbanded ten Highland regiments, among them the Fraser
Highlanders, Montgomery's Highlanders and the Royal Highland
Volunteers. Those regiments went to the front lines of every British
foreign war. By 1766, the Highland regiments had proven themselves to be among the best in Britain.

But why, after Culloden and the atrocities that followed, why
did so many Highlanders undertake to serve in the British army?
First, the Highland chieftains who might have opposed their signing on were either dead or in exile. Those who remained wanted no
part of any rebellion. Second, many Gaelic Highlanders were farmers in fact but warriors at heart. In the army they could sport their
kilts, carry their weapons and follow the bagpipes as their ancestors
had done for centuries.

The officers of the new regiments often came from their own
clans. These were their own tacksmen offering Highlanders a
chance to do as they had always done—to gain honour on the
battlefield. Finally, and perhaps most importantly, those who
enlisted would be fed and clothed. They would be able to send

money home to support their wives and children, and perhaps ultimately to create a better life for themselves and their families.

The creation of these regiments would have implications for Highlanders who, during the Clearances, emigrated to Canada. The retired soldiers got there before them. Those driven out of Scotland could often be sure of finding family and friends on the other side, clan members who had already established themselves in Britain's northern colonies.

The Clearances occurred most intensively over two main periods, a long one that ran from the 1780s to 1820 and a shorter one that lasted from 1842 to 1854. The great irony is that, during these periods, Highland regiments were distinguishing themselves in such places as the Crimea and India. They had begun this process during the Seven Years' War, which ended in 1763, and continued it through the American Revolutionary War, which ran until 1783.

Highland Brigade Camp Looking South, again by Francis Grose, 1801. Retired soldiers were among the first Highlanders to settle in Canada.

The Highland regiments did not come into their own without incident. Two examples will serve. In April 1779, with the Revolutionary War well begun, two detachments of Gaelic Highlanders belonging to the 42nd and 71st regiments were sent from Stirling Castle to Leith, the port at Edinburgh, to join their regiments in North America. At Leith, troops were told they would instead join the 80th and 82nd—two English-speaking regiments. The men refused, flatly declaring that they would serve only in their original corps.

Troops arrived at Leith to discipline the Highlanders by bringing them to Edinburgh Castle as prisoners. A fight ensued. The mutineers killed one captain and thirty-one soldiers before they were overpowered and carted off to Edinburgh. Three prisoners— two from the 42nd and one from the 71st—were brought before a court martial. They were charged with "having been guilty of a mutiny at Leith . . . and of having instigated others to be guilty of the same, in which mutiny several of his Majesty's subjects were killed and many wounded."

The three offered essentially the same defence. They had enlisted as soldiers in old Highland regiments wearing the Highland dress. Their only language was Gaelic and they neither spoke nor understood English. They had always worn the Highland dress and found wearing breeches so inconvenient as to be impossible. As a result, they could serve only in a Highland regiment. The three added that when they arrived at Leith, an officer informed them that they were now to join regiments that wore the Lowland dress, and under an officer who spoke only English.

No order from the commander-in-chief was read or explained to them, but an officer insisted that they must immediately join the Hamilton and Edinburgh regiments. A great number of the detachment protested, without any disorder or mutinous behaviour, that they were altogether unfit for service in any other corps than Highland ones, noting that they were incapable of wearing breeches as a part of their dress. At the same time, they declared their willingness to be regularly transferred to any other Highland regiment, or to continue to serve in those regiments into which they had been regularly enlisted. Nobody listened to their objections. The sergeant charged with explaining matters in Gaelic insisted again that they should board the ships immediately. They refused. The fighting commenced with disastrous results.

The court martial found the three prisoners guilty and sentenced them to be shot. But now came a surprise. Acting for His Majesty, the court gave them a free pardon, confident that they would atone for their atrocious offence. The three men and their fellows joined the Gaelic-speaking 42nd Regiment, where they later elicited praise for steadiness and good conduct.

The second incident arose in that same year, 1779. It involved the 76th Regiment, raised by one Alexander MacDonald, the 9th Baronet of Sleat. Having attended Eton and married an Englishwoman, this MacDonald lived mainly in London and Edinburgh. In 1773, he had failed to impress Samuel Johnson. On meeting the man while rambling the Highlands with James Boswell, Johnson observed: "He has no more the soul of a chief than an attorney who has twenty houses in a street and considers how much he can make by them."

Through 1778, the baronet raised a regiment of 750 Highlanders. He added Lowlanders and Irishmen to make the total 1,000. At Fort George, the "great drill square" or training area for Highland regiments, the men complained about overdue payment of salaries. Even so, early in March they made their way south towards

Leith through the mountains around Aviemore. They met Mac-Donald at Perth, but they marched while he went ahead by ferry.

The regiment continued through Fife to Burntisland near Leith. Not long before, the Seaforth Highlanders had revolted after hearing a rumour that they were to be sold into the use of the East India Company. A similar rumour now swept the 76th. The men protested to their officers. At morning parade, when they received no assurances, the regiment turned and, ignoring all pleas and threats, marched to the top of a nearby hill.

The men remained disciplined. They set up camp and appointed sentries. But they would not embark for Leith. They sent armed parties into the town for supplies, and paid cash for all they bought. The stand-off lasted for three days.

The officers summoned MacDonald from Edinburgh. He had to climb the hill and listen to the men's petitions. He paid the men what he owed them and quashed the false rumour about the East India Company. Their sense of honour satisfied, the Highlanders broke camp next morning and marched back down to Burntisland, where they boarded boats to Leith. A newspaper reporter wrote that "the behaviour, sobriety and good conduct of the regiment since they were raised reflects the highest honor on the . . . men." This exemplary mutiny was never reported. Nobody was punished. And the 76th Regiment sailed across the Atlantic to fight the American rebels.

Even after the Revolutionary War, the British government continued to raise regiments in the Highlands. The Reverend Donald Sage remembered the raising of the 93rd Highlanders or Sutherland Regiment, which began in 1799 when he was ten. In May 1800, two army officers came to Kildonan to enlist young men. To ingratiate himself with the community, the senior man, Major-

General William Wemyss, sent ahead to the manse of Kildonan "immense quantities of tobacco-twist and strong, black rapee snuff, together with the very suitable accompaniment of a large snuff-horn superfly mounted with silver, and having attached to it by a massive silver chain a snuff-pen of the same costly material."

The gentleman officer had put himself to unnecessary expense, Sage tells us: "Smoking was a luxury then utterly unknown and quite unappreciated by the men of Kildonan. What became of the General's supply I know not; but none of it was used, the old men contenting themselves with the light-coloured snuff which their fathers had used before them."

Those interested in joining the army assembled on the green to the west of the manse, most of them "tall handsome young fellows" who at a verbal summons presented themselves before General Wemyss, "that he might have for the asking the pick and choice of them." While the young men seemed keen enough, their parents had to be induced to part with their sons. The general promised two things—"first, that the father should have the leases of their farms, and next, that the sons, if they enlisted, should all be made sergeants. The first promise was to a certain extent fulfilled; the second, it is needless to say, could not possibly be fulfilled."

And so away they went, the young Highlanders, to wage war on behalf of the government that had slaughtered their ancestors. They themselves might survive. But as the Englishman James Wolfe wrote, "no great mischief if they fall."

PART TWO

———

OMENS
OF
RESISTANCE

6

—

Ship of the People

W E WERE VOYAGING SIXTY-SIX KILOMETRES WEST OF
Scotland's Outer Hebrides in the most remote part of the
British Isles. Winds here often reach gale force and only
twenty percent of ships that approach Hirta, the main island in
the archipelago of St. Kilda, ever manage to land a soul. We were
safe with Adventure Canada aboard the *Ocean Endeavour*, a two-
hundred-passenger expeditionary ship, but the day had dawned
grey, windy, and unpromising. Our hopes sank. But as morning
wore on, the winds died down and the sun came out. Did we dare
to dream? Early in the afternoon, thrilled with our good luck, we
piled into Zodiacs and zoomed ashore.

St. Kilda has dual World Heritage status for both natural and
cultural significance. Bronze Age travellers visited 4,000 to 5,000
years ago, and Vikings landed here in the 800s. Written history
reveals that a scattering of people (around 180 in 1700) rented land
here from the Macleods of Dunvegan, based on the Isle of Skye.
The people of St. Kilda lived on Hirta in a settlement (Village
Bay) of stone-built, dome-shaped houses, or "cleits," with thatched
roofs. Here, they developed a unique way of life, subsisting mostly
on seabirds.

Even today, most ships have trouble transporting people ashore on Hirta, the main island in the archipelago of St. Kilda. We managed to land using Zodiacs. But in the eighteenth century, getting here in open longboats meant taking your life in your own hands.

This was the period when, according to a 1697 visitor named Martin Martin, "the only means of making the journey [to St. Kilda] was by open longboat, which could take several days and nights of rowing and sailing across the open ocean and was next to impossible in autumn and winter. In all seasons, waves up to twelve metres high lash the beach of Village Bay, and even on calmer days landing on the slippery rocks can be hazardous. Cut off by distance and weather, the natives knew little of the rest of the world."

In the nineteenth century, as improved ships allowed for more frequent contact, St. Kildans became increasingly dissatisfied with their hard life. And in 1930, after a century of emigration, the last thirty-six St. Kildans evacuated to the Scottish mainland. That is another story. During our visit in June 2018, with the help of a scientist posted here to do an environmental study, I located the beehive cleit marking the spot where, for more than five years in the 1730s, Lady Grange had endured as "the prisoner of St. Kilda." This stone-built cleit, erected on the foundations of the original, reminded me that even before Culloden, clan chieftains were not always paragons of virtue and protectors of their people.

This beehive cleit is built on the foundations of the original. In the 1730s, Lady Grange lived here for over five years as "the prisoner of St. Kilda."

Two men sprang to mind: Alexander MacDonald, the 7th baronet of Sleat, and Norman MacLeod of Dunvegan, known even to his clansmen as "The Wicked Man." Both were involved in the imprisonment of Lady Grange and, even worse, in the mass kidnapping that came to be called the Ship of the People.

First, Lady Grange. Born Rachel Chiesley, she had married John Erskine, Lord Grange, around 1707 when she was twenty-eight. Described as a "wild beauty," she was headstrong and articulate. Over the next two decades, she gave birth to nine children. She and her lawyer-husband divided their time between a townhouse in Edinburgh and an estate at Preston, east of the city, where for years she ran the place as factor or manager.

After more than two decades of marriage, Lord Grange took a mistress and refused to give her up. The married couple separated acrimoniously. While rooting among the papers of her estranged husband, Lady Grange found letters implicating him in a Jacobite plot to overthrow the Hanoverian government—this during the long run-up to the Forty-Five. She threatened to blow the whistle. That would mean exposing not just Grange but some powerful fellow conspirators, among them MacDonald of Sleat and MacLeod of Dunvegan.

In 1732, after consulting those allies, Lord Grange had his irrepressible wife violently kidnapped and bundled off, ultimately to the inaccessible archipelago of St. Kilda. Here, Lady Grange endured in misery as the only literate, English-speaking mainlander except for the minister and his wife. She did a lot of drinking. Eventually, thanks probably to the minister, she managed to smuggle out two letters. But by 1740, when a would-be rescuer arrived, she had been removed and imprisoned elsewhere. She died in the northern reaches of Skye, still a prisoner, in 1745.

Meanwhile, in 1739, Alexander MacDonald and Norman Mac-Leod had masterminded a still worse offence, this one against their own people. For years they had complained of losing sheep and cattle to thieves. MacLeod, The Wicked Man, had a twenty-four-year-old nephew also named Norman. He lived on Berneray, a tiny island situated between North Uist and Harris. Late one October night, acting on orders, young MacLeod organized a mass kidnapping on Harris and Skye. In the dead of night, he led a gang of five in invading blackhouses and seizing ninety-six men, women and children—twenty of whom were between the ages of six and ten. He and his thugs bundled these innocent farmers onto a ship called the *William*, bound for the American colonies. There, the prisoners were to be sold as indentured servants to work on the cotton plantations.

The weather intervened. A storm drove the ship onto the rocks thirty kilometres east of Belfast, near Donaghadee in Ulster. Rescuers took the victims to local authorities and the dark plot came to light. On Skye, MacDonald of Sleat denied any role in the enterprise. But according to a 2016 report in the *Scotsman*, young Norman MacLeod insisted that he had the consent of all the lairds on Skye to remove "as many men, women and children as he could provide shipping for and carry them to America" or wherever else he pleased.

With a warrant issued for his arrest, MacLeod escaped and fled to the Netherlands. About forty of the kidnapped Scottish Islanders settled near Donaghadee, while a few journeyed back to Skye. The *William*, standing in for the whole episode, became known as Soitheach na Daoine, or the Ship of the People. Sir Alexander went to his grave denying any involvement, though in one letter, held at the Clan Donald archive on Skye, he wrote: "I never was so angry at myself as about this matter and I must regret my folly as long as I have my sences [*sic*]."

While both Alexander MacDonald and Norman MacLeod had conspired with Grange to overthrow the Hanoverians, neither chieftain sent forces to join the Jacobites that made a stand at Culloden. The first told his kinsman MacDonald of Clanranald, who did send men to fight, that the uprising was inopportune and had little chance of success. In the end, grateful that the Hanoverians had restored his estates after the forfeiture of 1715, he sent two companies of Highland clansmen to fight alongside the government troops.

MacDonald of Sleat and "Wicked Man" MacLeod of Dunvegan were outliers among their peers. The Ship of the People remained an isolated incident for more than two decades. Even after Culloden, the Highland way of life persisted, with people farming collectively and chieftains arbitrating any disputes. But after Culloden, the British government's fiendishly clever Abolition of Heritable Jurisdictions Act of 1747 began functioning to separate the chiefs from their clansmen.

Under these new English laws, the chieftains now owned the estates that had previously been regarded as collective property held in trust. First the chieftains themselves, and then the tacksmen, came to understand the implications of the shift. The farmers who worked the land, most of them, would never grasp—and when they did, would certainly never accept—that they no longer shared ownership of the lands on which their ancestors had toiled for generations.

Meanwhile, during visits to Glasgow, Edinburgh and London, chieftains learned from Lowlanders that they could make their estates far more profitable by devoting them not to tenant farmers but to sheep. If they found turning their kinsmen out of their homes unpalatable, all they had to do was sell their estates to Lowlanders and let them do the dirty work.

Consider the example of John Lockhart, a Royal Navy captain who in 1761 inherited the Ross-shire estate of Balnagowan, some forty-five kilometres north of Inverness. Born southeast of Glasgow in 1721, the son of a baronet, Lockhart was entailed to take the name Ross and so became John Lockhart-Ross. He married, withdrew from active service in the navy (at least temporarily), and set about improving his holdings by planting new crops and draining marshy land.

John Lockhart-Ross (1721–1790) by James Stanier Clarke. Lockhart-Ross showed the way forward for landlords bent on increasing profits.

From Balnagowan Castle he controlled the estate. He refused to renew the leases of absentee landlords and instead built new fences and raised the rents of his subtenants. Even more significantly, he leased extensive lands to the efficient Thomas Geddes, who became the first Lowland sheep-farmer to work on a large scale north of Inverness. Geddes introduced a new breed of sheep to the Highlands.

Farmers from the Scottish Borders had cross-bred their delicate "long hill" sheep with Merino, Lincolnshire and Spanish animals to develop a tough new Cheviot sheep. These "Great Sheep" not only produced more wool and meat but were hardy enough to withstand the rugged Highland winters. The British Wool Society sold them by the flock and urged landlords "to drive away all the present inhabitants"—all those inconvenient farmers. With a shepherd and a few dogs, they could "cover the mountains with flocks of wild, coarse-wooled, and savage animals" that needed only wide-open spaces covered with grass.

In 1760, sheep farmers had begun leasing grassy hills as far north as Perth, some 175 kilometres south of Inverness. Now, encouraged by the "improver" Lockhart-Ross, Thomas Geddes began bringing 200,000 sheep a year into the Highlands. He was reaping enormous profits and other landlords took notice. With the price of wool rising steadily, Highland landowners and chieftains realized they could get rich quick by evicting tenant farmers and devoting their holdings to Cheviot sheep.

They began "rack-renting," raising rents far beyond viability to drive their impoverished clansmen off the grassy glens of their forefathers and onto the rocky Scottish coast. They told their tenants to survive by fishing and gathering kelp. Initially, although reluctant to move, those who went, went peacefully. Some of them tried to eke out a living along Scotland's rocky coast. But these farmers weren't fishermen, and harvesting kelp is cold, wet, difficult, dangerous and far from lucrative, at least for the men wading in the water. Some of the "cleared tenants" journeyed south to Edinburgh, Glasgow or even London, hoping to land government-sponsored jobs building roads, bridges and later canals.

Others had no such hope. In 1824, a wealthy Edinburgh woman named Christina Stewart bought lands from the Duke of Argyll encompassing four townships in Morvern, directly north of the Isle of Mull. To create two large sheep farms, she set about clearing the 135 people who lived in those settlements, one of which—Inniemore or Unnimore—is now open to the public as Aoineadh Mor Historic Township. Among those cleared was the Gaelic-speaking Mary Cameron, who later recalled that when people "got the 'summons to quit,' we thought it was only for getting an increase of rent, and this we willingly offered to give; but permission to stay we got not."

As relayed in *Reminiscences of a Highland Parish* by Norman Macleod, Cameron was driven to sell her small sheep and then her one cow. "When shall I forget the plaintive wailing of the children deprived of the milk which was no more for them? When shall I forget the last sight I got of my pretty cluster of goats bleating on the lip of the rock, as if inviting me to milk them? But it was not allowed me to put a pail under them."

On the day of "flitting," as Mary Cameron called it, officers arrived and ordered her family to leave immediately. "The hissing of the fire on the flag of the hearth as they were drowning it reached my heart." Cameron's husband carried his aged mother on his back in a creel. Mary Cameron hugged a baby, and two little toddlers stumbled along as best they could. Neighbours brought their few sticks of furniture. "On the day of our leaving Unnimore, I thought my heart would rend. I would feel right if my tears would flow, but no relief thus did it find." She sat for a while on a hill "to take a last look at the place where we had been brought up. The houses were being already stripped." The Camerons made their way south to Glasgow and, with the help of their minister, found work in a cotton mill.

But many other Highlanders, having weighed their options, took to the emigrant ships. In the early 1770s, three vessels sailed from the Hebrides, bringing farmers to Prince Edward Island. But the best-known early voyage, and to it we shall return, was that of the decrepit old *Hector* in 1773.

7

Year of the Sheep

IN EDINBURGH WE STAYED FOR A WEEK, SHEENA AND I, in what remains of James Boswell's house, most of which was destroyed in a nineteenth-century fire. Located just off the Royal Mile, today's ground-floor studio apartment, called "the Castle Snug," has been completely refurbished. Yet it does contain several architectural features that evoke the eighteenth-century gentleman who resided here, among them exposed stone walls, a "shot window" and "three oval fanlights."

The Snug has one distinction: it was from here in 1773—the same year the *Hector* sailed from Ullapool—that Boswell and Dr. Samuel Johnson, England's foremost man of letters, left Edinburgh to ramble around the Highlands and Islands. The two travelled north along Scotland's east coast through St. Andrews and Aberdeen, and then swung west through Inverness before making their way onto the islands of Skye, Coll and Mull. Here and there, we crossed the paths of the two illustrious travellers. But in my mind's eye, they were always with us.

The conservative Johnson, an unlikely champion of Gaelic Highlanders, lamented that ancient traditions were being eradicated and complained that clan chieftains were acting not like guardians and protectors but rather like wealthy proprietors everywhere. As a result, he wrote, they "have already lost much of their influence; and as they gradually degenerate from patriarchal rulers to rapacious landlords, they will divest themselves of the little that remains." Johnson deplored the "epidemical fury of emigration."

James Boswell, engraving by Samuel Freeman. In 1773, Boswell toured the Highlands and Islands with Dr. Samuel Johnson. In his journal, Boswell wrote of witnessing "a dance called America" that celebrated Highland emigration.

The equally saddened Boswell, heir to a Lowland estate, offered an anecdote that would give contemporary historian James Hunter a title for his classic work, *A Dance Called America*. Boswell described how one evening, during their visit to Skye, "the company danced as usual. We performed, with much activity, a dance which, I suppose, the emigration from Skye has occasioned. They call it *America.* Each of the couples, after the common involutions and evolutions, successively whirls round in a circle, till all are in motion; and the dance seems intended to show how emigration catches, till a whole neighborhood is set afloat."

While Boswell and Johnson were travelling, enterprising businessmen circulated advertisements recruiting ever more passengers for Nova Scotia and Canada. One such ad spoke of a "substantial coppered Fast Sailing Ship," while another advocated sailing aboard "The Fine Brigantine *Good Intent.*" Such notices said nary a word about dysentery, smallpox, cholera or typhus, at least one of which invariably broke out during the weeks-long voyage. And the rack-rented Highlanders, discovering no better alternatives, kept signing on.

A few years after Boswell and Johnson visited the Highlands, a London bookseller named John Knox did the same. He reported that between 1763 and 1775, twenty thousand people sailed for the colonies. In one year alone, fifty-four emigrant ships departed from Scotland's western shores. Those who left during this early phase, twenty, thirty, forty at a time, often led by an educated tacksman— those were the lucky ones.

The more dramatic Clearances began in 1785, when the wife of Duncan Macdonell of Glengarry, known as "light-headed Marjorie," evicted more than five hundred tenants to make room for a sheep walk. Glengarry, one of the largest estates in the Highlands, stretched from the Great Glen that runs between Fort William and Inverness, westward to the rugged coast of Knoydart, which faces out towards the Isle of Skye.

Soon after Culloden, tacksmen began taking Glengarry subtenants to British North America, sailing with them from Fort

William. In 1782, Marjorie Macdonell leased a sheep walk on Loch Quoich, in the heart of Glengarry, to one Thomas Gillespie. She extended this lease on condition that 500 of her clansmen be removed. In 1785, Gillespie crammed 520 of these inconvenient crofters into the hold of a ship called the *McDonald*. It sailed for Glengarry in Upper Canada, where Macdonell Loyalists had settled after escaping the American Revolution.

Backed by her teenage son, Alastair Ranaldson Macdonell, Marjorie rid herself of still more tenants over the next few years. In 1788, when at last her husband died, young Alastair inherited the estates and increased the pace of evictions. As Charles MacKinnon writes in *Scottish Highlanders*, Alastair loved to play the Highland chief, and "inspired Sir Walter Scott with some of his least accurate ideas on Highlanders." Alastair "strutted proudly in full Highland dress, wearing broadsword, dirk and pistols, and was followed by his 'tail' of henchmen, bard, piper and bodyguard." To maintain his increasingly lavish lifestyle, he evicted more tenants and turned ever more lands over to sheep.

In *Waverley*, Walter Scott romanticized this Macdonell as the swashbuckling Fergus MacIvor, and Henry Raeburn painted an enduring portrait of the Highland peacock. The poet Robert Burns saw through the man, however, and lampooned him in his "Address of Beelzebub." Written in the voice of "the prince of devils," the ironic poem praises Macdonell for keeping the "Highland boors" in subjugation and urges him to act ever more harshly and to break their spirits.

Having evicted his hard-pressed clansmen from their lands, Macdonell went ballistic when he learned that, rather than increase his coffers by clinging to rocks and mining kelp, they were emigrating to North America. To retard their progress, he sought to prevent the construction of the Caledonian Canal. Designed to link three lakes in the Great Glen, the canal provided desperately needed employment and enabled people to sail between Inverness and Fort William—and onwards if they chose.

Colonel Alastair Ranaldson Macdonell of Glengarry by Sir Henry Raeburn. This greedy Macdonell managed to empty his estate of his clansmen.

Alastair Macdonell stole timber and bricks from construction sites. When caught and accused, he insisted that no Highland gentleman would make a fuss over a few bits of brick and wood that happened to be lying around. Having survived one court case after another, he died deeply in debt in 1828. By the mid-1800s, thanks mainly to the greed and selfishness of this one man, more than twenty thousand Macdonells were residing in Upper Canada and almost none in the lands of their forebears.

In these early days of the Clearances, and even through the depredations of "light-headed Marjorie" and her son, evicted tenants might grouse and grumble, but they tended to obey their chieftains and landlords. That began to change in 1792, which came to be known as Bliadhna nan Caorach, or the Year of the Sheep. Sir John Sinclair of Ulbster had bought land from the Earl of Caithness and brought the Great Sheep to northeastern Scotland. At Langwell, farther north than Balnagowan Castle, he demonstrated that these hardy creatures could thrive through the harshest of winters. And while he himself was a decent, fair-minded man, concerned with the welfare of the people, most of those who emulated him did not share his humane attitudes.

In the eastern part of the county of Ross, or Easter Ross, Sir Hector Munro evicted his last six tenants from his once-populous estate at Kildermorie and leased the land to Captain Allan and Alexander Cameron, brothers from Lochaber. The story is detailed in the *Transactions of the Gaelic Society of Inverness*. The brothers imported sheep to the area, fifty kilometres north of Inverness, and told local farmers to take their cows elsewhere.

Accustomed to allowing their cattle to roam freely, the locals paid no heed. The Camerons took to impounding, or "poinding," straying cows and refusing to release them until their owners paid a fine. In May 1792, this having happened several times, the farmers of Strathrusdale sent word to Ardross, five kilometres down the valley, calling for assistance.

The Ardross men, out cutting peat for fuel, downed tools and, led by Alexander Wallace, or "Big Wallace," answered the summons. At Kildermorie, the Camerons were out in force, though still outnumbered. One of them, Captain Allan Cameron, carried a loaded gun and a foot-long dirk. Big Wallace wrested these from him. The locals then made off with their own cattle.

The Camerons resorted to the courts, charging eight men with "riot, assault and battery" while forcibly relieving cattle from a poind-fold, and with "assaulting and beating the gentleman and his servants who had poinded the cattle." In September, the jury found the alleged assailants not guilty.

Meanwhile, more dramatic events had captured public attention. The *Transactions of the Gaelic Society* offers several conflicting accounts. The truth runs roughly as follows. On Friday, July 27, at a wedding in Strathrusdale, two men—Hugh Breck Mackenzie and John Aird—excited celebrants with the idea of rounding up all the sheep in the northern counties and driving them south across the River Beauly to near Inverness, and there setting them free to wander. They could communicate with everyone on Sunday, they said, by making announcements at parish churches.

Once the sheep were driven off, the instigators suggested, evicted tenants would be able to return to their homes and resume their old lives. This fanciful naivety caught the public imagination. On Sunday, calls went out at parish churches throughout Ross and Sutherland, and at sundry public houses. The following Tuesday, a couple of hundred people turned up at the designated location (Strath Oykel) and began rounding up sheep and driving them south. They hurt none of the animals and killed none—even though the herders began to grow hungry.

On Saturday evening, with six thousand sheep, the men reached Boath, at the east end of Kildermorie. Next morning, they were sending a party to retrieve the Cameron flocks when they got word that Sheriff Donald Macleod of Geanies was approaching to intercept them. He had gathered two dozen landowners in Dingwall, and with their support and that of British Home Secretary Henry Dundas, had summoned a regiment of Black Watch troops from Fort George, forty kilometres away. Almost all the rebellious sheepherders faded into the countryside.

The soldiers captured a dozen men. On September 14, the

sheriff brought the alleged ringleaders to trial in Inverness. He drew up an indictment charging that they had sought "to excite and instigate a number of persons to assemble and convocate . . . for the purpose of violently seizing and driving away the flocks of sheep belonging to various proprietors." These ringleaders had warned that "the curse of the children not yet born and their generations would [be on] such as would not cheerfully go and banish the sheep out of the country." Having convened "a number of persons armed with guns, bludgeons, and other offensive weapons for whatever purpose," they were guilty of "crimes of an heinous nature of a seditious and alarming tendency, subversive of law, order, and good government, and severely punishable."

Accounts differ as to the verdicts. According to *The Scots Magazine* of September 1792, probably the most reliable source, one charge was dismissed. One man was fined and jailed for a month. Another was jailed for three months. Two men were banished from Scotland for life, and two more—the instigators Hugh Breck Mackenzie and John Aird—were to be transported for seven years "beyond seas to such places as his Majesty shall appoint"—which meant, almost certainly, Botany Bay, Australia.

One observer applauded these sentences, suggesting that they "completely quelled the spirit of rebellion amongst the people in general, who soon discovered that they had been misled by artful and designing men to accomplish their own purposes."

But the sentences were never carried out because all of those who were imprisoned escaped inexplicably from Inverness jail. As another contemporary observed, the verdict and sentences "did not carry along with them the public opinion, which was probably the cause that the escape of the prisoners was in a manner connived at; for they disappeared out of prison no one knew how and were never inquired after or molested."

Later, stories emerged of how a jail door had been left open by the keeper while he was occupied in another part of the building. The government did offer a reward for the apprehension of Mackenzie and Aird, "upon their being secured in any legal jail in Scotland." But the two men had vanished into thin air.

The landowners returned their sheep to their respective pens. Lord Adam Gordon, commander-in-chief of the Scottish army, insisted that the Ross-shire Sheep Riot, as it came to be called, implied "no disloyalty or spirit of rebellion or dislike to His Majesty." But this uprising, largely symbolic and expressive, and certainly not a "riot" in any meaningful sense, was the first time that the Highlanders mounted any organized resistance to the landlords and their Clearances. That was the good news. The bad news, probably more significant, was that the chiefs and the lairds had determined that, when push came to shove, they could count on the support of the law and the military.

8

—

Road to Culrain

HROUGHOUT THE HIGHLANDS, THE MOST ASTUTE
tacksmen began leading a non-military resistance that took
the shape of emigration. In the two decades leading up to 1791,
from western Inverness and Ross alone, sixteen vessels sailed for
the British colonies carrying some 6,400 emigrants. In 1772, the
Catholic tacksman John MacDonald of Glenalladale bought land
on the Island of St. John, later known as Prince Edward Island, and
sailed there with "opprest people" from South Uist, Moidart and
Arisaig. He predicted that "emigrations are like to demolish the
Highland Lairds, and very deservedly."

Emigration slowed in 1776, as people became aware of the
American Revolution. The exodus to North America resumed in
1783, after the war ended—though now more people began opting
for northern rather than southern colonies. During the first three
years of the 1800s, some 10,000 people left the Highlands for Nova
Scotia and Upper Canada. In 1801 alone, from Fort William, eleven
ships sailed with 3,300 emigrants. Some merchants bought land in
Canada and, without seeing it, made a fortune sending people there
from Glengarry and Strathglass.

Showing callous indifference to human suffering, Alastair Macdonell of Glengarry packed so many of his people into emigrant ships that, by the time the Clearances ended, Canada was home to 20,000 Macdonells and the original Glengarry to almost none. For aggressive thoroughness, few could match Macdonell—though the Chisholm family became contenders. In 1801, urged on by his wife of six years, William Chisholm began clearing Strathglass, the broad valley that follows the River Glass south from Beauly, twenty kilometres west of Inverness.

Chisholm had married Elizabeth Macdonell, the daughter of Light-headed Marjorie. Having become Elizabeth Chisholm, she drove this endeavour. In 1801, that first year of Strathglass Clearances, 799 farmers sailed from Fort William for Pictou, Nova Scotia. The next year, 473 departed for Upper Canada and 128 for Pictou, while 550 sailed from Knoydart. In 1803, four ships sailed from Strathglass to Pictou, each carrying 120 people. In one of the vessels that sailed from Fort William, a severe fever took hold, bringing hallucinations, tremors and howling. Fifty-three people died of an epidemic during the voyage, and those who reached Pictou were quarantined in horrific conditions.

One man, Bishop Chisholm, wrote to Elizabeth Chisholm pleading for an end to the evictions: "Oh! Madam, you would really feel if you only heard the pangs and saw the oozing tears by which I am surrounded in this once happy but now devastated valley of Strathglass, looking out all anxiously for a home without forsaking their dear valley; but it will not do, they must emigrate." Mrs. Chisholm justified the expulsion of 5,390 in those first three years by telling herself that she needed the money to educate her son, Alexander, at Cambridge. By 1809, that well-educated individual had completed the job of ridding Strathglass of 10,000 clansmen.

A lonely few remained on lands owned by a far more humane widow named Elizabeth Wilson. The daughter of a Dr. Wilson of Edinburgh, she took pride in maintaining a prosperous tenantry until her death in 1826.

Four years after that, however, with most of his leases expiring, the new Chisholm chief asked to meet his tenants at the Cannich Inn, thirty kilometres south of Beauly. Instead of attending himself, he sent a factor who ordered the people from their lands, which he had already leased to sheep farmers from the south. One of those present, Colin Chisholm, wrote: "I leave you to imagine the bitter grief and disappointment of men who attended with glowing hopes in the morning, but had to tell their families and dependents in the evening that they could see no alternative before them but the emigrant ship, and to choose between the scorching prairies of Australia and the icy regions of North America."

On hearing of these proceedings, Lord Lovat, clan chieftain of the nearby Frasers, bought out one of the large sheep farmers on his property and divided that land to accommodate those evicted from the Chisholm estate. Looking to grow his clan, Fraser offered a boll of meal—about six imperial bushels, or 140 pounds—to any tenant who would take his name. The incomers were happy to do so. By 1878, there would be just one Chisholm tenant left in Strathglass.

But now, early in 1820, young Hugh Munro—the laird of Novar and an aspiring art collector—announced that he intended to clear his estates around Culrain in Easter Ross, thirty kilometres west of Dornoch. He proposed to evict as many as six hundred people from Strath Oykel, including one hundred who were aged or infirm. He meant to lease their lands to a Major Forbes of Melness for a sheep walk. The area was part of the green, fertile valley that, in 1792, had given rise to the Year of the Sheep.

Little more than a decade after that, during the Napoleonic Wars (1803–1815), this area had supplied more than 2,500 fighting men for the 78th Regiment, the Ross-shire Highlanders, also called the Ross-shire Buffs. As part of the 2nd Battalion, those men had fought in the 1806 Battle of Maida, a significant British victory in the toe of Italy. The following year, during the "Fraser Expedition," they were among those who seized and occupied Alexandria for six months.

In Egypt, at Al Hamed near Rosetta, three companies of Ross-shire men were taken prisoner and held in miserable conditions. Others lost their lives in 1809 to illness in the Netherlands, when the Walcheren Campaign brought heavy losses through "Walcheren fever." The men fought again in Belgium at Merksem in 1814 and did not return home until the following year.

Surely the landlord would take all this military service into consideration? Apparently not. Hugh Munro had steadily increased rents and in some cases more than tripled them over a few years. When the stylish young laird announced his intentions, the tenants—who had never fallen into arrears—offered to pay an additional 5 percent, thinking this might change his mind. Major Forbes, however, was offering an increase of more than 200 percent for those lands and Munro would not relent.

On February 2, 1820, his law-agent turned up in the valley carrying writs of removal. These ordered everybody who lived along the River Oykel around Culrain to be ready to leave by Whitsunday, the seventh Sunday after Easter, or May 21. Many of these people had sent their sons to war on behalf of the government and many of those young men had died in southern Italy and Egypt. The soldiers who had returned home, young family men now, were outraged by the proposed seizure of their ancestral lands. Nor was Munro making any offer of resettlement.

When the laird's agent arrived in the area, a hostile crowd sent him packing. He and his witnesses "were maltreated and pillaged of their papers," according to a letter of complaint from Sheriff Donald Macleod of Geanies, published in the *Inverness Courier*. "They were pursued off the bounds of the property," he wrote, "threatened that if they returned their lives would be taken and themselves thrown into the Kyle of Firth." One of the witnesses, he added, "who had run away from the terror, was pursued and struck with stones to the danger of his life."

Landlords from Dingwall to Inverness, fearing that insurrection might spread, backed Hugh Munro in demanding that Sheriff Macleod enforce the law. Macleod, who in 1792 had put down the Ross-shire Sheep Riot, wrote to Lord Advocate Robert Dundas, asking him to send a small army from Fort George, suggesting a force of five hundred foot soldiers and three cannons.

When this request was rejected, the seventy-six-year-old sheriff raised his own force locally. And on March 2, 1820, with forty constables, twenty-five recalcitrant militiamen (who loaded their guns with blank cartridges) and a scattering of gentlemen and servants, this resolute figure set out in his carriage to travel fifty kilometres north from Dingwall to serve the requisite writs of eviction. In Dingwall, a rumour circulated that a troublemaker from Sutherland, one of the survivors of the Strathnaver Clearances, had been travelling around Strath Oykel, urging people to resist and promising help.

Sheriff Macleod hoped to win over the Highlanders with vague promises of resettling the locals at the Cape of Good Hope in South Africa. But when he reached Culrain, he found scores of people gathered on the road and in the surrounding hills. Most of them were women or, as the sheriff later insisted, men dressed in women's clothing. Still more men were sheltering behind stone walls that lined the road. Boys blew whistles and more people came hurrying, some setting out from across the river, which was part of Sutherland.

Sheriff Macleod stepped out of his carriage, waving his writs and yelling at people to disperse. He shouted that they would be resettled at the Cape of Good Hope. The women hollered back that they would rather die here on their ancestral turf than in America, much less in South Africa.

Later, on March 11, 1820, the *Scotsman* newspaper would write of the Culrain riots: "On notice being given to these poor creatures to remove, they remonstrated, and stated unequivocally, that as they neither had money to transport them to America, nor the prospect of another situation to retire to, they neither could nor would remove, and that if force was to be used, they would rather die on the spot that gave them birth than elsewhere."

A woman carrying a stick struck the first blow and so began hand-to-hand combat. The constables wielded ash-sticks and, from their horses, the gentry swung at women's heads and faces with their riding crops. Militiamen fired into the air, then gathered around to protect the old sheriff, swinging their muskets. One militiaman, who had apparently disobeyed the secret order to load blank cartridges, shot a woman in the chest. Down she went. Her female comrades attacked in a frenzy.

The militiamen surrounding the old sheriff backed away down the road. The furious people of Strath Oykel overturned his abandoned carriage and ripped it apart, while also tearing to shreds the writs of removal. They pursued the gentry and their protectors six kilometres down the river to Ardgay. The sheriff and his men holed up at the inn and remained there, recovering, for a week.

The people went home, assuring one another that the laird, Hugh Munro, must now change his mind. Their minister, Alexander Macbean, felt torn. He denounced the sheriff for arriving with an invading army. But he threatened the people with damnation if they continued in this rebellion. He travelled the valley arguing that resistance could only lead to more violence and destruction. Another influential gentleman, Thomas Dudgeon, countered this by swearing to stand with the people while he had a drop of blood within him.

But Macbean's warnings of hellfire carried the day. Seven of the most influential tenants, worn down and frightened by their minister's threats, signed a letter requesting a meeting and promising to accept the writs of removal. On March 14, they went with Macbean to the Ardgay Inn and there humbly accepted the papers. Their subtenants followed their lead. The gentry nodded and congratulated themselves.

But one year later, eight kilometres north of Culrain, in April 1821 at Gruids, the abused tenantry would rise up yet once more—this time in territory owned by the Staffords of Dunrobin Castle. When the sheriff's officers arrived with writs of removal, the *Inverness Courier* reported, they "were literally stripped of their clothes, deprived of their papers, and switched off the bounds of the property."

This time, the Lord Advocate sent out the 41st Regiment from Fort George. For a day and a night, the farmers of Gruids watched the redcoats from the hills. Finally, they recognized the inevitable, accepted the writs, and marched the fifty kilometres to where the Marquess of Stafford sent them—the coastal town of Brora. There, they set about eking out a livelihood from the rocks and the waves, though many despaired and took instead to the ships.

9

—

Dunrobin Castle

E VERYTHING HERE IS LIKE A FAIRY STORY," HARRIET Beecher Stowe wrote to her husband in September 1856. "The place is beautiful! It is the most perfect combination of architectural and poetic romance, with home comfort." Stowe, the celebrated American author of *Uncle Tom's Cabin*, was describing Dunrobin Castle, which is situated in the Sutherland Highlands some eighty-five kilometres north of Inverness. The place is splendiferous, no question.

The first time Sheena and I visited, in 2016, I had just begun researching the Clearances and had only a vague idea of what Dunrobin represented. Like Stowe before me, I was dazzled by the magnificence of the place. Would you believe 189 rooms? And a history dating back to at least 1401, when the Norse-Gaelic Lords of the Isles built a square keep here with walls six feet thick? In one splendid room after another, we admired paintings of this duke and that lady, not quite sure who was who. In the Music Room we found a surprise—a gorgeous full-body portrait of the Irish chieftain Hugh O'Neill (1550–1616), whose resistance politics could hardly be more out of place.

The splendiferous Dunrobin Castle has 189 rooms and a history dating back to 1401. Since the Clearances, it is the most politically incorrect edifice in the Highlands.

The next year, while staying at the nearby Golspie Inn, we visited Dunrobin Castle for the second time. I had a much better grasp of what and who merited my attention. During the Rising of 1745, a Jacobite army stormed and seized Dunrobin. The 17th Earl of Sutherland narrowly escaped through a back door. He sailed to Aberdeen, joined the army led by the Duke of Cumberland, and subsequently regained his castle. In 1765, his eleven-year-old granddaughter, Elizabeth Sutherland, inherited Dunrobin and its extensive estates. Twenty years later she married the wealthy politician George Granville Leveson-Gower, also known as Lord Stafford, who later became the 1st Duke of Sutherland.

At this time, Lord Stafford enjoyed an income of £300,000 a year. The countess had brought into the marriage her 4,494 square kilometres of Sutherland. In 1803, Stafford inherited still more estates from his uncle, the Duke of Bridgewater. Together, this well-connected pair—Lord and Lady Stafford—were among the richest couples in Britain.

Dunrobin Castle contains portraits of both and paintings also of their son, the 2nd Duke of Sutherland, and his wife, the Duchess Harriet. Their daughter, Elizabeth Georgiana Campbell, Duchess of Argyll, was the one who, in 1854, played host to Harriet Beecher Stowe, filling her head with denials and obfuscations about the Clearances while squiring her around London and, later, Dunrobin.

Elizabeth, Duchess-Countess of Sutherland by George Romney, 1782.

In the gift shop, I picked up an illustrated, large-format paperback entitled *Dunrobin Castle: Jewel in the Crown of the Highlands.* The text does not ignore what the Sutherlands did. But it portrays Lord Stafford as a "do-gooder" who was "shocked by the primitive conditions of his wife's tenantry." The book quotes another baronet explaining that Stafford was one of those reformers "willing to dedicate his life and fortune to making other folk do something they found desperately disagreeable for the sake of what he believed to be their future good."

Using his enormous personal wealth, "he destroyed the old ways of life in Sutherland by uprooting the pastoral inhabitants of the hills and glens and moving some of them to housing on the coast where they could earn better money working in industries which he himself had financed." That housing includes what are now stone ruins clinging to the dangerously wind-swept cliff edge at Badbea Clearance Village, where farmers were invited to fish and pick kelp.

Lord Stafford, we learn, "was too much influenced by [economist James] Loch, and the clearance work was carried out at great speed by his agents whose harshness is still remembered." Stafford "lost a great deal of money in his 'philanthropic' indulgences" but created "a modern communications system in Sutherland, and while he was hated at first, he came to be respected by many at his death, though there are still Scots who can see no good in him and many regard him as an enemy of Gaeldom."

That would be why the locals have repeatedly tried to topple the towering, one-hundred-foot-tall statue that Stafford erected of himself just north of the nearby town of Golspie. Many of the five thousand people he evicted from Sutherland glens "were forced to emigrate and this accounts for the wide scattering of Scots throughout the British Empire. It was their hardy characteristics and imaginative minds which contributed so much to the building of that empire."

So you see, Stafford was right to do what he did. It all worked out in the end.

As we explored Dunrobin Castle and its magnificent gardens, I couldn't help feeling that one man, above all, deserves to be commemorated here. That man, a stonemason named Donald Macleod, is remembered only by a rough stone cairn at the side of a two-lane highway that winds north to the Strathnaver Museum near the coastal town of Bettyhill. As for Dunrobin Castle itself, by the time we left, I considered it the most politically incorrect edifice in Scotland. Why so?

The stonemason Donald Macleod is remembered by this modest cairn off a two-lane highway that winds north to the Strathnaver Museum near Bettyhill.

In 1811, Lord Stafford was serving as a member of Parliament when the British government passed a bill offering to pay half the cost of building roads in northern Scotland. The north had none to speak of because the Romans, who had occupied England from AD 43 to 410, never gained control of Scotland. Stafford and his wife had recently hired three wealthy, well-educated men—Patrick Sellar, William Young, and James Loch—to suggest ways to "improve" their land holdings and make them still more profitable.

His three emissaries advised Lord and Lady Stafford to move people away from the broad and fertile river valleys—Strathnaver, Strath Brora and the Strath of Kildonan—and to convert these regions into giant sheep farms. The people could be sent to allotments and put to work fishing and mining kelp on the coasts of Sutherland. The Staffords, Patrick Sellar wrote, "were pleased humanely to order" this new undertaking.

The interior of Sutherland would be given over to shepherds and Cheviot sheep, and tenant farmers would be removed to the rocky coast and "placed in lots of less than three acres, sufficient for the maintenance of an industrious family, pinched enough to cause them to turn their attention to the fishing." This benevolent action would "put these barbarous Highlanders into a position where they could better associate together, apply themselves to industry, educate their children, and advance in civilization."

In 1813, the Staffords—also known as the Sutherlands—offered their tenants new lands on the cliffs north of Helmsdale at rocky, windswept Badbea. The farmers had a choice. They could either become herring fishers and kelp pickers or they could emigrate. Ninety-six opted immediately to depart for faraway Rupert's Land (a massive expanse encircling the east, south and west of Hudson Bay). They crossed the water to Stromness and sailed on the emigrant ship *Prince of Wales*. After finding Badbea uninhabitable, others followed. In the two decades ending in 1831, the Staffords slashed the population of Kildonan from 1,574 people to 257.

How did they manage this? In 1814, Patrick Sellar gave orders to burn hill-grazing areas so there would be no food for the tenants' cattle and the people would have no choice but to depart. Soon he was ordering the burning of villages. In May of that year, 430 people were evicted and forced to move to the coastal town of Brora. Sellar himself personally directed the clearances. To force the people out, he had the roofs of their houses pulled down and the timbers set alight to prevent rebuilding. Such is the sanitized version.

As it happened, a courageous young stonemason named Donald Macleod witnessed Sellar in action. Born in the 1790s, Macleod had grown up in a traditional blackhouse listening to worried discussions about the worsening conditions for Highland farmers like his own family. Between 1772 and 1791, nearly seven thousand people had left the counties of Inverness and Ross. At this point, those who emigrated had faced pressure but had not been forcibly evicted. They had simply been ordered to move from their viable ancestral holdings onto miserable plots of land on the famously blustery Scottish coast.

Patrick Sellar (1780–1851) acted for the Duke of Sutherland in clearing Strathnaver, Strath Brora and the Strath of Kildonan.

Yet even on those barren, rocky shores, the displaced farmer was not to be his own man. He was to become a fisherman, yes. But he was also expected to pick kelp, seaweed trapped among the rocks, an activity that could provide more profits than sheep. These profits would go mostly to the laird, of course. And so, during the brief kelping season in April and May, men who had once been farmers stumbled around on rocks in the freezing cold waves gathering green weeds for poverty wages.

This kelp-gathering required a massive labour force. Landlords expressed dismay when, despite their efforts to populate the coast, those they sent there thwarted their good intentions by retreating to Inverness or Glasgow, or else by joining the military or even emigrating. To maintain the flow of profits from trading in kelp, one laird insisted that "if the [fertile farming] country has any inhabitants at all, they must be expelled."

In the spring of 1814, Patrick Sellar ordered all the tenant farmers to quit Strathnaver, that rich farming valley along the River Naver, where for generations their forefathers had tilled the soil. A few days after sending the first notice, Sellar ordered the pasture to be burned so the people would have to move their cattle. During previous removals, farmers had been permitted to carry off the door frames and timbers of their houses for use at their new allotments. This time, with most of the able-bodied men away from home, seeking pasturage for their cows, Sellar waved off that consideration and ordered groups of strong men to oust the aged, the infirm, the women and the children.

Sellar himself had recently gained control of these lands and he meant to turn them into profitable sheep farms. The tenants had expected that, according to precedent, they would be allowed to remain a while in their ancestral homes, salvaging their crops while slowly they relocated. They were shocked into disbelieving silence when Sellar and his henchmen began knocking down their homes and setting them to the torch. Anything they were unable instantly to remove, the marauders destroyed.

Sellar personally directed this orgy of destruction, as Macleod and other witnesses later attested. One old man stumbled off among the trees and rocks and wandered, disoriented, before succumbing to the elements. Several small children did not survive.

"To these scenes," Donald Macleod wrote—first in newspapers, later in pamphlets and a book—"I was an eye-witness and am ready to substantiate the truth of my statements, not only by my own testimony, but by that of many others who were present at the time. In such a scene of general devastation, it is almost useless to particularize the cases of individuals; the suffering was great and universal. I shall, however, notice a few of the extreme cases of which I was myself eye-witness."

Macleod wrote of John Mackay's wife, Ravigill, who while trying to pull up and preserve the timbers of their house, fell through the roof. "She was in consequence taken in premature labor, and in that state was exposed to the open air and to the view of all the by-standers." A man named Donald Munro, sick in bed with a fever, was expelled from his house and left vulnerable to the wind and the rain. Donald Macbeath, an old man, bedridden, had the roof of his house torn off, and lay in the elements until he expired.

Patrick Sellar and William Young and their hired thugs put three hundred houses to the torch, even as Macleod and a few other able-bodied men struggled to remove the sick and the helpless before fire engulfed them. Macleod would never forget the cries of women and children, the bawling of cows, the barking of dogs. Sellar had the roofs of the houses pulled down and the timbers set ablaze to prevent rebuilding. "I was present," Macleod wrote, "at the pulling down and burning of the house of William Chisholm, [in the town of] Badinloskin, in which was lying his wife's mother, an old bed-ridden woman of nearly 100 years of age, none of the family being present. I informed the persons about to set fire to the house of this circumstance and prevailed on them to wait until Mr. Sellar came. On his arrival, I told him of the poor old woman, Margaret Mackay, being in a condition unfit for removal. He replied, 'Damn her, the old witch, she has lived too long—let her burn.'"

Later that night in June 1814, Donald Macleod climbed a hill and counted 250 blazing houses. "Many of the owners," he wrote later, "were my relatives and all of whom I personally knew; but whose present condition, whether in or out of the flames, I could not tell. The fire lasted six days, till the whole of the dwellings were reduced to ashes or smoking ruins. During one of those days a boat lost her way in the dense smoke as she approached the shore; but at night she was enabled to reach a landing place by the light of the flames."

FOUR DECADES later, the celebrated Harriet Beecher Stowe read what Donald Macleod had written and was moved to write about the Sutherland Clearances. She had received an account, she explained, containing some "ridiculous stories about the Duchess of Sutherland" that had been circulating in America. "There were dreadful accounts of cruelties practiced in the process of inducing the tenants to change their places of residence," she wrote. "The following is a specimen of these stories."

Harriet Beecher Stowe (1811–1896) knew nothing of the Highland Clearances when she denounced eyewitness accounts.

Here she quoted a passage by Donald Macleod, which he had first published in the *Edinburgh Weekly Chronicle* in 1840, and then in a booklet, *History of the Destitution in Sutherlandshire*. She quoted the passage that began, "I was present at the pulling down and burning of the house of William Chisholm."

Stowe took advice from Elizabeth Campbell, the Duchess of Argyll and the granddaughter of the original Lady Stafford, who had orchestrated the clearances. On her advice, the celebrated American author had consulted Patrick Sellar's fellow conspirator, Mr. James Loch. This gentleman assured her that "the only thing like a fact stated in the newspaper extract" is that Mr. Sellar was accused of acts of cruelty. He had challenged this account, Loch added, by suing the sheriff substitute who affirmed the story and "obtained a verdict for heavy damages." He neglected to mention that, the testimony of several eyewitnesses notwithstanding, he had engineered the court's verdict. The sheriff left the country, he said, and both he and Sellar "are since dead."

Stowe quoted James Loch as adding that, thanks to Lord and Lady Stafford, Sutherland was flourishing: "nothing could exceed the prosperity of the country during the past year; their stock, sheep, and other things sold at high prices; their crops of grain and turnips were never so good, and the potatoes were free from all disease; rents had been paid better than was ever known. . . . As an instance of the improved habits of the farmers, no house is built for them that they do not require a hot bath and water closets."

In truth, all this was fatuous nonsense. A journalist set the record straight in the *Northern Ensign*, insisting that Sutherland had slid backwards in population and land values, and had "no shipping or commerce, no post offices, no banks, not a newspaper or a press or a bookshop." Nevertheless, Harriet Beecher Stowe relayed Loch's report as gospel in her 1854 book *Sunny Memories of Foreign Lands*. At the same time, this world-famous darling of the abolitionist movement—her *Uncle Tom's Cabin* had sold 300,000 copies—asserted that Donald Macleod's eyewitness accounts of the Clearances were fabrications. According to Stowe, the stonemason was a fraud and a liar.

Two years after *Sunny Memories* appeared, Donald Macleod sat shaking his head over the book in the town of Woodstock, 145 kilometres southwest of Toronto. From Edinburgh, where he had worked latterly as a bookseller, he had recently crossed the ocean after losing his wife. Now nearing seventy years of age, Macleod had made his way to extended family in this bustling town in what is now Ontario. Along the way he had consulted with the activist-journalist Donald Ross, who had written so eloquently about several Clearances before emigrating to Nova Scotia. Ross had encouraged him to respond to Stowe's vicious libel.

And so, in the autumn of 1856, Macleod sat at a kitchen table perusing the relevant section of Stowe's book. She had quoted him at length: "Fire was immediately set to the house, and the blankets in which [the dying woman] was carried out were in flames before she could be got out. She was placed in a little shed, and it was with great difficulty they were prevented from firing it also. The old woman's daughter arrived while the house was on fire and assisted the neighbours in removing her mother out of the flames and smoke, presenting a picture of horror which I shall never forget, but cannot attempt to describe. Within five days she was a corpse."

That scene from 1814 haunted him still, though he had tried to put it behind him. In 1818, he had married Betsy Gordon, the bright-eyed daughter of Charles Gordon, a man highly respected in Farr and all along the north coast of Sutherland for his religious and moral character. Having apprenticed with his own father as a mason, Donald Macleod had taken to travelling south every summer to work around Inverness or even Edinburgh, where he could earn better wages. In winter he returned to Rossal Place at Bettyhill to live among family and friends.

As a result, he had witnessed countless scenes of destruction and devastation, including one that, in 1820, culminated in the death of his worthy father-in-law. That admirable man had left six orphans in a state of destitution—for before he drew his last breath, he had seen everything he owned destroyed and his house razed to the ground.

With his wife, Macleod had taken in the six children. Two years later, because his wife needed his help at home, he gave up his summer travels and worked locally for less money. If he had been less outraged by injustice and of a more crouching disposition, he might have moved south and survived there indefinitely. But seeing oppression and persecution flourish around him, and having learned that Lowlanders endured no such treatment, Macleod proved unable to hold his tongue. He became a marked man, and his powerful enemies—Patrick Sellar chief among them—yearned to make an example of him.

For seven years, after the death of his father-in-law, Donald Macleod kept his tormentors at bay, answering one false charge after another. If people owed him money, they might pay or they might not. He could obtain no legal redress. The struggle came to a head in 1827, when Macleod was summoned to court to pay a substantial bill (worth roughly $800 today). He described arriving to find Patrick Sellar sitting at a raised table and decked out in a scarlet robe, white wig, black scarf and scarlet hood.

Sellar said, "Well, Donald, do you owe this money?"

"I would like to see the pursuer before I enter any defence."

"The pursuer is before you."

"I thought you were my judge, sir."

"I shall both pursue you and judge you. Did you not promise me on a former occasion that you would pay this debt?"

"No, sir. I did not."

Sellar the judge called out to the constable: "John Mackay, seize the defender."

The constable collared him like a criminal and for some hours kept him prisoner in an adjoining room. Then Sellar the judge summoned him once more.

"Well, Donald, what have you to say now? Will you pay the money?"

"Just the same, sir, as before you imprisoned me. I deny the debt."

"You, Donald Macleod, are one of the damn'dest rascals in existence. But I shall make you pay this sum, whatever receipts you may hold—and I'll get you removed from the estate."

"Mind, sir, you are in a magisterial capacity."

"I'll let you know what—" And he offered a volley of execrations.

"Sir, your conduct disqualifies you from your office. Under the protection of the law of the land, and in presence of this court, I put you to defiance."

Red-faced and furious, Sellar threatened Macleod with eviction, removal and banishment, then ordered him away from the bar: "Get out!"

Sellar immediately took steps to make good on his threats. But Macleod refused to turn and run. He wrote a "memorial" to Lord and Lady Stafford, humbly laying out his case, and noting that he had six helpless orphans in his care. He explained that he had been unjustly and illegally imprisoned and ordered to pay money he did not owe. He called for an investigation, alleging that he would answer the accusation of his enemies by undeniable testimonials of honest and peaceful character.

As a result, on the very day he had been ordered to vacate, one of the under-factors verbally relayed a communication from the Staffords telling him that for now he could remain in his house. He should continue to work as usual, repairing houses and providing fuel, until Commissioner James Loch arrived to adjudicate his case.

On learning of this, Patrick Sellar grew alarmed. Macleod had denounced him and several other factors for their barbarous treatment of his fellow Highlanders, exposing their infamous deeds to public reprobation. What? Would they now be shamed before all of Scotland? By this rebellious miscreant, Donald Macleod? No. They would make him an example to deter others. Sellar and his friends, among them the parish minister, wrote letters to James Loch. And, as Macleod would write, the result would prove the weakness of a just cause in the face of cruel, despotic factors and graceless ministers. Macleod's case had been judged and decided before the commissioner left London.

The charade went on. Macleod's "memorial" to Lord and Lady Stafford was returned with a communication that Mr. Loch, on his next visit to Sutherland, would examine his case and decide. The parish schoolmaster, a relation of Macleod's wife, Betsy, relayed in confidence that Loch had already decided the case. The schoolteacher had it from good authority that if they were smart, the Macleods would leave the area as soon as possible.

Donald Macleod rejected this advice. James Loch arrived and conducted another sham trial. He reserved judgment in seeming good humour. Macleod pressed to know his decision but in a soothing tone of voice, Loch said, "You will get to know it before I leave Sutherland. Make yourself easy."

Macleod received this as good news and carried it home as such. His wife remained apprehensive. One month later, on October 20, 1830, her dark forebodings became a nightmare reality. Donald Macleod was sixty-five kilometres away, working in Wick. At three o'clock in the afternoon, as his family was finishing a meal, a messenger arrived with an order to quit the premises, followed immediately by eight men. These did not stop to talk. They dragged his wife, Betsy, and the children out of the house. Then, ignoring the wails of protest, they flung furniture, bedding, and possessions out the door. They extinguished the fire in the fireplace and nailed up the doors and windows while his wife stood watching helplessly, an infant sucking her breast, three children by her side, all of them younger than eight.

Rain began falling before the men left. Betsy stayed a while at the house, gasping in shock and astonishment. Then she gathered her children and hurried to seek shelter at the house of a friendly neighbour, only to learn, to her stunned dismay, that she was not welcome. She tried another house with the same result. Messengers had passed this way, warning all those who lived nearby against affording shelter or assistance to the family of Donald Macleod.

The locals were so intimidated that, even with a storm coming on, they did not dare to help their distressed friend. Betsy gathered blankets and covered the children as best she could, then led them across bog and mire to the house of Macleod's great aunt. Fearing another rejection, she placed the baby in the arms of her seven-year-old son. She stood waiting in the rain with the two smaller children while he went to the door. Finding it open, the boy bolted inside and, advancing upon his astonished relative, laid the infant in her lap. He then went back outside, took the other two children and, without waiting for an invitation, led them into the house and sat them down before the fire.

The man of the house faced a conundrum. He could not think of turning the children out of doors, yet he dreaded the ruin that threatened should he shelter the Macleods. His wife called him a coward and refused to put out the children or leave the house. Her husband decided that if he was not there, he could hardly be punished. He left and spent the night with a neighbour.

Betsy Macleod had already set out into the wind and sleet. To travel any distance in such a violent storm meant risking death by falling over one of the cliffs or precipices that encircled the township—or even into the sea, as others had done. Yet she had no choice. Eventually, with the help of a good friend of her husband, she secured the assistance of William Innes, a gentleman of some influence in the district. Innes gave Betsy permission to occupy an empty house he owned at Armadale, just a few miles from their former home.

When Donald Macleod arrived next day from Wick, called home by a premonition, he was engulfed by a wave of rage that might well have driven him to murder. He listened to the admonitions of his wife, collected the children and brought them to Armadale. Then, from his former home, he salvaged what he could.

Having settled his family into the borrowed house, Macleod learned that obtaining fuel for the fire would be a problem. People feared the wrath of Patrick Sellar and declined to sell or give him peats. Eventually, he made a clandestine arrangement. After paying for the peats, he would be allowed to collect them himself, under cover of darkness, so that nobody would be any the wiser.

His work as a mason still took him from home, and the heavy labour of peat-carrying often fell to his poor wife. That winter came on with unusual severity, bringing blizzards and tempests unknown in the Lowlands. Betsy had to walk miles through snow, wind and rain with heavy peats on her back. Some of the neighbours managed to mitigate her hard lot, though always by stealth, for fear of incurring the vengeance of the factors.

Peats drying in the sun in Shetland. As a young mother, Betsy Macleod was driven to walk miles in the winter carrying similar peats on her back.

All through that winter and the next spring, Patrick Sellar and his henchmen sought to induce the gentleman Innes to withdraw his protection and turn the family out of the Armadale house. He refused. But at last, Macleod decided to take steps for removing himself and his family forever from those scenes of persecution and misery. Late in the spring of 1831, he went to Edinburgh and found work, with a view to bringing his family south as soon as he had saved enough to cover expenses.

Soon after he departed, his enemies resumed their persecutions. Patrick Sellar turned up at his borrowed house unannounced. He threatened Betsy Macleod, warning that if she did not instantly remove herself, he would take steps that would astonish her, the nature of which she would not know until they fell upon her. He added that he knew Donald Macleod was now in Edinburgh and could not aid her in resisting.

The poor woman, knowing she could expect no mercy, and fearing for her very life, moved with the children into the tiny house of Macleod's mother, near the parish church. There, kindly received, she hoped to find shelter and respite until her husband returned to take her and the children away. This was the week of the Easter sacrament. Betsy was anxious to partake of that ordinance in the house where her forefathers had worshipped, before she left it forever.

But on the Thursday before that solemn occasion, Sellar again terrified her by suddenly turning up with threats and imprecations. He alarmed Macleod's mother so much that his wife and children had again to stumble out into the night. They sheltered nearby at the home of a courageous friend, and next day, Betsy Macleod bade adieu to her native country and friends, leaving the sacrament to be received by her oppressors.

After two more days of terrible toil, she arrived with the family at Thurso, having trudged and carried for nearly sixty-five kilometres. These protracted sufferings so damaged the health of this once strong and healthy young woman that instead of the cheerful and active helpmate she formerly was, she became, except at short intervals, a burden to herself, with little or no hope of recovery. She saw doctors and consumed a great many medicines with little effect. The injuries she had suffered in body and mind were too deep for even her good spirits and excellent constitution. For some years, Betsy Macleod survived as a living testament to the oppression of the Highlanders. But then she passed away.

In Edinburgh, the articulate Donald Macleod found work as a bookseller. He wrote of all he had seen, but at first could find no outlet for his work. In the early 1840s, as public opinion began to change, the *Edinburgh Weekly Chronicle* published twenty-one of his letters. Macleod expanded these into his *History of the Destitution in Sutherlandshire*. That was the work Harriet Beecher Stowe had seen fit to malign with her *Sunny Memories of Foreign Lands*.

Now, in autumn 1856, Donald Macleod, the former stonemason from Rossal Place, Bettyhill, resolved to answer the celebrated, know-nothing author. People had expressed interest. He would bring together everything that he remembered in a work called *Gloomy Memories: The Highland Clearances of Strathnaver*. Rousing himself, he put pen to paper.

For the rest, Patrick Sellar did stand trial for setting fire to the house from which Margaret Mackay had to be carried, and for evicting two elderly people who could scarcely walk. Exposed to the chill northern air, they had died. Sellar was charged with manslaughter but acquitted, no surprise—though even Lady Stafford judged him "exceedingly greedy and harsh with the people." She continued with her own clearances, though she did dismiss Sellar. He became a successful sheep farmer and owner of one of the largest estates in the district.

Commissioner James Loch published a long apologia for Sellar and other "improvers" entitled *An Account of the Improvements on the Estates of the Marquess of Stafford in the Counties of Stafford and Salop, and on the Estate of Sutherland.* This was the work he later conveyed to Harriet Beecher Stowe, who swallowed it whole.

One far-seeing social scientist would have none of it. In 1834, anticipating twentieth-century denunciations of the Highland Clearances as an instance of ethnic cleansing, Simonde de Sismondi published an essay on landed property in which he used the Clearances as his main example of the destructive impact of capitalism on the old rural order: "There is something so absurd and revolting," he wrote, "in interpreting as a form of progress the destruction of the happiness, of the liberty, of the very existence of a race in the interests of wealth."

PART THREE

ATLANTIC
ARRIVALS

Nova Scotia, circa 1773

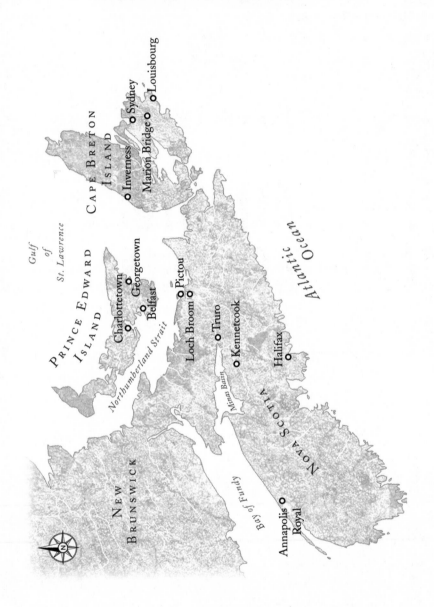

10

Voyage of the *Hector*

VISITORS TO PICTOU, NOVA SCOTIA, CAN TODAY explore a replica of the sailing ship *Hector* tied up at the dock, the Hector Heritage Quay. This is a full-size copy of the most famous "coffin ship" ever to arrive from Scotland—though people did not speak of "coffin ships" until the mid-nineteenth century. Thomas D'Arcy McGee (1825–1868)—that eloquent Irishman and Canadian Father of Confederation—suggested the term during one of his dramatic speeches. But given that eighteen deaths occurred during the *Hector*'s historic Atlantic crossing, the tiny wooden vessel richly deserves to be so identified.

In 2018, when I arrived at Heritage Quay and saw the replica for the first time, the hair on the back of my neck began to tingle. Another Thin Place. It whirled me back to the spring of 1773. In the distance I see Highlanders striding over the hills to Ullapool. Camerons, Grants, Frasers, Mackays, they all come striding through mountains and valleys to the original *Hector*. They arrive ten or fifteen at a time, some having walked eighty kilometres or more, carrying their possessions on their backs and their babes in their arms. Besides single men from here and there, six extended families come from the nearby Coigach Peninsula, ten from east Inverness-shire around Beauly, and fourteen from Sutherland, notably the Assynt area.

At the Hector Heritage Quay in Pictou, Nova Scotia, visitors can board an exact replica of the original *Hector*, which sailed here from Ullapool in 1773.

The people set up camps along the coast of Loch Broom to wait for the *Hector*'s arrival. They talk and laugh and assure one another that they are doing the right thing, the only thing. They are off on the adventure of a lifetime, away to the New World. Of course they are anxious. But mainly they feel excited. When the rains begin they huddle in makeshift shelters, though even the cold and the wet cannot quell the excitement of the many children among them.

On July 10, when the *Hector* sails into the harbour, the waiting Highlanders erupt in a spontaneous cheer. They see a few passengers, collected in Greenock near Glasgow, waving from the deck. Can this really be happening? With the ship standing a quarter mile offshore, sailors begin rowing the emigrants to the ship, one or two families at a time, bringing their bags and wooden chests bulging with everything they own.

At last, when almost everyone is aboard, people notice that one kilted figure stands lonely onshore. The Mackay piper. Word spreads: the piper failed to pay his fare in advance and does not have the money to pay it now. A commotion ensues, becomes a kerfuffle: the departing Highlanders must have a piper! Surely the man should sail for free? Captain John Speirs and recruiter John Ross stand firmly opposed, but after several passengers agree to share their food with the piper, the two nay-sayers relent and allow him aboard. And so, early in the second week of July 1773, the *Hector* sails out of Loch Broom bound for Pictou, Nova Scotia.

According to Donald MacKay, a descendant of Pictou County settlers, most of the voyagers were "obscure, illiterate crofters and artisans . . . who spoke [only] Gaelic." In *Scotland Farewell: The People of the Hector*, MacKay notes that one of the few passengers who spoke both Gaelic and English was a young schoolteacher named William Mackenzie, and fortunately he left a record. Mackenzie reported that those who boarded the *Hector* found they could scrape slivers from her rotting hull with their fingernails. After weeks of keen anticipation, reality began sinking in.

The *Hector* was a decrepit, three-masted vessel much smaller than expected—just eighty-five feet long and twenty-two wide. She weighed two hundred tons. And she sailed from Loch Broom, according to three different passenger lists, with 189 passengers—23 families and 25 single men. To say that the ship was overflowing is a gross understatement. And this would become the rule with vessels assigned to the business of emigration. Invariably, they had seen better days. Over-insured, they were often more valuable to their owners if they sank.

Passengers ran short of food and water and death rates would often reach 30 percent. Sharks would follow the coffin ships because so many bodies were thrown overboard. Britain would not enact legislation to protect emigrant passengers until 1803, and for decades unscrupulous ship owners continued to provide too many people with too little to eat. But hunger was far from the worst of it.

In 2018, while visiting the replica at Heritage Quay, I descended the ladder into the hold and stepped to the middle of the ship where, at just over six feet in height, I could finally stand upright. I could hardly believe my eyes. What with the captain, the two mates, the sailmaker, the carpenter, the cook and several seamen, as well as John Ross and three ex-soldiers who had fought in the colonies, some two hundred people were crowded onto this ship. Almost all of them would spend most of the voyage hunkered down here below decks, so close together they could reach out and touch each other. And, oh, the stacked bunks: men, women and children—thirty of them under two years of age—would sleep on rough pine boards with twenty-four inches between their own bunks and those above. Scarcely enough room to roll over.

Eighteen-year-old William Mackenzie, hired to serve as schoolmaster, lost his journal but later created a passenger list from memory (corroborating and adding detail to another by William Mackay). Mackenzie became friendly with two fellow voyagers in their early forties: Alexander Cameron and Alexander Fraser. In 1746, at Culloden, these two had stood with a throng of boys who witnessed the slaughter at the Battle of Culloden.

A few years after the government troops cleared out, Fraser had married, become a family man and settled into farming at Beauly. He had operated a whisky still on the side, until the day the "gaugers," or taxmen, seized his horse and cart. They plundered his whisky, then adjourned to an inn and drank themselves stupid. As the gaugers slept, Fraser got a stable-boy, a relative, to release his horse and cart, which he promptly drove home to Beauly. Next day, he sold them in a neighbouring parish. But he was so angry—and probably fearful of the law—that when recruiter John Ross passed through town, he became the first man to sign up. He sailed with his wife and five children.

Another passenger, a brawny, twenty-seven-year-old blacksmith named Roderick (Rory) Mackay, had recently chanced upon a police seizure of whisky. He attempted to make off with this booty but got caught and taken to the Tolbooth jail in Inverness. He became friendly with one of his jailers, pulled out a bit of money, and sent the man off to buy ale and whisky. When the jailer returned with his arms full of bottles, Mackay ducked behind him and sprang out the open door of his cell. He then locked it after him and, while his "friend" howled his dismay, made off with the key—which he brought as a souvenir onto the *Hector*. Today, it can be found in the public archives in Halifax.

The wealthiest passenger on board was John Patterson, a twenty-five-year-old carpenter who had inherited real estate in Greenock. Like Mackenzie, he spoke both English and Gaelic. At Pictou, the dynamic Patterson would become a merchant, a trader, a builder, and official founder of the hamlet. By the time he died, he was known as the Father of Pictou.

But now, in 2018, I found myself spinning back 245 years to stand among the scores of people crammed into squalid darkness below decks. No portholes, no toilets, just slop buckets and a complete lack of privacy and a worsening stink of urine, vomit, and excrement. As the *Hector* emerges into the open Atlantic it begins to buck and roll. More and more passengers are heaving into buckets. A few days out, men begin drinking, some of them heavily, and then start roaring at each other, pushing and shoving and finally fighting. People are groaning with dysentery, vomiting and defecating in the darkness, others trying desperately to get out of the way. Children are crying, even the big ones, and babies are howling in their mothers' arms. And always there is the stench— the unbearable, intolerable, worsening stench.

Now people recognize smallpox, an epidemic that brings fever, thirst, aching limbs and more dysentery. A mother and daughter have brought the disease aboard at Greenock. Ironically, they will recover to live long lives. But as the ship beats west, smallpox and dysentery kill eighteen people, almost all of them children. Parents weep as they consign their dead babies to the deep.

The *Hector* sails on across the roiling sea, rolling and rocking through three weeks, four weeks, five, six, seven. The water tastes foul and people are running out of food. Some have brought oatcakes. Early in the voyage, when those cakes went mouldy, people had set them aside. One man, Hugh Macleod, kept those rancid cakes. Now, when he offers them around, they don't taste bad at all and may even save a few lives.

One evening, Captain Speirs claims that the voyagers are two weeks out of Pictou. Passengers grow excited. But in the middle of the night, the ship begins heaving and rolling worse than ever before. The *Hector* has sailed into a hurricane. Gale-force winds force the Hector to do an about-face and sail eastwards. The violence is unbelievable. After a week of madness, the storm begins to relent. Captain Speirs points the *Hector* towards Nova Scotia. Lacking navigational aids, he can only estimate their location. Down in the hold, passengers decide they have had enough. Convinced that the storm has carried them nearly home to Scotland, they choose a few men to approach the captain. They will go to him in the wheel-house and tell him they can take no more. They will implore him, they will beg him if necessary, to turn the ship around once more and take them home. Their pleas will fall on deaf ears.

That 1773 voyage of the *Hector* marked the beginning of large-scale Scottish emigration to Canada—although by then Scots had a history of visiting Nova Scotia. That history dates back officially to Sir William Alexander (1567–1640), a Scottish courtier and poet who became a favourite of King James I of England (and James VI of Scotland). In 1621, having observed the emergence of New England, New France and New Spain, Sir William conceived the notion of establishing a New Scotland. From King James, he secured a grant to "Nova Scotia," encompassing all the lands between New England and Newfoundland. The King also deemed a tiny area out front of Edinburgh Castle to be part of Nova Scotia, so that various noblemen, by paying him a small sum, could stand in the colony, at least metaphorically, and "take sasine" or receive a chunk of rock representing newly granted estates comprising six-teen thousand acres each.

Between 1622 and 1628, Sir William tried and failed four times to establish a settlement in Nova Scotia. Finally, in 1629, his son, William Alexander, the first Earl of Stirling, planted seventy set-tlers at Port Royal (near present-day Annapolis Royal). Nominally colonized, "New Scotland" became by charter an extension of mainland Scotland. It remained so for only three years, as King Charles I signed a treaty in 1632 returning Port Royal to France. And the Scottish settlers departed.

More than a century later, between 1755 and 1764, the British deported 11,500 Acadians from Nova Scotia (leaving 2,600). This was during the Seven Years' War, after the French-speaking settlers refused to swear an oath of allegiance to Great Britain. The British had then replaced them with 8,000 American colonists, many of whom were of Scottish or Scots-Irish heritage.

The entrance to Edinburgh Castle. To the right of the entrance, invisible at this scale, visitors can see a plaque marking the area as part of Nova Scotia.

In the late 1750s, speculators from the southern colonies began buying up tracts of land in Nova Scotia with a view to parcelling them out to settlers at a profit. In 1762, a group of enterprising Americans, among them Benjamin Franklin, formed the Philadelphia Company and bought 200,000 acres along the north shore—lands encompassing Pictou Harbour. In 1767, they hired the hundred-ton *Betsey*, a small brigantine, to carry passengers north. But when the ship sailed from Rhode Island in May, she carried only six families, a total of forty settlers. They brought three servants— two of them African-American slaves and a convict working off his sentence.

That convict was employed by Robert Patterson, who came originally from Renfrew, Scotland. After a career in the British army, Patterson had settled in Maryland to work as a surveyor. He brought his wife and five children, who ranged in age from nine years to three months. Seeking opportunity, he had come to Nova Scotia, where he would become known as Squire Robert—though not without earning that sobriquet. Just over a century later, in 1877, one of Robert's descendants, Rev. George Patterson, would evoke the arrival of the *Betsey* in *A History of the County of Pictou, Nova Scotia*.

"Picture the loneliness of the little band," he wrote, "and [we] need not wonder that their hearts sank within them at the prospect of the toils and dangers before them." Here they found not a series of rolling hills but a forest of towering trees. "After they landed," the Reverend continued, "Mrs. [Robert] Patterson used to tell that she leaned her head against a tree, which stood for many a year after, and thought if there was a broken-hearted creature on the face of the earth, she was the one. As she looked upon her little ones left shelterless in the cruel wilderness . . . she could only cling to her husband with the cry, 'Oh, Robert, take me back!'"

Robert Patterson declined to do so and in 1767 went to work with an axe, clearing land and building shelter. Six years later, when passengers from the *Hector* waded ashore on a sunlit afternoon, they found the American settlers installed along the coast, their log houses built. Their numbers had changed little since the last official count, in 1769, when 120 American settlers occupied the Pictou area: 11 families, 2 single men, and a few African-American slaves. Together, they possessed 6 horses, 16 bulls, 16 cows, 37 sheep, and 10 pigs. And they had built a rough store.

———

BACK IN Scotland in 1773, the year of the *Hector*'s ghastly voyage, the touring Dr. Samuel Johnson deplored the worsening "epidemic of emigration." He blamed the chieftains and regretted that the clans retained little of their original character: "their ferocity of temper is softened, their military ardour is extinguished, their dignity of independence is depressed, their contempt of government subdued, and the reverence for their chief abated. Of what they had before the late conquest of their country, there remains only their language and their poverty." Dr. Johnson lived until 1784—not long enough to know that, during his tour with Boswell, he had seen only the first ripples of a wave that would develop into a roaring tsunami. He had been appalled by what was just the beginning.

Most of the Highlanders who sailed in 1773 had been driven to abandon their homes by impossible rent increases, those first harbingers of what would become violent Highland Clearances. The neglect of the estates of Cromarty and Lovat, forfeited to the crown after Culloden, drove more than a hundred inhabitants to resort to the *Hector*. These Frasers, Mackays and Grants had never really recovered from the post-Culloden plundering of their crops and cattle.

Three years before the *Hector* sailed, when rents were rapidly rising, the *Falmouth* and the *Annabella* had brought colonists from the Hebrides to Saint John Island—renamed Prince Edward Island in 1799. They were two of fifty-four emigrant ships that sailed to British colonies in 1770, mostly to the Carolinas. But in 1772, after a fierce winter, more than two hundred Roman Catholics had joined those emigrants on Saint John Island. Then came four hundred Macdonells from Glengarry, Glenmoriston, Glen Urquhart and Strathglass.

This mass exodus, part of the aftershock of Culloden, would shudder to a halt in 1776 as Highlanders got wind of the American

Revolution. By then, 23,000 emigrants had sailed for the colonies—roughly one-tenth of the population of the Highlands and Islands. What was causing this outflow? The answer was obvious, according to the *Edinburgh Advertiser* of 1773: "oppression by rising rents above what the lands can bear." The newspaper attacked landlords for encouraging evacuation to expand their holdings cheaply and avoid supporting starving tenants. It accused tacksmen of seeking to maintain leadership positions by departing with their tenant-followers.

Late in 1772, Glasgow businessman John Pagan had begun advertising for farmers and others "inclined to settle upon easy terms in the Province of Nova Scotia in North America." Pagan offered an extraordinary deal to the first twenty families that applied—ownership of 150 acres per couple, plus 50 more per family member, at a rate of six pence per acre (compared with three shillings per acre, or six times as much, in the Carolinas). An escalating but still low price would follow, and everyone would have two years to pay off this debt.

Travel costs, also relatively low, had to be paid in advance. Pagan noted that partners in the enterprise included Dr. John Witherspoon, a leading Scottish Presbyterian minister who had become president of a New Jersey college. Before long, Witherspoon would become a prominent revolutionary, and even a signatory to the Declaration of Independence, but who could foresee that? In his newspaper ads, Pagan claimed that usually the voyage to Nova Scotia took about four weeks (in truth seven or eight), but that he would supply the ship for twelve weeks.

He added that the land grant included twenty miles (thirty-two kilometres) of coastline and was well suited to growing grain and raising cattle. He forgot to mention that the Philadelphia Company had been struggling to attract settlers to the forty thousand acres he and Witherspoon had bought for a song, and that the newcomers would receive lands situated not along the coast but several miles inland, in the heart of a primeval forest.

The scheme did inspire skepticism, and a lively debate ensued in the newspapers. From New Jersey, Witherspoon insisted that he was providing a service, and that those who found it difficult "to subsist on the soil in which they were born, may easily transport themselves to a soil and climate vastly superior to that." Pagan focused on practicalities and early in 1773, unhappy with the lukewarm response to his ads, he hired the veteran recruiting agent John Ross to go to work out of Ullapool. Three years before, Ross had served the same proprietors in dispatching two hundred Highlanders to Boston on the *Hector*.

This time, Ross undertook to sign up 250 emigrants and to remain in Pictou to supervise their settling. He was offering free passage, one year of free provisions and land for a farm. He rode out on horseback to beat the drum, ranging from Dornoch in the north to Inverness in the east. Early in March, Pagan advertised that the Greenock-based *Hector* would sail by mid-May for Pictou and New England. That deadline came and went, but towards the end of June, having taken on a dozen Lowlanders in Greenock, the *Hector* sailed for Ullapool on Loch Broom, a northward voyage of more than five hundred kilometres, to collect the main body of emigrants.

These were the Highlanders who, having endured seven weeks of living hell aboard the *Hector*, only to sail into a terrifying hurricane, had sent a few men to approach Captain John Speirs and convince him to take them home. But the emissaries found the captain adamant. He had contracted to deliver the passengers to Nova Scotia and this he would do. His job depended on it. The passengers beat a retreat. The captain spent two weeks regaining his previous position, and then two more in completing the voyage. Food and water and even mouldy oatcakes were almost gone when, after eleven terrible weeks at sea, a sailor in the rigging called, "Land ahoy!"

As the battered ship approached the forest that lined the Nova Scotia coast, the piper on board dug out his bagpipes. He set about blowing his instrument, according to the earliest account, "with might and main, its thrilling tones for the first time startling the denizens of the endless forest and its echoes resounding through the wild solitude." On September 15, 1773, after a storm-tossed voyage from hell—rotten food, foul drinking water, dysentery, smallpox, and the deaths of eighteen people, mostly children—the *Hector* sailed into Pictou Harbour at Browns Point, immediately west of the present-day town.

On going ashore, the people of the *Hector* got one last shock. They had expected to settle along the coast, and there to occupy thirty kilometres of prime farmland. Instead, recruiter John Ross directed them to proceed five kilometres into the heavily wooded interior. The rolling farmland they had been promised did not exist. Instead, they faced rough, uncleared forest. And when, according to the earliest account, they compared that foreboding reality with the recruiting agent's promises and avowals, "many of them sat down in the forest and wept bitterly."

11

—

A Discovery of Logs

TO THE TWENTY-FIRST-CENTURY EYE, THE LITTLE LOG church at Loch Broom, Nova Scotia, is properly austere. Obviously, the minister would stand behind that simple lectern on a wooden stage raised two feet above the floor while the congregation sat facing him on rough benches. To worship here was serious business. A memorial cairn out front explains that this replica stands at the site of Pictou County's first church, erected in 1787—fourteen years after the *Hector* people arrived. Forty feet long by twenty-five feet wide, that original, too, was built of logs. Here, about three kilometres by water from Pictou, the first services were conducted in Gaelic.

To the left of the church, a plaque pays homage to the *Hector* people, and notably to Alexander Cameron, born in Scotland's Loch Broom in 1728. Cameron saw two older brothers killed at the Battle of Culloden in 1746. Here in Nova Scotia, he named his land grant Loch Broom and, as a pioneer farmer, turned the engulfing forest into farmland. A community leader, Cameron lived to the age of 103. He is buried eight kilometres south of this site at Durham Pioneer Cemetery, under a grave marker that, in relation to almost all the others, faces "the wrong way."

This is an on-site replica of the little log church at Loch Broom.

Cameron had spent his first winter in a lean-to at Browns Point, gazing across the harbour at a hillscape reminiscent of his home. Come spring, he and his wife moved there and named it Loch Broom. They built a log house and in it raised eight children. His friend and fellow Culloden witness, Alexander Fraser, eventually settled not far away on the lower Middle River.

The *Hector* Highlanders had stumbled onto the Nova Scotia shore without supplies or shelter of any kind. With winter coming on, the new arrivals were far too late to plant crops. And the promised free provisions were nowhere to be found. The newcomers struggled through the first few weeks thanks mainly to that scattering of American settlers who had arrived before them and to unexpected assistance from a handful of First Nations people.

Late in the autumn of 1773, more than half the *Hector* people, notably those with small children, decided to spend the looming winter in the established settlements of Halifax, Truro and Windsor. There, some hoped to purchase more promising lands, while others would work as labourers or servants. Among those who left temporarily was Alexander Fraser. Having lived comfortably at Beauly, west of Inverness, he found the early going a tough slog. At one point, he cut down a birch tree and boiled the buds to feed his family. When that failed, he visited the field of one of the Americans and filched some potatoes. A neighbour told on him, but as Donald MacKay writes in *Scotland Farewell*, "the pious old Yankee said only that he thanked God the potatoes had been there to feed Fraser's family."

Alexander Cameron (1728–1831) is one of many *Hector* people buried in the Durham Pioneer Cemetery, which is eight kilometres south of the Loch Broom church.

Fraser took his wife and children to Truro to find work, and his son would recall carrying his little sister on his back for three days, with only the tail of an eel to eat. The next spring, back at Pictou, the family planted seed potatoes, covering them over with earth, only to get so hungry that they dug them up and ate them. Not long afterwards, Fraser's wife was driven to killing the family's only laying hen for food.

Another passenger, the widow Margaret Fraser, had lost her husband during the voyage from Scotland but had also given birth to a daughter—the youngest passenger on the ship. With that baby girl on her back, Margaret trudged sixty-five kilometres to Truro, where she remarried and launched a second family.

At Pictou, seventy-eight settlers remained—twenty-three men, fourteen women, and forty-one children. They refused to traipse into the thick forest to their allotted sites, as land agent John Ross insisted they should. Instead, recognizing that they needed to fish to survive, they squatted near the coast on fertile lands bounded by rivers. From the New Englanders, the adults learned how to wield an axe. They built log huts and lean-tos of branches and bark.

The *Hector* had left and sailed south as planned, with the captain promising to return with provisions. When the ship did arrive back, company agents—now led by the American Robert Patterson—told them they would receive no free provisions because by refusing to move inland, they had broken the terms of their contracts. Those settlers who had a bit of money bought provisions for a while, while others traded clothes and belongings.

But for some, the situation soon grew desperate. Colin Douglas and Donald Macdonald, family men from the Beauly area, resolved to act. During the voyage, Douglas had lost two children to smallpox. Now, Macdonald's youngest child had fallen ill. Together with Roderick Mackay, the resourceful blacksmith, these two went to the store. They seized and tied up Patterson and a second agent and took what food their families needed. In the woods, to preclude reprisal, they hid their victims' guns.

Patterson sent a messenger to the garrison at Halifax, calling for soldiers to come and quell the rebellion. The commander there sent word to Truro, telling the militia to march on Pictou and punish the miscreants. The man in charge responded: "I will do no such thing. I know the Highlanders and if they are fairly treated there will be no trouble with them." When no insurrection ensued, the retiring governor in Halifax, Lord William Campbell, ordered the company agents to give the Highlanders food. Patterson let the matter drop and reported later that the three men who had plundered the store repaid every penny they owed.

Meanwhile, the Mi'kmaq became excellent allies. Long before the arrival of the *Hector*, about nine hundred of them had settled along the north coast. In 1759, they had raided Dartmouth, across the harbour from Nova Scotia, and Annapolis Royal, three hundred kilometres southwest of Pictou. For years, they had been at war with the Abenaki from across the Bay of Fundy and with Mohawks from the St. Lawrence Valley. At one point, a war-party of Mohawks had launched a late-night assault on Mi'kmaqs sleeping on Caribou Island immediately off Pictou. They set out swimming from the mainland but got caught in the current and drowned. On another occasion, Abenaki travelling in two war canoes surprised a party of Mi'kmaq fishermen and slaughtered all but two of them, who hid beneath a pile of seaweed.

Some Mi'kmaqs concluded treaties with British governor Charles Lawrence, who retracted his promise to recognize their claim to lands along the Northumberland coast. In 1763, the Mi'kmaq were still demanding that no white settlements be permitted in the area. But when the *Hector* people arrived a decade later, some native peoples came to their aid. With the American settlers James and John McCabe, who knew how to hunt, canoe and snowshoe, two of the Mi'kmaqs, Lulan and Patlass, taught the newcomers woodland skills.

Lulan "rented" use of his corn patch to Donald Fraser and saved John Patterson from drowning after he went through the ice in Pictou Harbour. Patlass learned how to play checkers and became waterfront champion. Tensions did arise on occasions, as when a group of Mi'kmaqs pushed into one house and demanded that a settler's wife cook supper for all of them. She complied, but her husband, George Morrison, after arriving home and hearing the tale, rushed off, accosted the perpetrators and laid a beating on them.

For the most part, as an earlier settler, John Robinson, wrote, the local Mi'kmaqs were "a friendly, harmless, well-behaved people, ready to do any little service for you they can, such as assisting you in crossing a river . . . but they cannot be prevailed on to assist in any sort of labour. They are stout and active, well made, of a yellow complexion, their faces and noses are broad, their eyes usually black, and their teeth remarkably white. They have long black hair and rub their bodies with bear's grease to prevent the musshetoes from biting them."

In the later 1770s, as the *Hector* people began to flourish, the Mi'kmaqs started to decline in number, mainly because they had not previously been exposed to alcohol, smallpox and tuberculosis. In 1775, 900 Mi'kmaqs lived around Pictou. One century later, their number had dwindled to 250. They hunted and trapped in winter and fished and farmed in summer. In 2011, Pictou County had a population of 45,600, including 23,000 people of Scottish origin (just over 50 percent). The Mi'kmaq numbered 1,600 (3.5 percent).

In 1776, three years after the *Hector* people stumbled ashore, hungry and destitute, fifteen farm families arrived who were even more desperate than they were—sixty-seven people in total, early victims of the American Revolution. Originally Scottish Lowlanders, and nicknamed the "Dumfries Settlers," they had been wealthy enough two years before to charter a ship to carry them from southern Scotland to Saint John Island.

A First Settlement, engraving by William Henry Bartlett, captures the situation.

They had brought farming equipment, provisions, even a library, and settled around Georgetown. Late in 1775, with the Revolution looming, American fishermen convened in the island harbour. Before heading south to join the rebels, they got drunk and went on a rampage, ransacking Georgetown of valuables.

The Dumfries Settlers had survived the ensuing winter only thanks to the existence of a French settlement a few miles away. With the French, they traded Scottish woollens for potatoes. After trudging homeward through heavy snow, the men trembled to enter their homes, fearing to find their children dead of starvation. Come spring, a plague of rodents that they called "mice"—probably rats—devastated their planted crops. On hearing that conditions were better at Pictou, they crossed the narrow Northumberland Strait and waded ashore. They arrived with few goods but proved a valuable addition to the settlement as they brought large-scale agricultural expertise.

Meanwhile, in Great Britain, which ruled the waves but continued to expand its navy, shipbuilders had almost exhausted the forested lands that produced the timber they needed for wooden vessels. Finding themselves in a New World where heavily treed land was astonishingly abundant, the *Hector* people recognized their opportunity. After clearing enough space to accommodate rough log homes, they turned to felling the sixty-foot oaks and white pine that lined the streams and floating them downriver to the coast. From Truro, they brought in expert hewers who helped them trim the trees.

Late in 1775, in an old ship provided by the governor of Saint John Island, they sent their first cargo of squared timber to the Scottish port of Greenock. With that, those early settlers laid the foundations for a timber trade that would sustain the colony for decades, while acting also as a magnet for further settlement. They became the first to establish an enduring Scottish colony, a beachhead, on soil that would one day form part of Canada.

By 1776, however, tensions were rising throughout Nova Scotia. The Pictou settlers could hardly fail to hear the drumbeat of revolution emanating from the south. Most American settlers were ready to join the Revolution and make Nova Scotia a rebel colony. Former New Englanders at Onslow, next door to Truro, refused to take a British oath of allegiance. At Truro, all but three Americans refused. In contrast, the newly arrived Highlanders remained loyal to the Crown. Many of them would have had relations in the Highland regiments that evolved after Culloden, and some may themselves have served.

In the summer of 1776, an old familiar supply ship, the *Molly*, sailed into Pictou's East River. Two *Hector* men, Roderick and Donald Mackay, rowed out with a load of barrel staves and found themselves taken prisoner by American pirates who had seized the ship. A few men from the *Molly* had already rowed up the river to plunder Roderick's forge of valuable tools and iron. They returned with their booty but instead of unloading, proceeded to get drunk— and so failed to see the iron-heavy rowboat sink beneath the waves under its own weight.

Next day, the privateers released the Mackays and their first prisoner, the ship's captain, and sailed away. A newly arrived British warship gave chase and followed the *Molly* into Baie Verte in what is now New Brunswick. The pirates abandoned the ship and fled into the woods, where several of them died of starvation.

Roderick Mackay, incensed at having been plundered, joined the British war effort. With his wife and two children, he made his way to Halifax. As a skilled blacksmith, he soon found work at the shipyard, and there he remained until he retired, twenty years later. As his first contribution, he forged a massive chain to prevent pirates from entering Halifax Harbour.

Many other Scottish immigrants fought on the British side— either in the 82nd Regiment garrisoned at Halifax or else in the 84th, the Royal Highland Emigrants Regiment, led ultimately by Captain Allan MacDonald, husband of the Jacobite heroine Flora MacDonald. She herself would make her way north from North Carolina and spend the harsh winter of 1778 at Fort Edward (Windsor).

Soon after 1784, following the British defeat in the Revolutionary War, close to fifty thousand Loyalists retreated northwards— more than thirty thousand of them flooding into Nova Scotia, New

Brunswick and Prince Edward Island. Estimates vary, but most were probably Highlanders, and this proved to be a shaping wave of immigration. Of the nineteen thousand Loyalists who settled in peninsular Nova Scotia, two thousand were disbanded British soldiers and their families.

Many of those disbanded Scots gravitated to Pictou County, heart of the now-flourishing timber trade. The government, grateful for the loyalty of the first arrivals, granted thirty-five families title to the lands on which they squatted. By 1803, when Thomas Douglas, the Earl of Selkirk, visited Nova Scotia to survey Scottish settlements, he could report that each year, twenty 400-ton vessels were leaving Pictou for British ports loaded with timber. Two years later, that number increased to fifty—and many of these ships returned with still more Highland immigrants.

Some were fleeing hardship. Others came seeking to own land. By 1803, according to Selkirk, the *Hector* immigrant known as Squire William Mackay had "built a new stone house, exactly a good comfortable farm house in Scotland." He had cleared a hundred acres and kept twelve cows and thirty sheep. The "old settled Highlanders," Selkirk observed, "have in general cleared as much as they want and do little more—being not ambitious of making money so much as living comfortably."

When colonies farther west, notably in Upper Canada, began advertising a gentler climate and a still-more-comfortable future, many Scottish immigrants preferred to remain in Nova Scotia for two reasons. First, proximity to Europe helped maintain contact with the Old Country. Second, the area was predominantly Highland Scottish—Catholic in some areas, Presbyterian in others. These newcomers wished to retain a collective identity and to build a life in the New World that closely resembled the one they had left in the old one, complete with churches, schoolhouses and a sense of community.

The descendants of those first settlers were highly esteemed by those who moved farther west. In 1923, for example, when Nova Scotians wrote to the St. Andrew's Society of Toronto indicating that they wished to erect a monument to mark the arrival of the *Hector* 150 years before, the society—appreciative of "the human load that spread into all the provinces and did much valiant work on the upbuilding of the Dominion"—sent a significant contribution.

12

—

The Pictou Connection

WE LEAVE SOMETHING OF OURSELVES BEHIND WHEN we leave a place," Pascal Mercier writes in *Night Train to Lisbon*. "We stay there even though we go away. And there are things in us that we can find again only by going back there." So it is with many of those connected to the *Hector*, even across generations. And that impels me, before leaving the *Hector* people, to whirl through time with at least one of the first families as it maintained the Pictou connection into the twenty-first century.

We begin with the feisty Mackay brothers, Roderick and Donald, who arrived on that first voyage. Their oldest brother, Alexander, was the one who, having fought with the Fraser Highlanders at Louisbourg and at the Plains of Abraham, alerted his siblings to the possibilities in Nova Scotia. Alexander Mackay was said to be the strongest man in James Wolfe's army at Quebec. In 1759, he was the second soldier to clamber up the cliff and onto the Plains.

He was wounded in the leg at that battle—an injury that kept him initially in Beauly when the Fraser Highlanders disbanded in 1763. Complications from that injury, followed by uncertainties related to the American Revolutionary War, kept Alexander in Scotland longer than he intended. But in 1784, at age fifty-six, he sailed for Pictou with his wife (Nellie Calder), four children, his sister and her husband.

Roderick (Rory) Mackay, who during the revolution had worked in Halifax as a blacksmith, greeted Alexander on arrival and noticed that he was still limping as a result of his injury. The Mackay brothers settled south of Pictou along the East River on farms of 300 to 500 acres. They left much of their land uncleared, but were among those who drew admiring remarks from Lord Selkirk when he passed this way in 1803. Selkirk wrote that most settlers had cleared as much land as they needed and that "many of the older settlers are now building, or have got, neat framed houses." In *Scotland Farewell*, author Donald MacKay observes that in fact painted frame houses remained rare and most habitations were of "squared or unsquared logs with roofs of birch bark or boards."

The *Hector* people, the Mackays among them, built their log cabins on high ground using hewn logs for the floor. Usually they added a door with wooden hinges, two small windows and a bark-and-shingle roof. They put a rough-stone chimney at one end of the house and made fire with a flint and old logs. To farm they used axe, hoe, sickle, and a "crooked-foot" spade developed in the Scottish Highlands. They could carry a bushel of potatoes—always their first crop—on their backs in creels of thin wood. They ate shellfish and salmon, and the Mi'kmaqs taught them to make soup from nettles and herbs. On special occasions the men donned kilts, but usually, like the New Englanders, they wore homespun trousers and moccasins.

The son of Alexander Mackay, also named Alexander, arrived at Pictou with his family when he was fifteen. By the time he entered his twenties, he was renowned as the strongest, fastest man in Pictou County. On one occasion, people sent for him when nobody dared to approach a bull that had gone wild. Farmers had trapped the beast in a barn. Alexander Mackay arrived, stationed himself in readiness, and ordered the barn door opened. When the bull emerged, Alexander grabbed it by the horns, heaved it onto its back, and held it down until the creature grew quiet and still.

Another time, Alexander chased down a caribou calf, astonishing even the Mi'kmaqs, who appreciated the animal's speed. He traded the calf for a heifer, and the new owner, the wily Squire William Mackay, sent it as a gift to Governor John Wentworth—who rewarded him with a land grant of 2,000 acres. Alexander continued to mow hay with much younger men into his nineties and died in 1866 at age ninety-seven.

Here things get complicated and we draw on a family history developed by Toronto lawyer Ted Betts. Young Alexander's great-granddaughter, Catherine Mackay (1872–1976), married a George Ross. Their daughter Freda Ross (1905–2001) married George Elmer Langley. Their daughter, Diane Elmira Langley (born 1946), married lawyer Gordon Betts—and these two became the parents of Ted Betts (born 1969), a partner (and head of infrastructure and construction) at Gowling WLG law firm in Toronto.

People joke that everybody in Nova Scotia is descended from someone who arrived on the *Hector*. Toronto lawyer Ted Betts has documents to prove it.

Betts enjoys noting the longevity that marks his maternal line: his mother is thriving, his grandmother lived to almost 97, his great-grandmother to 102, and his great-great-grandmother to 104. His relations descended from *Hector* people include Murray G. Ross, who served as president of York University from 1959 to 1970; and Dr. G. Ross Langley, a prominent physician and medical researcher who was awarded the Queen Elizabeth II Golden Jubilee Medal.

In the early 1950s, Ted Betts's grandmother Freda purchased "a red-painted shack" near Pictou. A farmer had used a tractor to haul the one-room building onto a point at Toney River, eighteen kilometres northwest of the township and overlooking Northumberland Strait. The family called the shack the "Red Cottage." In the mid-1970s, after a stint in Vancouver, Betts's parents moved to Toronto and began spending summers at Toney River. In 1977, the family bought their own cottage there. "That is where I proposed to my wife," Betts says, "where one of my brothers proposed to his, and where another brother got married."

That cottage, Toney River and Pictou County "are still deeply bred in our bones," he notes, "just as they are for my cousins who travel from Calgary every summer, two of whom have now retired in Toney River." The Red Cottage, now painted white, is still in the family—and sign-posted. Ten of Betts's relations, all of them connected to the *Hector*, have built cottages nearby. "We take our kids around to a different part of the county or the province every year," Betts says, "and every couple of years make sure we get back to see the *Hector*."

13

PEI Beachhead

FORTY KILOMETRES EAST OF CHARLOTTETOWN, ON A quiet road just outside the community of Belfast, visitors to Prince Edward Island can today find a magnificent wood-framed Presbyterian church that is one of the oldest in the province. This white edifice features a four-stage bell tower and a weathervane and several pointed-arch Gothic windows. The building occupies the footprint of the original log church built by the first settlers to arrive here in 1803—Highlanders who came with Thomas Douglas, Lord Selkirk.

From the church, if you travel four kilometres to the coast and Lord Selkirk Provincial Park, you can visit the cove where, like the Acadians before them, those first settlers—escapees from the Highland Clearances—came ashore in 1803. The history-minded will ignore the nearby golf course. Here you can explore the small Acadian-Scottish Ancient Burial Ground, where most of the gravestones have become illegible, and look out over a red sand beach towards Point Prim. If you squint and drift back through time, you can see a small sailing ship called the *Dykes* dropping anchor off this cove.

This magnificent Presbyterian church, one of the oldest in Prince Edward Island, encompasses the footprint of a log church built by the 1803 Selkirk settlers.

During its approach, the young earl on board judged that the south coast of Prince Edward Island had "a pleasant appearance as compared with C. Breton." In his journal entry for August 8, 1803, he described low cliffs interspersed with bays, and pine trees intermixed with hardwoods. Five days before, when the *Dykes* had emerged from the mid-Atlantic fog within sight of Cape Breton Island, the excited Selkirk had taken a few men and gone rowing around some tiny, bird-rich islands.

Then, two evenings later, with the ship becalmed near Cape North, he had again gone rowing, and this time ventured ashore, where he discovered only scrubby woods and gullies cut by little rivers. Now, with four men, Selkirk again jumped into a small boat, bent on taking a closer look at PEI. Six weeks before, he had set out from Scotland to launch the most ambitious resettlement scheme ever undertaken in any British colony. Altogether, on the *Dykes* and its two sister ships, the *Polly* and the *Oughton*, Selkirk was bringing eight hundred emigrants to a New World he himself had never seen. Nobody could say he lacked ambition.

Born in 1771 at Kirkcudbright in the Lowlands, the fifth son of an earl, Thomas Douglas had never expected to inherit the family estate, much less to launch a landmark emigration project. At the age of fourteen, with four brothers standing between him and the earldom, he had ventured north to study liberal arts and the law at the University of Edinburgh. Arriving into a city still ablaze with the Scottish Enlightenment, home to intellectuals like economist Adam Smith and the late philosopher David Hume, young Douglas had co-founded a small group called the Friday Club, which spent a lot of time discussing how to help "the oppressed."

With one fellow member, Walter Scott, he became lifelong friends. Later, as a pre-eminent novelist, Scott would remember Douglas as "one of the most generous" men he had ever known. After university, the upper-middle-class Scott joined the Faculty of Advocates, while the aristocratic Douglas—reserved, carrot-red-haired and standing over six feet tall—went travelling. At twenty, he sojourned in post-revolutionary Paris, and the following year he spent several months exploring the north of Scotland, where the Highland Clearances had begun displacing thousands. The year was 1792—the Year of the Sheep. He visited Ross and Cromarty, where tenants were beginning to mount some resistance. Of that he approved.

But like Boswell and Johnson two decades before, Thomas Douglas was appalled by the actions of the landlords. And he would not forget. Still in his early twenties, still powerless, he rounded out his education with the Grand Tour of Europe typical of his class. He spent a year in Naples under the tutelage of a British ambassador, and in Paris he became friends with Charles-Maurice de Talleyrand-Périgord, one of the most versatile diplomats in European history. Then, incredibly, during a terrible three-year period that began in 1794, all four of his older brothers died in quick succession—two of yellow fever and two of tuberculosis.

Back in Scotland, unexpected heir to the family estate, Douglas prepared himself by acquiring a farm and, to the astonishment of all, working it like a tenant. In 1799, when his father died, the twenty-eight-year-old became the 5th Earl of Selkirk—and one of the wealthiest men in Scotland. Concerned still about the effects of the Highland Clearances, the young earl turned to public affairs—specifically to emigration. Would-be settlers had sailed to Nova Scotia out of Kirkcudbright as early as the 1620s.

But the first to establish a permanent Scottish settlement, as Selkirk well knew, were those Highlanders who in 1773 had sailed from Loch Broom in the *Hector*. Selkirk worried that some of those settlers had drifted south from Nova Scotia into the now independent United States of America—a pattern repeated all too frequently. Selkirk detested the very idea of losing people to the States because of a boyhood experience that arose during the American Revolution.

In 1778, when he was seven, Tommy Douglas had been at home in Kirkcudbright when American privateer John Paul Jones—originally a Scot who had been born nearby—sailed into the harbour that lay off the family estate at St. Mary's Isle. Hoping initially to kidnap the fourth earl and hold him for ransom, the American sailors discovered that the man was away on business and settled for making off with the family silver. They avoided bloodshed and brutality, but looking back as an adult, Selkirk remembered that raid as "a momentous event in my life. I was terribly frightened . . . and when I was but a youth I developed an antipathy for the United States due almost solely to the buccaneering of John Paul [Jones]."

Tommy Douglas, later Lord Selkirk, was seven in 1778 when the piratical John Paul Jones made off with Lady Selkirk's silver. Douglas detested Americans ever after.

Just a few years before, the newly minted earl had analyzed the flow of emigration from Great Britain. Precise numbers proved hard to find, but Selkirk discerned that every year, thousands of people were emigrating from the British Isles to the United States. Nobody could expect to reverse that flow, but Selkirk wondered if he could channel emigrants towards colonies loyal to Britain, and so provide people with a bright future while strengthening the empire abroad.

Selkirk looked first to Ireland. Not long before, in 1798, the British government had harshly quelled a rebellion driven by hunger, high rents and desperation. Selkirk had crossed the channel to Ireland, studied the situation and returned to propose a radical cure. The solution, he argued, was to offer the rebellious Irish a chance to emigrate to the New World and to assist them in resettling—perhaps at Red River in the west? This the Colonial Office flatly refused, dismissing the Irish as intractable.

Disappointed but not discouraged, Selkirk revised his plan. This time he focused on the Scottish Highlanders, who were being cleared none too gently from their ancestral lands. As a target area, he proposed Upper Canada, specifically the Falls of St. Mary (Sault Ste. Marie). The Colonial Office countered, suggesting a "maritime situation."

From a fellow Scot, Selkirk had learned that Prince Edward Island showed agricultural promise. It meant a shorter voyage from Scotland and no great overland journey after disembarkation. He proposed to include Prince Edward Island as part of a larger scheme. Encouraged by the Colonial Office, he bought swaths of land on the island at a low price and set about encouraging many of those he had convinced to emigrate to Upper Canada to move instead to Prince Edward Island, where a scattering of Highlanders had already settled.

Selkirk signed up a hundred families—more than 750 people. Most came from the Isle of Skye and had planned to sail for North Carolina. The young earl, thinking ahead to establishing a beachhead for future departures, recruited people from Argyll, Ross and Inverness, and hoped to spread them across the northern colonies. But in February 1803, with Napoleon Bonaparte sabre-rattling in France, the Colonial Office withdrew its support for the scheme. Anti-emigration sentiment was growing. If young Highlanders departed, where would the government find soldiers to fight its battles? Having already recruited his settlers and contracted for ships and supplies, Selkirk needed to reduce expenses. That meant postponing his more ambitious plans and confining this first enterprise to Prince Edward Island.

Meanwhile, needing troops, the government passed a Passenger Vessels Act to discourage emigration with a tax that would triple or even quadruple the cost of passage to North America. This act would come into effect on July 1, 1803. But that enabled Selkirk, who was sailing in late June, to fill his ships with a final fifty emigrants from North and South Uist. If some of his passengers were relatively well off, these people were not. They had been driven from their inland crofts to live and gather kelp along the coast. Unfortunately, the market for kelp had dried up and families were facing starvation. Selkirk brought them aboard the *Dykes* and sailed west.

After an Atlantic crossing featuring "continual cold fog," Selkirk had at last come within sight of "a settlement of two *steadings*— with a good appearance of cultivation." These Cape Breton farms provided Selkirk with his first concrete image of a North American settlement. Now, as with four men he rowed along the south coast of Prince Edward Island, he saw marshes, sandy bays and red cliffs twenty feet high. After going ashore, he found evidence of a great fire, passed "the vestiges of two Indian Whigwams," and complained that mosquitoes "made a vehement attack on us, and were much worse than the little black flies which we met at Cape Breton."

As evening came on, the men started back to the ship, but the *Dykes* had changed course and the night grew dark. "We pulled on for several hours without discovering her," Selkirk wrote. With a thunderstorm erupting over the island, the men "made for the shore to kindle a fire and show where we were." They were just about to land when they heard a big gun fire from seaward. They took again to the oars, and "after that the guns continued at half hour intervals till we reached the ship—past midnight."

Next day, when the *Dykes* sailed into Hillsborough Bay, just southeast of Charlottetown, Selkirk saw to his consternation that one of his other ships, the *Polly*, had arrived first—and that, contrary to his intentions, passengers were "hutting themselves in Whigwams." He had hoped to arrive before them to prepare "some kind of barracks." As well, his agent "was proceeding to fix the people in two or three large villages instead of ten or twelve small ones"—a process he would have to reverse. Debarking from the *Dykes*, Tommy Douglas, Lord Selkirk, made his way to shore and, at what is now Lord Selkirk Campground, stepped into Canadian history.

14

A Dance Called America

OR THE MAJORITY OF EMIGRANT HIGHLANDERS, THE "dance called America" involved a single life-changing transition—the leaving of Scotland. For those who went first to the southern colonies and remained loyal to the British Crown during the American Revolution, that dance entailed two wrenching departures—one from the Highlands or Islands, the second from the revolutionary states. For a few, the dance became more elaborate still and featured a third separation, one that brought them full circle. A case in point is Jacobite heroine Flora MacDonald, who in her twenties became a Scottish heroine by helping Bonnie Prince Charlie escape a pursuing army bent on his destruction.

Flora had been born in 1722 on South Uist at the settlement of Milton, where today a lonely cairn marks the location of the house. Her father, Ranald, was a tacksman who sublet small holdings for their owner, the clan chieftain. Her mother was the daughter of a Presbyterian minister whose ancestors included the founder of the MacDonalds of Sleat, as well as Somerled and Robert the Bruce. Flora's father died the year after she was born and his "tacks" went eventually to his eldest son, Angus. In 1728, her mother took another husband, Hugh MacDonald, of a different branch of the family.

In 1773, Jacobite heroine Flora MacDonald entertained James Boswell and Dr. Samuel Johnson. The following year, she and her husband sailed for America.

Young Flora spent a lot of time visiting Lady Clanranald in Nunton on the island of Benbecula, a short distance north across a narrow channel. Here she learned social graces and added English to her native Gaelic. According to biographer Hugh Douglas, those who later met her "could not discern by her conversation that she spent all her former days in the Highlands."

In 1744, Flora resided with relatives in Argyll for ten or eleven months. When she returned to Milton early the next year, she found the islands roiling with news that yet another uprising was imminent. Jacobites had already rebelled four times—in 1689, 1708, 1715 and 1719. The most notable so far was that of 1715, when the son of the exiled Stuart king, the so-called Old Pretender, had failed in a major attempt to regain the throne. Now his son—the Young Pretender, or Bonnie Prince Charlie—was trying again.

In Chapter 4, we summarized the catastrophic defeat that ensued at the Battle of Culloden on April 16, 1746. The Bonnie

Prince ran for his life and Flora played a central role in guiding him to safety. That story has been told and retold. Caught and imprisoned for fifty-one weeks, Flora then became a folk hero thanks to the appearance of an allegorical, thirty-page pamphlet called *Alexis, or the Young Adventurer*. It told the story of the courageous Heroica, who showed great resourcefulness in helping a prince to escape his dastardly pursuers.

During a visit to Skye in 1750, after the British government had declared an amnesty, Flora accepted a marriage proposal from Allan MacDonald, who was in line to become the chief factor of Lord MacDonald of Sleat. Flora settled into life as a tacksman's wife. Through the 1750s and '60s, while living on Skye at Kingsburgh, she gave birth to seven children.

Highlanders were now under siege from rack-renting landlords, most of whom were English Anglicans or Lowland Presbyterians. They had begun emigrating in large numbers, mainly to the American colonies. They were lured by promises of a better climate and cheap land, and encouraged by those landlords who hoped to make a killing by replacing crofters with sheep. Flora and her husband talked of joining the "dance called America" but delayed while caring for Allan's aging father.

They were still residing at Kingsburgh in September 1773 when James Boswell and Dr. Samuel Johnson came rambling around the Highlands. Both gentlemen were appalled by the scale of the Scottish exodus and tired of hearing, as Boswell wrote, of "racked rents and emigration, and finding a chief not surrounded by his clan."

At Kingsburgh, the fifty-one-year-old Flora and her husband entertained the two visitors royally. The sharp-eyed Boswell drew a word-sketch of Allan MacDonald: "He had his tartan plaid thrown about him, a large blue bonnet with a knot of black ribband like a cockade, a brown short coat of a kind of duffil, a tartan waistcoat with gold buttons and gold button-holes, a bluish philibeg [kilt] and tartan hose. He had jet black hair tied behind, and was a large, stately man, with a steady sensible countenance."

Flora installed Dr. Johnson in the bed where Bonnie Prince Charlie had once slept. The Englishman insisted that Flora tell him the story of her singular adventure and encouraged Boswell to take notes. Johnson was saddened to learn that, her father-in-law having recently died, she and her husband were preparing to join their extended family in North Carolina. Later, he described her as "a woman of soft features, gentle manners, kind soul and elegant presence." And he added, using words that would one day be engraved on her memorial at nearby Kilmuir, that hers was "a name that will be mentioned in history, and if courage and fidelity be virtues, mentioned with honour."

One year after the visit of Boswell and Johnson, in August 1774, Flora and her husband made their first departure, sailing from Campbeltown in Kintyre. They brought their two oldest sons and eight servants, three of them women, all indentured for five years. This was common practice for tacksmen who could pay transportation costs. After a miserable two-month voyage, the party landed at Cape Fear, North Carolina. Established immigrants welcomed Flora as a celebrity symbol of Scottish bravery, and the moment Allan strode off the ship in his Highland finery—the same he had displayed for Boswell—he stepped into the role of clan leader.

The Revolutionary War would not be declared until April 1775, but skirmishing had already begun. Wilmington was bubbling with unrest. Stiff-necked puritans were especially outraged by Great Britain's Quebec Act of 1774, which recognized a language other than English (French) and the right to practice a religion other than Protestantism (Roman Catholicism).

Flora's half-sister, Annabella, had immigrated in 1772 and settled with her husband at Mount Pleasant, three hundred kilometres inland from Wilmington and fifty northeast of Charlotte. The newcomers had other relatives in the vicinity, and after an extensive search bought a 425-acre farm at Cheek Creek (Pekin), a hundred kilometres east of Mount Pleasant. Their daughter Anne and her husband, Alexander MacLeod, lived halfway between the two homesteads.

Early in 1776, Flora and the women servants turned to cleaning, cooking, making clothes and candles, growing vegetables, and caring for geese, ducks and hens. Her husband, their two sons, and five male servants were preparing to tackle the seventy acres of the farm that were ready for the plough. But now war loomed. Thanks partly to the prestige of his wife, Allan MacDonald was widely regarded as the leading Highlander in the region and a key figure in the struggle to retain British control of North Carolina. He was made a lieutenant colonel, while his oldest son, Alexander, became a captain, and his younger one, James, received a junior commission.

Allan recruited Loyalist volunteers. He got word that seven regiments of men were sailing from Cork, Ireland, in four ships. These volunteers would not actually sail until mid-February. But communications were so poor that Allan MacDonald set out that month to meet up with a force that was still weeks from arrival. He had hoped to raise an army of 3,000. But he marched east with half that—1,500 men armed with 650 guns and 80 broadswords.

Thirty kilometres north of Wilmington, in the woods at Moore's Creek Bridge, the rebel forces had set a trap, removing planks and greasing timbers that supported the bridge. On February 27, when in the early morning light eighty sword-wielding Scots mounted a splendid Highland charge, they were cut down by withering fire or else driven into the black waters of the creek.

The Loyalists retreated but 850 were captured. Many were released on parole, but the leaders were marched off to jail, among them Flora's husband and twenty-year-old son, Alexander. On learning what had happened, Flora MacDonald took to her bed. Years later, she published a third-person account describing how she had plunged into misery and sickness on "being informed that her husband and friends were all killed or taken. [She] contracted a severe fever and was deeply oppressed with straggling parties of plunderers from their army, and night robbers, who more than once threatened her life, wanting a confession where her husband's money was. Her servants deserted her, and such as stayed grew so very insolent that they were of no service or help to her."

With her son James, who had escaped the patriots, she stayed on at the homestead though she no longer felt safe. When she recovered from her fever, Flora felt driven "to visit and comfort the other poor gentlewomen" whose kinfolk were in prison with her husband, because "they blamed him as being the author of their misery in raising the Highlanders." She set out, as Hugh Douglas tells us in *Flora MacDonald: The Most Loyal Rebel*, to ride around the country, visiting one family after another. On one of these outings, she fell from her horse and broke her right arm, and so was confined to her home for months. She became more vulnerable than ever. Thieves made off with books and family treasures, including an exquisite, four-piece set of silver given to her by admiring Jacobite sympathizers in London.

With her husband incarcerated, his fate unknown and her

safety at home in jeopardy, Flora MacDonald moved several times. For some months, she resided with her daughter Anne, who had her fourth child in 1776. Patriots plundered property, burned down houses, and robbed and terrorized Loyalists. Dragged from one prison to another for eighteen months, Allan MacDonald could only protest and petition Congress.

Loyalist families were fleeing northward out of North Carolina. In October 1777, Flora received word that Allan had negotiated his release and secured a prisoner exchange. From Philadelphia, he had made his way to New York City and, while raising a company of "gentlemen volunteers," was trying to arrange for her to join him there.

British forces had taken New York the previous year. A cousin, Alexander MacDonald, was urging Allan to travel north to Nova Scotia, to take up his commission with the Royal Highland Emigrants. He delayed, waiting for Flora. After much back and forth, her son-in-law, Alexander MacLeod, obtained a flag of truce that enabled Flora, her daughter Anne, and her four grandchildren to flee. They sailed in a small boat from Wilmington to New York, by water roughly 1,100 kilometres "in the dead of winter," as she wrote later, "being in danger of our lives for the most of a voyage by a constant storm."

In April 1778, she reached New York and rejoined her husband after a separation of two years and two months. In August, from Nova Scotia, Allan received an ultimatum from his military superior, ordering him to take charge of his regiment or his pay would be cut. In October, he made his way north to Fort Edward at Windsor, Nova Scotia. There, on a hill overlooking Minas Basin, a four-cornered wooden palisade enclosed several buildings: a barracks, officers' quarters, a bakery, kitchens, stores and a two-storey wooden blockhouse, the last of which is all that remains today. Allan secured permission for Flora to join him.

Late in the autumn of 1778, four years after she departed Scotland, Flora MacDonald sailed north from the southern colonies— a second wrenching departure. By the time she reached Halifax, she "was very nigh death's door by a violent disorder the rough sea and long passage had brought on." She stayed in Halifax for eight days, "on account of my tender state." On the ninth day, she set out for Fort Edward, sixty-five kilometres northwest, travelling through woods and snow by horse-drawn sleigh.

On day five, she reached the fort, where accommodations were rough and rudimentary. Flora joined Allan in the officers' quarters— a spartan log dwelling, bitterly cold: "There we continued all winter and spring, covered with frost and snow, and almost starved with cold to death, it being one of the worst winters ever seen there."

When summer came, Flora took another bad fall, dislocating the wrist of her good arm. The regimental surgeon did his best, but forever afterwards Flora had trouble with both arms. She was now fifty-seven and as the year wore on, she began to dread the thought of another winter at Fort Edward—and to think wistfully of her old life on Skye. In October 1779, with war still raging to the south and her husband obligated to remain where he was, Flora sailed back across the Atlantic—her third and final leave-taking in the dance called America.

For Flora MacDonald, that dance had proven unfortunate. After landing in England, Flora took ill, suffering "a violent fit of sickness which confined me to my bed in London for half a year." Jacobite friends cared for her and in the spring of 1780, she travelled north to Edinburgh and then to Skye. For the next few years, she lived mostly at the MacLeod-owned Dunvegan Castle with the family of her daughter, Mrs. Anne MacLeod. But she also shuttled among relatives on the Long Island.

After the war ended in 1783, Allan MacDonald received his land grant—seven hundred acres near Kennetcook, Nova Scotia. He cleared woodlands and built a house, hoping to send for Flora and create a new home. But he received far less money for his military services than he had hoped, and in 1785, he returned to Skye.

One of their sons, John, who had astonished everyone by amassing a small fortune in Sumatra, relieved them of any financial worries. They settled into a home on Skye near four of their five surviving children. In 1789, as she wound up a series of autobiographical letters at the request of Sir John MacPherson, Flora wrote of having casts on both her arms and of how her husband's long confinement had resulted in his losing the use of his legs—"so that I may fairly say we both have suffered in our person, family and interest, as much as if not more than any two going under the name of refugees or loyalists, without the smallest recompense."

Flora MacDonald is buried at Kilmuir Cemetery on Skye, near where she landed with Bonnie Prince Charlie.

On March 4, 1790, Flora MacDonald went to the grave. She was buried at Kilmuir Cemetery on the north Skye coast, less than two miles from where, in 1746, she had landed with the prince. She is commemorated, more than two centuries after she died, in song, dance, poetry and stone. In Canada, visitors to Fort Edward can walk where once she walked. And in so doing, we can honour the intrepidity of the woman who, in her twenties, risked her life to save the most wanted man in Europe; and who, in her fifties, as Hugh Douglas points out, faced "disaster with bravery which made her as great a heroine as when she was rescuing Prince Charlie."

PART FOUR

BARBAROUS CLEARANCES

15

Croick Church

THE VOYAGE OF THE *HECTOR*, THE PRINCE EDWARD Island settlement of Lord Selkirk, and even the dance called America evolved in response to the earliest Highland Clearances. That first phase of evictions reached a violent crescendo in the Sutherland Clearances which centred around Dunrobin Castle. The second phase, which became even more violently ugly than the first, began in the 1840s and spawned a still greater flight to Canada. One of the key locations, the antithesis of Dunrobin, is the modest Croick Church.

Today you can reach that little building by driving west from Dornoch for just under forty kilometres. You follow the A949, a two-lane highway that takes you to Bonar Bridge. Cross the Dornoch Firth onto the A836 to Ardgay, turn right and follow a smaller, nameless road that winds west along the River Carron. You drive through Dounie and past Gruinards Farm and Cottages, the centre of the area formerly known as Greenyards, or Greenyard.

To those already interested in the Clearances, those names may be familiar. Finally, there you see it, the little white church where the people of Glencalvie took refuge after they were evicted from their homes. According to a plaque outside, they sheltered "in the lee of the church building rather than in the church itself, which to them might have been sacrilegious." Today, the church remains always open. Sheena and I entered to read the names and messages scratched in the glass of the east window. But first we paused in the churchyard and looked around at the empty rolling hills.

In 1845, when they were driven from their homes, the people of Glencalvie marched almost ten kilometres to shelter beside Croick Church.

In those hills in 1842, not ten kilometres from where we stood, eighty-eight people lived as their ancestors had done, communally farming a total of twenty acres. Most of them bore the surname Ross. They resided in nineteen heather-roofed cottages, one made of stone, the others of turf. Elderly single women occupied three of those dwellings. They paid no rent and supported themselves by grazing a few sheep or goats. The other cottars contributed to the rent, which they raised by growing barley, oats and potatoes, and herding cattle and sheep. A reporter from *The Times of London* would write that these people "are exceedingly attached to the glen. Their associations are all within it. . . . Their hearts are rooted to their hearths."

In February, the people of Glencalvie learned that estate manager James Gillanders had posted an advertisement offering to sell their lands. Community leaders approached Gustavus Aird, their twenty-eight-year-old minister. Since arriving in January of the previous year, the devout Aird had endeared himself to the people of Glencalvie. On March 14, Aird wrote to James Gillanders, telling him that Major Charles Robertson had promised there would be no evictions. The major, then serving with the British army in Australia, was the son and heir of the aging landowner, William Robertson. He had written to Aird: "So long as they paid the rent they were then paying, he would not think of turning out so many people, and I really think that if he were in the country that he would still be of the same feeling."

Not only that, Aird wrote, but the tenants stood ready to match any offer that might come from an outsider. If Gillanders declined, "these eighty-eight souls will then be set adrift, without knowing where to go or look for shelter. At home there is almost no prospect of their procuring any place; and to emigrate would prove to most of them but total misery, as, after reaching any of the colonies, they would not have the wherewithal to support themselves."

Gillanders responded on March 21. After "tender consideration," he had decided to leave the people in place, provided they gave "a full rent for the farm, which I do not consider they pay at present." He invited them to join in bidding for the land. Aird communicated this response and the Glencalvie Rosses declared themselves ready to pay the increase. They asked Aird to arrange a meeting for Monday, March 28. But on Friday the 25th, without further notice, the people learned that sheriff-officers were riding into the valley carrying writs of removal.

The farmers were "to flit and remove themselves, bairns, family, servants, subtenants, cottars, and dependents, cattle, goods, and gear." They were to leave their modest homes empty so that "the Pursuer or others in his name may then enter thereto and peaceably possess, occupy and enjoy the same in time coming." Any resistance would incur a fine, payable to Mr. Robertson of Kindeace, of £10—equivalent today to £960 (Can$1620)—to these people, an astronomical sum.

The women of Glencalvie gathered at the bridge that crossed the River Carron and built a peat fire. They greeted the arriving officers in a friendly manner, asked to see the writs of removal and, on receiving them, promptly threw them into the blaze. The officers turned around and rode back to Tain, forty kilometres away.

Young Gustavus Aird, badly frightened, knew they would be back in force. He begged the people to relent, to receive the officers civilly: "Say to them, Gentlemen by what hour must we be gone? Collect your cattle, your furniture, carry your sick, your children, and come in a body to the nearest town south. If you break the law, you make it impossible for any like your minister to say a word for you."

The following Monday, a grey day, a sheriff-substitute named Cameron approached Glencalvie with a band of constables. Gustavus Aird intercepted them some distance upriver and showed Cameron the letter Gillanders had sent promising the people a chance to bid. The government official expressed displeasure but waved his men onward just the same. Soon, they heard the Glencalvie people blowing whistles, summoning allies. In the roadway, half a mile from the bridge, a small group of men and women stood waiting, armed with cudgels. On spotting Gustavus Aird, these fell back.

A cold rain began to fall. At the bridge, a great crowd had assembled, tenants and subtenants from Glencalvie and neighbouring western Greenyard. They had built a smouldering peat fire. Later, Cameron would claim that two hundred people had gathered, most of them women. As the constables approached, the locals yelled at Gustavus Aird to leave them: "You have no business in such company!" Aird narrowly prevented a woman from hauling the sheriff-substitute from his horse.

Speaking Gaelic, Cameron hollered for silence. Then he said that he deeply regretted that "so many people should be turned adrift, but by resisting the law you are only injuring yourselves." Cameron spoke of a letter that Aird had received from Gillanders, and claimed that the latter "could not show his face if he turned you out." At this, people laughed and jeered. Cameron insisted, "I don't believe you'll be turned out, and I'll do all I can to prevent it, if you'll take the summonses and not break the law."

The people let Gustavus Aird cross the bridge. They pointed to a cottage and urged him to get out of the rain. Cameron dismounted and made to follow, but the crowd prevented him. Losing patience, he called the constables forward with the writs. The journalist from the *Times*, having hurried to Glencalvie on learning that evictions were imminent, reported that some of the women took the summonses mockingly, as if beginning a dalliance, and that all consigned the papers to the fire.

With his men, Cameron withdrew upriver to a gamekeeper's cottage. He sought the identity of those he called ringleaders—a man in a white hat and a woman with a stick in her hand. Nobody could identify any such figures. Cameron retreated to Tain and from there, the sheriff himself, a Mr. Jardine, sent a demand that the young people of Glencalvie should come to town to be examined by magistrates. They replied that they would come if the sheriff promised they would not be put in "the sharp-pointed house" or the Old Tolbooth jail in Edinburgh.

After that exchange, nothing. A calm descended. The aging Robertson, now on his deathbed in London, may well have denied Gillanders permission to use violence. The peace extended through the rest of that year and then through the so-called Disruption of 1843, when Gustavus Aird became one of 450 evangelical ministers to break away from the established Scottish church to form the Free Church of Scotland. For the people of Glencalvie, this meant abandoning the greystone church five kilometres away at Croick to attend services on a hillside, or else in an abandoned wool shed.

But then, in 1844, following the death in London of old William Robertson, sixth laird of Kindeace, James Gillanders got clearance from the new laird in Australia to proceed as he believed would be most profitable. Gillanders invited three Glencalvie leaders (some reports say four) to meet him at Tain. Believing he was accepting their latest offer, they went, only to be handed writs of removal. Gillanders told them they had until next spring to clear out. He would evaluate their stock and pay them fair market value. And they had permission to take away the timber of their houses, which served for door frames.

Blind-sided, stunned, the three Rosses accepted the writs and went home. Gustavus Aird undertook to assist them. Yet he also told his flock they should obey the law. Aird sent letters to all and sundry describing the situation and seeking funds to help with resettlement. A committee of "northern gentlemen"—among them, Donald Ross, an activist-journalist based in Glasgow—established the Glencalvie Fund. Spokesman Charles Spence, a supreme court solicitor, sent a passionate communication to John Delane, editor of *The London Times*, complaining that ninety Ross-shire cottagers were being evicted and had nowhere to go.

Spence wrote that nineteen people had so far donated the equivalent of a few thousand dollars "for the relief of these poor people." He hoped "that they may yet be saved from the necessity of camping in the CHURCHYARD, as the aged could not be expected to survive the effects of exposure to damp and cold in such a situation, especially laboring as they are under heavy depression of spirits produced by expulsion from the land of their fathers, where for centuries they have been located." He hoped also that "the sympathy of the public will yet help to cheer the sufferers amidst their cloudy prospects."

The *Times* editor, to his credit, responded by sending out "a gentleman of experience and talent"—what today we would call an investigative reporter. In mid-May, having taken rooms at the Inn of Ardgay, this anonymous "commissioner"—probably Donald Ross—filed a series of dispatches sympathetic to the evicted. In the first, dated May 15, 1845, he invoked the Sutherland Clearances of 1820, regretting that "the heartless course, with all its sequences of misery, of destitution, and of crime, is again being resorted in Ross-shire."

He wrote with controlled fury of "the almost inconceivable misery and hopeless destitution in which, for the expected acquisition of a few pounds, hundreds of peaceable and generally industrious and contented peasants are driven out from the means of self-support, to become wanderers and starving beggars." He set the scene, describing the remote parliamentary district of Croick as twenty miles (thirty kilometres) long, ten to fifteen miles (fifteen to twenty-five kilometres) wide, and "consisting chiefly of hills of heather and rock, peopled only in a few straths and glens." The district "was formerly thickly peopled, but one of those clearances many years ago nearly swept away the population, and now the whole number of its inhabitants amounts, I am told, to only 370 souls." These lived in three straths or glens: Amatnatua, Greenyard and Glencalvie.

"It is the inhabitants of Glencalvie, in number 90 people," he wrote, "whose turn it is now to be turned out of their homes, all at once, the aged and the helpless as well as the young and strong; nearly the whole of them without hope or prospect for the future." He described Glencalvie as comprising "bleak rough hills, whose surface are almost all rock and heather, closed in on all sides, leaving in the valley a gentle declivity of arable land of a very poor description, dotted over by cairns of stone and rock, not, at the utmost computation, of more than 15 to 20 acres in extent." For this piece of indifferent land, with a right of pasturage on the hills, he wrote, the tenants were paying an "incredible" rent. He quoted respectable farmers as saying they did not know how the people raised such an amount.

"Eighteen families have each a cottage in the valley; they have always paid their rent punctually, and they have contrived to support themselves in all ordinary seasons. They have no poor on the poor roll, and they help one another over the winter. I am told that not an inhabitant of this valley has been charged with any offence for years back. During the war it furnished many soldiers; and an old pensioner, 82 years of age, who has served in India, is now dying in one of these cottages, where he was born."

In 1843, when Gillanders sent men to serve summonses of removal, the tenants had been fully paid up. "For 500 years their fathers had peaceably occupied the glen, and the people were naturally indignant. Who can be surprised that, on the constables going amongst them with the summonses, they acted in a manner which, while it showed their excitement, not the less evinced their wish to avoid breaking the law? The women met the constables beyond the boundaries, over the river, and seized the hand of the one who held the notices; whilst some held it out by the wrist, others held a live coal to the papers and set fire to them. They were afraid of being charged with destroying the notices, and they sought thus to evade the consequences. This act of resistance on their part has been made the most of."

One of the tenants told him that in 1843, on hearing they were to be turned out because they did not pay enough rent, the people offered to pay fifteen pounds a year more, and then to match any offer. "The following year [1844], however, the four chief tenants were decoyed to Tain, under the assurance that Mr. Gillanders was going to settle with them, they believing that their holdings were to be continued to them. The notices were then, as they say, in a treacherous and tricky manner, served upon them."

After serving the tenants, the officers obtained "a decreet of removal" under which, if the people refused to leave, they would be put out by force. At this point, they negotiated an agreement that they could remain until May 12, allowing them time to find other quarters. They would receive a hundred pounds on quitting, be paid for their stock and be free to carry away the timber of their houses. Later, the date of removal was extended to May 25.

Now, even this stood revealed as a deception. "In speaking of all, the four principal tenants only are meant," the *Times* reported, "for, according to the factor, these were all he had to do with; but this is not the case even in regard to the four principal tenants. Two only, a father and son, have got a piece of black moor, near Tain, 25 miles off, without any house or shed on it, out of which they hope to obtain subsistence. . . . Another old man with a family has got a house and a small lot of land in Edderton, about 20 miles off." Only these had obtained places where they might hope to eke out a living.

"A widow with four children, two imbecile, has obtained two small apartments in a bothy or turf hut near Bonar Bridge, for which she is to pay £2 rent, without any land or means of subsistence. Another, a man with a wife and four children, has got an apartment at Bonar Bridge, at £1 rent. He goes there quite destitute, without means of living. Six only of eighteen households, therefore, have been able to obtain places in which to put their heads; and of these, three only have any means of subsistence before them. The rest are hopeless and helpless."

The people of Glencalvie had distributed their furniture among the cottages of their nearest neighbours, the reporter declared. Then they marched out of the glen in a body, with two or three carts carrying children, many of them infants, and other carts containing their few possessions. "I am told it was a most wretched spectacle, to see these poor people march out of the glen in a body, with two or three carts containing their bedding and their requisites. The whole countryside was up on the hills watching them." The reporter saw them himself, seated on the banks of the River Carron, listening to the recital of psalms—"the women all neatly dressed in net caps and wearing scarlet or plaid shawls; the men wearing their blue bonnets and having their shepherds' plaids wrapped about them."

The writer asked: "For what is this virtuous and contented community to be scattered and driven into destitution? I confess I can find no answer." He speculated that landlords acted out of "fear of the New Scotch Poor Law," which required them to help support the indigent on their lands. But the laird of Kindeace, he wrote,

"NEVER GAVE ONE FARTHING, the poor supported their own helpless poor, the wealthy let them do so unassisted."

At first, not realizing that the people followed the counsel of their minister, Gustavus Aird, the visitor marvelled that the Glencalvie people were so docile. He speculated that "these poor Highlanders" had been so broken in spirit that not a murmur, not a remonstrance, escaped them in the completion of this "most heartless wholesale ejectment." Were any such clearances attempted in England, he told his readers, "I leave you to conceive the excitement . . . the mob procession, the effigy burning, the window-smashing." Later, awakened by spending a few days among them, he wrote that "it is owing to the influence of religion alone that they refrain from breaking out into open and turbulent resistance of the law."

Looking out from the inside of Croick Church. Some of those who took shelter here scratched messages in the windows, and many of them made their way to Huron County, Ontario.

The weather turned wet and cold and, as feared, the people were forced to retreat to the church at Croick, many of them sheltering in the churchyard under a tarpaulin stretched over poles. They kindled a fire and children clustered around it, and two "dejected looking mothers" placed cradles containing infants close to the flames. The reporter counted twenty-three children in the churchyard, "all under the age of ten, and seven of them were ill." He saw a few young adults, but most people were over forty.

Within a week of their arrival, the farmers had disappeared from the churchyard. Most left no records of where they went, although some made their way as refugees to Huron County, Ontario. Before they left, using their second language, English, some scratched a few words in the windows of the church—despairing messages that, some 170 years later, two Canadians stood reading in transcription at Croick Church: "Glencalvie people was in the church here May 24, 1845 . . . Glencalvie people the wicked generation . . . Glencalvie is a wilderness . . . ship them to the colony." We could not decipher every word but no matter. What had happened here was perfectly clear.

16

—

The Most Hated Man in Scotland

I N THE MID-NINETEENTH CENTURY, COLONEL JOHN Gordon lived in the fabulous Cluny Castle in Aberdeenshire. He owned six slave plantations in the West Indies and was said to be "the richest commoner" in Britain. Gordon became "the most hated man in Scotland" not because he was a slave-owner, and not because he was wealthy, but because he stayed that way by ruthlessly squeezing the lifeblood out of poor tenant farmers eking out a living on his massive land holdings—estates that included, as of 1838, the entire island of Barra.

In *Clanship to Crofters' War*, historian T.M. Devine describes Gordon as the prototypical Highland estate owner, a man who "bought partly *because* rentals were low and the land was poor in the hope of transforming its prospects and so making huge gains in the long term." In 1838, by outbidding the infamous Patrick Sellar in what today would be considered a bankruptcy sale, Gordon acquired key sections of the vast Clan Ranald (MacDonald) estate in western Scotland.

That estate included lands on the Scottish mainland and in both the Inner and Outer Hebrides—among these last, Benbecula,

South Uist and Barra. These three islands, linked to the Clan MacNeill for hundreds of years, had been consolidated with the more northerly lands of the MacDonalds in the early 1600s. Two centuries later, the clan chieftain Reginald George MacDonald— famous for swaggering around in Highland dress at the court of King George IV—lived so far above his means that he drove his estate first into trusteeship and then into insolvency.

Cluny Castle in Aberdeenshire was home to Colonel John Gordon when he began driving people out of their blackhouses and into penury and wretchedness.

Enter Colonel John Gordon, who acquired not the entire estate but the three outer islands, where a potato famine began taking a toll in the mid-1840s, reducing people to penury. The Reverend Norman Macleod wrote: "The scene of wretchedness which we witnessed, as we entered on the estate of Col. Gordon, was deplorable, nay, heart-rending. On the beach the whole population of the country seemed to be met, gathering cockles . . . I never witnessed such countenances—starvation on many faces—the children with their melancholy looks, big looking knees, shriveled legs, hollow eyes, swollen-like bellies—God help them, I never did witness such wretchedness."

By 1848, the rents paid by these people had earned Gordon a return of less than 66 percent on his investment. Meanwhile, he had been compelled to expend £8,000 in famine relief. The colonel had not attained his splendiferous lifestyle by letting this sort of thing continue. He acted, and today one result of his handiwork can be discovered on the east side of Barra at an archaeological site that was once a thriving village.

You won't find "Balnabodach" listed in the guidebooks or even on maps of the Outer Hebrides. But if on Barra you drive seven kilometres north out of Castlebay on the one-lane highway that encircles the island, the A888, you should be able to spot a series of ruins on the eastern side of the road, down the hill as you approach Loch Obe. You may have to scramble a bit (think trial and error), but you can make your way through marshy ground to stone ruins that once were Barra blackhouses. To wander among them, careful not to do damage, is to get as close as anyone can to those who lived here once upon a time.

Here, along a freshwater stream that tumbles down the hill to the loch, people have lived off and on for centuries. The loch connects to the open sea by a four-hundred-metre channel that once afforded excellent protection against sea raiders. Peat deposits provided fuel for fires, and cows and sheep could graze on the gentler slopes. In 1996, according to an Isle of Barra website, archaeologists discovered a barbed flint arrowhead dating from around 2,000 BC. And people who lived here during the Iron Age, between 200 BC and AD 200, left nearly 250 pieces of pottery, as well as flint tools and pumice stones used for scrubbing animal skins.

Here we see the ruins of Balnabodach on the Isle of Barra. John Gordon had people violently evicted and shipped to Canada.

By the time of Scotland's first census, in 1841, Balnabodach was home to eight households and twenty-six people. They lived in Barra blackhouses built during the previous century, with thick walls and single doors in one long side. Families made do with an earthen floor and cooked and slept around the fireplace at one end. The largest house, designated House A, once had a wooden dresser in one corner. Here, the family displayed their finest pottery, which comprised brightly coloured "sponge ware" from the Scottish mainland and crockery from Stoke and Newcastle in England.

Archaeologists found an abundance of bowls, useful for eating broth, gruel and porridge. They turned up a clay pipe, some glass beads and copper buttons, an iron chisel and knife, and a sharpening stone. They also found a copper thimble outside the front door and could imagine a "woman of the household sitting on a sunny summer day, mending an item of clothing and dropping her thimble between the cracks in the stone." In an atypical flight of fancy, they surmised that the woman might well have been Anne Macdugald or her sister-in-law, Flory Macdugald.

This they extrapolated from the 1841 census, when Hector Macdugald and his family probably lived in House A, which had a small room added onto one end not as a byre for animals but for human habitation. While most of the households were listed as crofters, one was a cottar (who farmed another tenant's land) and another a pauper—eighty-year-old Neil Macdugald. These families kept a few sheep and did some fishing, but mainly they subsisted by growing potatoes and barley.

In the mid-to-late 1840s, the horrendous potato famine that devastated Ireland also wreaked havoc in the Outer Hebrides. It starved Islanders on Barra and South Uist and, less acceptably still, rendered them unable to pay their rent. Colonel John Gordon decided to solve this problem by evicting the wretched crofters and shipping them to Canada. He identified Balnabodach as one of the Barra townships to be cleared and in 1851 turned loose his hired thugs.

According to oral tradition, these well-paid hooligans forced the tenantry into boats in the safe harbour. One young woman was out milking the family cow by the loch when Gordon's agents dragged her off with nothing but the clothes on her back. A few people ran into the hills and were hunted down by dogs. They were hauled aboard in handcuffs.

A Protestant minister named Beatson led the evictions in Barra and the tiny island of Mingulay, which were Roman Catholic. An eyewitness named Roderick MacNeill, remembering in the present tense, described Beatson as "the most vigilant and assiduous officer Colonel Gordon has. He may be seen in Castle Bay, the principal anchorage in Barra, whenever a sail is hoisted, directing his men like a gamekeeper with his hounds, in case any of the doomed Barra men should escape." One such man "took shelter on an Arran boat which Beatson boarded in a fury, demanding his surrender. The master [one John Crawford] lifted a hand-spike and threatened to split the minister's skull, man of God or no, if he did not get ashore with his dogs."

MacNeill, evicted from Mingulay, had never been the same since "my people were scattered, some of them in Australia, some in Canada, and some mouldering in the dust. Oh, the turns of the hard world! Many a trick does it play, and so it was with me. My new house was burned over my head, and I burned my hands in rescuing my dear little children. Oh, the suffering of the poor folk, the terrible time that was! The land was taken from us though we were not a penny in debt, and all the lands of the township were given to a Lowland farmer. He had always wished to have them, and he was not content until he got them."

Small boats ferried the Barra people to a ship called the *Admiral*, which then sailed forty kilometres north to Lochboisdale in South Uist. There, on August 11, 1851, a different agent—the hot-tempered John Fleming—invited local tenants to a compulsory public meeting, threatening absentees with a severe fine (forty shillings). The meeting devolved into a surprise press-ganging, as thugs forced people into boats and then onto the ship that lay waiting to carry them to Canada. Forget gathering possessions: they were going aboard here and now.

Two days before, Fleming had written from South Uist to an emigration officer in Quebec. For the last three weeks, he had been "superintending the emigration of about 1,500 souls from this country to Canada." He had just learned "with regret" that due to the unexpected illness of Colonel Gordon, nobody had previously notified anybody in Quebec.

Fleming wrote that he had already sent two ships—the *Brooksby* and the *Montezuma* filled with passengers in late July, and the *Perthshire* on August 5. He expected "the *Admiral* to be cleared out a few days hence." He described the South Uist emigrants as having worked "at draining, ditching, road making, &c., and I trust they may be advantageously employed when they reach Canada in similar work, or at railway operations. . . . Of the Barra people, part have found employment at similar work, and part have supported themselves as fishermen, of which they have considerable skill."

Fleming noted that a thousand people had been sent out two years before, "and send home encouraging accounts to their friends here." Colonel Gordon was providing a free passage, clothing and shoes, and hoped that "these that are now leaving the land of their fathers may earn a competency in the land of their adoption."

Two resources enable us to envision the truth of these events. The first, a relatively recent study, "The Jaws of Sheep" by James A. Stewart Jr., was published in *Proceedings of the Harvard Celtic Colloquium* for 1998. The other we have already encountered: *Gloomy Memories* by Donald Macleod. In the 1850s, Macleod had emigrated to Woodstock, Ontario, some 150 kilometres west of Toronto. Whenever he travelled between Woodstock and Toronto, at about the halfway point he would pass through the town of Dundas. There he interviewed numerous former Islanders, survivors of Gordon's 1851 Clearances.

"Hear the sobbing, sighing and throbbing," he wrote later. "See the confusion, hear the noise, the bitter weeping and bustle. Hear mothers and children asking fathers and husbands, where are we going? hear the reply, *Chan eil fios againn*—we know not." One eyewitness, Catherine Macphee of Lochdar, near the north end of

South Uist, described the evictions as "loathsome work." She told Macleod: "I have seen big strong men, champions of the country-side, the stalwarts of the world, being bound on Loch Boisdale quay and cast into the ship as would be done to a batch of horses or cattle, the bailiff and the ground officers and the policemen gath-ered behind them in pursuit."

One powerful Highlander, Angus Johnstone, "resisted with such pith that they had to handcuff him before he could be mas-tered, but in consequence of the priests' interference his manacles were taken off and (he was) marched between four officers on board the emigrant vessel." The forced evictions went on for more than three weeks. One morning, Macphee said, "we were suddenly awak-ened by the screams of a young female who had been recaptured in an adjoining house, she having escaped after her first capture. We all rushed to the door, and saw the broken-hearted creature, with dishevelled hair and swollen face, dragged away by two constables and a ground-officer."

Almost 170 years later, while exploring South Uist in 2017, I thought about that young woman's first capture. Roughly ten kilo-metres north of the ferry dock in Lochboisdale, we came upon the ruins of a tacksman's house in Upper Bornish Clearance Village. Earlier that day, after visiting the birthplace of Flora MacDonald, we had gone to the Kildonan Museum and picked up an archaeo-logical guide pointing the way to notable ruins. It spoke rather grandly of a "Kildonan Trail" but we found ourselves greeting cat-tle as we beat across pathless, marshy ground to the ruins of this neglected village. In the eighteenth century, the guidebook said, Upper Bornish comprised half a dozen households, the people living mostly "in long houses shared at times with livestock."

Men, women and children who lived here in Upper Bornish Clearance Village were tricked into attending a meeting, dragged onto a ship and then sent to Lower Canada.

The tacksman among them, the senior tenant, was the only one who had a separate byre for sheep and cattle. Decades came and went, people lived and died, and in August 1851, the poor farmers whose ancestors had toiled here for centuries were among those commanded to attend a public meeting at Lochboisdale, where a sailing ship called the *Admiral* stood at anchor. When I read that the penny dropped.

I remembered the eyewitness narrative of Catherine Macphee, who reported that many of those who turned up for the Lochboisdale meeting had been "seized and, in spite of their entreaties, sent on board the transports." Later she heard the screams of that young woman, who had escaped once only to be recaptured. Among the ruins, I stood reflecting. Given its proximity to Lochboisdale, this village, Upper Bornish, might well have been where that young woman came from. I stood in silence gazing skyward.

Some of those who were put aboard the *Admiral* broke away and swam to shore. Macphee added that "Fleming led the police and officers in pursuit of them, combing the curling hills to the north of the loch, beating the fugitives down with truncheons and bringing them in irons to the quay." From Benbecula, located immediately to the north of South Uist, Fleming brought carts filled with bound men over the sand at low tide. He sent raiders to storm cottages as dawn broke, but even then some people escaped. "Were you to see the racing and chasing of policemen," Macphee said, "pursuing the outlawed natives, you would think that you had been transported to the banks of the Gambia on the slave coast of Africa."

She grew emotional at the remembrance: "I have seen the townships swept, and the big holdings made of them, the people being driven out of the island to the streets of Glasgow and the wilds of Canada, such of them as did not die of hunger and plague and smallpox while going across the sea. I have seen the women putting their children in the carts which were sent from Benbecula and Lochdar to Loch Boisdale while their husbands lay bound in the pen, and were weeping, without power to give them a helping hand, though the women themselves were crying aloud, and the little children wailing like to break their hearts."

Families were separated. On Barra, many people had fled into the rolling hills. Most were tracked down by dogs and taken, but not all. The daughters of one John MacDugall, for example, aged twelve and fourteen, were left alone on Barra after the rest of the family was shipped off to Quebec.

Between 1848 and 1851, Colonel John Gordon cleared more than 2,000 people from the Outer Hebrides. On five ships, he transported almost 1,700 people to Lower Canada, where 600 were accepted as paupers and were supported by the colony. Hundreds of others were reduced to beggary. A few were buried on Grosse Île, site of an immigration depot near Quebec City.

Gordon's promises of work and land proved empty. More than seventy people who had voluntarily boarded the *Admiral* wrote a deposition asserting that they had done so "under promises to the effect that Colonel Gordon would defray their passage to Quebec; that the Government Emigration Agent there would send the whole party free to Upper Canada, where, on arrival, the Government agents would give them work, and furthermore, grant them land on certain conditions." They declared, further, that they "are now landed in Quebec so destitute that if immediate relief be not afforded them, and continued until they are settled in employment, the whole will be liable to perish with want."

Many who proceeded to Upper Canada made their way to the township of Dundas. "They were in rags," said a newspaper, "their mourning weeds were the shapeless fragments of what had once been clothes." The *Dundas Warder* of October 2, 1851, reported: "We have been pained beyond measure for some time past, to witness on our streets so many unfortunate Highland emigrants, apparently destitute of any means of subsistence and many of them sick for other attendant causes. There will be many to sound the fulsome noise of flattery in the ear of a generous landlord who had spent so much to assist the emigration of his poor tenants. They will give him the misnomer of benefactor, and for what? Because he has rid his estates of the encumbrance of a pauper population."

That same editorial described the funeral of a refugee child. "It was pitiful the other day, to view a funeral of one of these wretched people. It was, indeed, a sad procession. The coffin was constructed of the rudest wood. . . . Children followed in the mournful train; perchance they followed a brother's bier, one with whom they had sported and played for many a healthful day among their native glens. . . . There was a mother too, among the mourners, one who had tended the departed with anxious care in infancy and had doubtless looked forward to a happier future in this land of plenty. The anguish of her countenance told too plainly these hopes were blasted, and she was about to bury them in the grave of her child."

On Nov. 26, 1851, the chief emigrant agent in Quebec, A.C. Buchanan, responded to Colonel Gordon's agent, John Fleming, with a cool-headed but ferocious dressing down. Between August 28 and October 18, he wrote, five ships had arrived from Gordon's estates carrying 1,681 passengers. These were *Brooksby*, 285; *Montezuma*, 442; *Perthshire*, 437; *Admiral*, 413; and *Liskeard*, 104. Five adults and three infants had died while sailing or in quarantine.

"These parties presented every appearance of poverty," he wrote, "and, from their statement, which was confirmed by the masters of the several vessels, were without the means of leaving the ship, or of procuring a day's subsistence for their helpless families on landing, and many of them, more particularly the party by the *Perthshire*, were very insufficiently supplied with clothing."

Buchanan laid out an account, noting that Gordon owed £152, in addition to which "there is a charge for a week's rations served out to the passengers on leaving the vessel, for which this department is held responsible, in the event of Colonel Gordon's declining to settle it."

Buchanan noted that because the Quebec populace spoke French, "this city and neighbourhood afford no opening of any extent for the employment of the destitute emigrants who arrive in large numbers and at a particular season of the year. It is in the interior and western portions of the province only that employment for labourers and artisans is to be procured, and these must be reached before the pauper can find any means of support. Therefore, to convey to this port emigrants possessing no resources whatever, and without a provision of some kind for their progress westward, is to subject them to great distress and certain discouragement."

Clearly furious, Buchanan continued at length. The provincial government could not afford to carry the freight for "those who are interested in the removal from Great Britain of paupers and other unprofitable portions of the populations." He asked Fleming to tell Colonel Gordon that "the mere transfer to this port of an indigent tenantry, without an alteration in any respect in their condition, gives no reasonable ground for expecting their subsequent successful progress."

On the other hand, if "the landlord who is interested in the reduction of the population of his estate should extend his assistance so far as to carry forward his emigrants to the occupation of land, or should secure their advance to advantageous employment, the sure result would be incitement to industry and exertion, and the strongest desire on the part of all to obtain a similar opportunity of benefiting themselves."

Buchanan closed by referring "to the wholly different circumstances under which a party consisting of 986 persons were sent out in the past spring by Sir James Matheson, from the island of Lewis. These emigrants were provided with a passage to this port, food and clothing, and on arrival were supplied with a week's rations and a free passage to their ultimate destination. They had embarked in the early part of the season, and nearly the whole landed here in July, when an unusual demand for labourers existed in almost every section of the province. About 400 proceeded to Sherbrooke, Eastern Townships, where those able to work obtained employment on the Montreal and Portland Railroad at ample wages. The remainder went forward to Toronto, where they, also, immediately obtained suitable employment."

At the end of the year, in a report to head office in England, the medical superintendent in Quebec, G.M. Douglas, wrote of those Highland emigrants sent out by Colonel Gordon: "The supply of provisions and water seems to have been good and liberal; but I never, during my long experience at the station, saw a body of emigrants so destitute of clothing and bedding; many children of nine and ten years old had not a rag to cover them. Mrs. Crisp, the wife of the master of the *Admiral* (which vessel brought out 413 of the number), was busily employed all the voyage in converting empty bread-bags, old canvass, and blankets, into coverings for them.

"One full-grown man passed my inspection with no other garment than a woman's petticoat. Great care and precaution seemed to have been taken of their health on the voyage by the medical men in charge, especially Dr. Patterson of the *Perthshire*, who caused the ship's allowance to be issued sparingly at first, as many families had for months previous to embarking subsisted solely upon shell-fish and sea-weed picked up on the beaches and rocks of their island. I learned on inquiry that the ordinary payment for the day's labour of an able-bodied man in South Uist was one pound of oatmeal, and that constant labour even for this miserable pittance was not to be obtained."

As to the money spent on provisions provided to the destitute souls he had dispatched to Quebec, Colonel Gordon, comfortably ensconced at Cluny Castle, never repaid a penny. Colonel John Gordon. The most hated man in Scotland.

17

Raasay, North Uist and Skye

T HE UPWARD-POINTING ARROW AT ROAD'S END SAID simply, "3.2 kilometres." To reach this spot, we had driven our rental car 5.7 kilometres along a winding, rutted and overgrown one-lane track that hugged the side of a small mountain. Luckily, we had encountered no vehicles and no cyclists—in fact, nothing but ornery sheep that stood defiant in the middle of the road while we hammered away on our horn. But now even that jolting progress had been halted. We could drive no farther.

Maybe they are just curious. But to people hiking up the trail towards the clearance village of Hallaig, the sheep certainly seem to have an attitude problem.

We were on the eastern coast of the tiny island of Raasay, which is situated between the Isle of Skye and the Scottish mainland. Our destination was Hallaig, one of the better-known sites of the Highland Clearances. Hallaig is famous because Sorley MacLean (1911–1996), arguably the greatest poet ever to write in Gaelic, gave that name to his most celebrated poem.

MacLean was born no great distance from that once-thriving settlement, now a ruin in which jumbles of rocks indicate where houses stood. Between 1852 and 1854, an Edinburgh gentleman named George Rainy cleared the entire populace of Raasay— twelve townships, ninety-four families. He had recently acquired the island from the debt-ridden MacLeod of Lewis and Raasay, also known as MacLeod of the Lewes. One of the townships Rainy cleared was Hallaig, which lay directly beneath the highest hill on the island, Dun Cana.

Sorley MacLean's relations had lived on this island for generations. In 1773, not far from Hallaig, James Boswell went hiking with some locals and visited a township called Screapadal. He called at a MacLean family farmhouse and later, describing it, presented a classic blackhouse: "It was somewhat circular in its shape," he wrote. "At one end sheep and goats were lodged; at the other, the family. The man and his wife had a little bedstead. The place where the servants lay was marked out upon the ground with whinstones and strewed with fern. The fire was towards the upper end of the house. The smoke went out at a hole in the roof, at some distance and not directly above it, as rain would hurt it." Boswell thought to add, "The farmer here had no children, and he and his wife spoke only Erse [Gaelic]."

Eighty years later, this township, like Hallaig, would be made a jumbled ruin. Most of the people from Raasay journeyed to the colonies that later became Canada. Sheena and I, having travelled the other way, left our car when we could drive no more and followed a dirt track slowly upwards. The hike seemed longer than 3.2 kilometres, but eventually we reached a cairn created in memory of "Sorley MacLean, the people of Hallaig and other cleared crofting townships."

This cairn below Hallaig celebrates the Gaelic-language poet Sorley MacLean. Most of the people cleared from Raasay made their way to Canada.

On the cairn, you can read MacLean's famous poem in the original Gaelic or in English translation by Seamus Heaney. To me, it is reminiscent of "Fern Hill" by Dylan Thomas, one of my all-time favourites: "Time, the deer, is in Hallaig Wood / There's a board nailed across the window / I looked through to see the west / And my love is a birch forever."

Raasay, again, lies immediately east of Skye. To the west of that vastly larger central island, somewhat farther away—call it fifty kilometres—one finds North Uist and South Uist, two islands of the Outer Hebrides. If we were to draw a straight line from Hallaig on Raasay to Dunvegan on Skye and extend it, that line would pass very near Sollas on North Uist.

In 1849, the activist Donald Ross—hard at work with the Glasgow Association in Aid of the Poor—got wind of violent evictions happening in Sollas. Two years before, the second eldest son of Macdonald of Sleat—Godfrey William Wentworth Bosville-Macdonald—had inherited his father's Scottish estates and became the 4th Baron Macdonald. During the previous century, the seventh baron had become infamous for the Ship of the People—that foiled 1739 attempt to kidnap farmers and sell them into slavery in the American colonies.

More recently, between 1838 and 1843, certain Macdonald chieftains, having incurred serious debts, had driven 1,300 tenants from North Uist and replaced them with sheep. Now, in 1849, the 4th Baron Macdonald had decided to evict another 600 people (110 families) from the settlement of Sollas on that island. He had debts exceeding £200,000 (today: more than Can$6.5 million) and three different sheep farmers had expressed interest in the fertile lands around Sollas.

Here, for generations, people had lived on a sandy bay. Lord Bosville-Macdonald proposed to send them to Canada. Not surprisingly, as Thomas Samuel Mulock reported in the *Inverness Advertiser*, the people did not wish to leave the rolling hills, their boats and their neat houses. An eloquent, strong-minded Irishman, Oxford-educated, Mulock is the primary source for later accounts of the Sollas Clearances, including those by Alexander Mackenzie and Ian Fraser Grigor. Mackenzie would emerge as the most comprehensive compiler of clearances accounts, but all three of those narratives contribute to the reconstruction that follows.

When ordered to depart, the people of Sollas were already suffering because the potato crop had failed several years in a row, as it had in Ireland, reducing this area to near famine. At times, families had lived for weeks on shellfish they gathered along the shore. Some men had worked on drainage ditches, but instead of paying them, the factors applied their earnings to their arrears. Lord Bosville-Macdonald, who was living large in England, ordered Sollas to be cleared by May 15, 1849. The inhabitants requested more time so they could sell cattle, kelp and other effects in the summer market. They received no answer. They continued sowing corn and potatoes until May 15 and beyond, and turned as usual to cutting peat.

On July 14, when a sheriff arrived with two assistants, the surprised farmers drove them off. They did the same two days later to Bosville-Macdonald's factor, a bold fellow named Patrick Cooper, who had arrived with twenty officers. On July 17, three hundred people flying black warning flags repulsed a third visitation. The people claimed (rightly) that it was too late in the season to sail for Canada. Before they could settle, winter would engulf them and they would have neither means nor money to survive.

Near the end of July, under two sheriff-substitutes, Colquhoun and Shaw, a stronger force embarked for North Uist from Inverness, comprising several officers, a minister named MacRae and three dozen constables. On arriving by steamer at Armadale on Skye, Colquhoun sent a messenger ashore to ask what to do in case of resistance. From his castle, the laird referred the matter to his factor, Patrick Cooper, who sent word that, "if the agreement to go to Canada, or elsewhere, as emigrants, was not signed by the Sollas tenants, their houses should be pulled down, roof and stance."

After proceeding to Lochmaddy on North Uist, Colquhoun and a few men rode fifteen kilometres west to Sollas, announced their intentions, and arrested two men for previous resistance. Next day, he and his party marched on Sollas in the rain. They encountered three hundred people who jeered at pleas from the factor and the minister and refused to sign an agreement to emigrate. The constables pushed and shoved their way forward and began their evictions, kicking down doors, throwing out furniture and seizing cattle and peat. People from nearby townships, with women in the lead, charged the police but were driven back.

In his *History of the Highland Clearances* (1883), Alexander Mackenzie drew on newspaper reports by Mulock in quoting an eye-witness sympathetic to the landlord: "In evicting Macpherson, the first case taken up, no opposition to the law officers was made. In two or three minutes the few articles of furniture he possessed—a bench, a chair, a broken chair, a barrel, a bag of wool, and two or three small articles, which comprised his whole household of goods and gear—were turned out to the door, and his bothy left roofless.

"The wife of the prisoner Macphail [who had been carried off to Lochmaddy the previous day] was the next evicted. Her domestic plenishing was of the simplest character—its greatest, and by far its most valuable part, being three small children, dressed in nothing more than a single coat of coarse blanketing, who played about her knee, while the poor woman, herself half-clothed, with her face bathed in tears, and holding an infant in her arms, assured the Sheriff that she and her children were totally destitute and without food of any kind. The Sheriff at once sent for the Inspector of the Poor and ordered him to place the woman and her family on the poor's roll."

Colquhoun's second in command, a sheriff-substitute named Shaw, refused to evict the old and infirm people who lived in the next house. Shaw also declined to throw out eight other families, insisting that the notices of eviction had been incorrectly prepared.

Colquhoun arrived at the home of John Mackaskill, a crofter and weaver with a wife and nine children. The crowd on a nearby hill began to shout as the police advanced to demolish the house, assisted by a dozen men hired from the south end of the island. Infuriated by this fact, the locals began throwing stones. The police stormed into the house and started flinging furniture out the door. They cut the web off the loom, and Mrs. Mackaskill rushed to the door with an infant in her arms, wailing that her children were being murdered: *"Tha mo chlann air a bhi' air a muirt."* By throwing more stones, the locals cleared the intruders from the roof of the house. But then, in two divisions, the police charged and scattered the resistance.

Even today on North Uist, sheep can be seen wandering the stone ruins that once were houses in which farm families lived and loved while working the land.

The invaders resumed their destruction. It reached a climax at a house filled with women. As the police dragged one woman out the door, Mulock reports, "she threw herself upon the ground and fell into hysterics, uttering the most doleful sounds, and barking and yelling like a dog for about ten minutes. Another, with many tears, sobs, and groans put up a petition to the Sheriff that they would leave the roof over part of her house, where she had a loom with cloth in it, which she was weaving; and a third woman, the eldest of the family, made an attack with a stick on an officer, and, missing him, she sprang upon him, and knocked off his hat. So violently did this old woman conduct herself that two stout policemen had great difficulty in carrying her outside the door."

With resisters regrouping, Colquhoun had second thoughts. These people were bent on remaining even if he destroyed their houses and crops. At that point, his employer would be legally bound to feed them through the winter—a prospect that might get him fired. He called a truce, and told the people that, if they signed an agreement to leave next year, before the end of June, they could remain until then. Enough people accepted this offer that the invaders could withdraw without losing face. He left most of the houses roofless and ruined and made off with the cattle, claiming them against arrears.

In Inverness, four men were charged, tried and found guilty of "deforcing," or disarming, police officers. They were sentenced to four months in jail—essentially, time served—after the jury unanimously recommended "the utmost leniency and mercy of the Court, in consideration of the cruel, though it may be legal, proceedings adopted in ejecting the whole people of Sollas from their houses and crops without the prospect of shelter, or a footing in their fatherland, or even the means of expatriating them to a foreign one."

Over the next couple of years, the 4th Baron Macdonald cleared Sollas completely, removing all 603 inhabitants. Late in 1852, the last of these sailed to Campbeltown in Kintyre, where they joined other refugees from Harris and Skye on the frigate HMS *Hercules*. On Boxing Day, that vessel sailed from Campbeltown for Hong Kong to become a hospital ship. She carried 756 civilians bound for South Australia and Victoria, most of them refugees from Macdonald's estates. Battered and delayed by a hurricane, the ship did not reach Queenston (Cobh) in Ireland until early January. Epidemics of smallpox and typhus then swept the ship, necessitating a three-month quarantine. Sixty-six people died. Officials sent home seventeen orphaned children and assigned others to a dozen different ships sailing wherever, sometimes breaking up families.

Having dealt with Sollas to the west, Lord Bosville-Macdonald—or rather his trustee, with his agreement—targeted two villages less than thirty kilometres from his ancestral home at Armadale on Skye: Boreraig and Suisnish. Nobody had expressed any interest in renting these lands, but they were well situated in the south of the island and looked promising. In September 1853, having visited these settlements, Donald Ross wrote in the *Northern Ensign* of "heartrending" evictions. The tenants of both were descended from "a long line of peasantry on the Macdonald estates, and were remarkable for their patience, loyalty, and general good conduct."

In the late 1840s, the Isle of Skye was one of the Highland regions hardest hit by the potato famine. In response, influential landlords had created the Highland and Island Emigration Society, designed to foster large-scale emigration to Australia. There, the landlords explained, the evictees would be able to apply their experience with cattle and sheep. Second choice: Canada. The chairman of the society, Sir Charles Trevelyan, argued that charity and relief were inflicting moral damage on the populace. The only remedy was emigration, "and people will never emigrate while they are supported at home at other people's expense."

From the Highlands and Islands, the unabashedly racist Trevelyan proposed to drive out thirty to forty thousand people. He wanted to rid the land of "the surviving Irish and Scotch Celts" and replace them with racially superior peoples. Trevelyan hailed the prospect "of flights of Germans settling here in increasing number—an orderly, moral, industrious and frugal people, less foreign to us than the Irish or Scotch Celt, a congenial element which will readily assimilate with our body politic."

On Skye, Macdonald's trustee had first issued summonses to ten families and arranged passage for them aboard the ill-fated HMS *Hercules*. After that disaster, perhaps the trustees in Skye would relent? No. In April 1853, around the time the *Hercules* finally sailed from Cobh for Adelaide, those left in Boreraig and Suisnish received notices of eviction. They were to remove their cattle and themselves. After petitioning repeatedly, they learned that they would receive land elsewhere on the estate—"portions of a barren moor," Donald Ross writes, "quite unfit for civilization."

In mid-September, Macdonald's ground officer arrived at those settlements with a body of constables. They "at once proceeded to eject in the most heartless manner the whole population," Ross writes, "numbering thirty-two families, and that at a period when the able-bodied male members of the families were away from home trying to earn something by which to pay their rents, and help to carry their families through the coming winter."

Despite the wailing of the women and children, the constables did their dirty work without compunction or hesitation, heaving out furniture and dragging out those so frail and infirm that they could not walk. Ross writes: "The scene was truly heart-rending. The women and children went about tearing their hair and rending the heavens with their cries. Mothers with tender infants at the breast looked helplessly on, while their effects and their aged and infirm relatives were cast out, and the doors of their houses locked in their faces."

Small children gathered in groups, weeping and howling, but to no avail. With the men away working, the constables proceeded with impunity, hauling the women outside and laying waste to their dwellings. Donald Ross detailed all this in *Real Scottish Grievances*, a pamphlet published in 1854. He details several examples, of which one, edited for length, suggests the tenor of the rest.

Flora Matheson, a ninety-six-year-old widow, lived with her son, Alexander Matheson, on a small lot in Suisnish. Her widower son, a father of four, had gone south to work the autumn harvest. He took his oldest boy, leaving his mother in the house with three children. "When the evicting officers and factor arrived," Ross writes, "the poor old woman was sitting on a couch outside the house. The day being fine, her grandchildren lifted her out of her bed and brought her to the door. She was very frail; and it would have gladdened any heart to have seen how the two youngest of her grandchildren helped her along; how they seated her where there was most shelter; and then, how they brought her some clothing and clad her, and endeavored to make her comfortable."

The sun was shining, a gentle breeze wafted over the hills, and the sea (Loch Slapin) glittered with millions of little waves. It looked like a lake of silver, gently agitated. The hills and fields blazed with blooming heather, multi-coloured wildflowers and yellowing corn. The children brought their grandmother a cup of warm milk and some bread from a neighbour's house. Just as the children started inside to prepare a frugal meal, a prolonged barking of dogs set them to running over the fields to see what was happening.

They arrived back looking scared and horrified. The furniture and possessions of their nearest neighbours, just over the hill, lay strewn about on the ground. Their young friends were screaming and crying, and strange men were putting bars and locks on the doors. The old woman knew what this meant. But what could she do? The children thought that if they could only get their aged grannie inside before the evicting officers arrived, they would stave off eviction—for, as their father had assured them, who would interfere with a defenceless old woman of ninety-six?

But already the officers were upon them. They blocked the doorway and then began throwing out articles from within. The children watched, horrified, as the men barred and padlocked the door. They were locked out. Their father and older brother were miles away, who knew where? Their mother was dead, and their frail grandmother, who could not walk unassisted, sat help-less before them. Wrote Donald Ross: "We cannot comprehend the feelings of the poor children on this occasion; and cannot find language sufficiently strong to express condemnation of those who rendered them houseless. Shall we call them savages? That would be paying them too high a compliment, for among savages conduct such as theirs is unknown."

The children cried until they were hoarse. As evening came on, the temperature fell. Their neighbours had also been evicted. None could offer shelter. The children investigated a nearby sheep-cot: small and damp, it had no door, no fireplace, no bed. But it would provide some protection from the weather, and the children con-vinced their grandmother to set out for it, several hundred yards away. They helped her creep along across the field, sometimes on her hands and knees, until finally they reached the shelter.

Here the old woman and her grandchildren remained, day after day, until finally her son arrived home. Not surprisingly, he was horrified. In December, after he had lived for a while with his family in the cold and damp, he was seized with violent cramps.

Then came a cough, and then his limbs and body swelled up, and then he died.

The inspector of the poor, who had served as chief officer in the evictions, got wind of the death. Neighbours threatened him with prosecution for neglect of duty and he removed the old woman to another house. He also removed the children: by this time, two were seriously ill and a third could hardly walk. The inspector left the ailing children fourteen pounds of meal and three of rice for three weeks. He allotted the grandmother two shillings and sixpence per month, but made no provision for fuel, lodgings or nutrition.

"When I visited the house where old Flora Matheson and her grandchildren reside," Donald Ross wrote, "I found her lying on a miserable pallet of straw, which, with a few rags of clothing, are on the bare floor. She is reduced to a skeleton and from her own statement to me, in presence of witnesses, coupled with other inquiries and examinations, I have no hesitation in declaring that she was then actually starving. She had no nourishment, no cordials, nothing whatever in the way of food but a few wet potatoes and two or three shell-fish. The picture she presented, as she lay on her wretched pallet of black rags and brown straw, with her [face] as black as soot, and her long arms thrown across, with nothing on them but the skin, was a most lamentable one—and one that reflects the deepest discredit on the parochial authorities."

"There was no one to attend to the wants or infirmities of this aged pauper but her grandchild, a young girl, ten years of age. . . . But for accidental charity, and that from a distance, Widow Matheson would long ere this have perished of starvation."

Three men of that settlement, Suisnish, were later charged with deforcing officers of the law. They were jailed first at Portree and then marched on foot to Inverness, more than 115 miles

(253 kilometres) away. Macdonald's men came by carriage "at the public expense," Ross wrote, and lived right royally, never dreaming but that they would obtain a victory and get the three captives sent to the penitentiary "to wear hoddy, break stones, or pick oakum for at least twelve months."

The accused, however, through the influence of friends, secured the services of a leading solicitor named Rennie, "who was able to show to the jury the unfounded and farcical nature of the charges made against them. His eloquent and able address to the jury" turned up in the *Inverness Advertiser*. Rennie depicted the case as "one of a fearful series of ejectments now being carried on through in the Highlands; and it really became a matter of serious reflection, how far the pound of flesh allowed by law was to be permitted to be extracted from the bodies of the Highlanders. Here were thirty-two families, averaging four members each, or from 130 to 150 in all, driven out from their houses and happy homes, and for what? For a tenant who, he believed, was not yet found.

"But it was the will of Lord Macdonald and of Messrs. Brown and Ballingal, that they should be ejected; and the civil law having failed them, the criminal law with all its terrors, is called in to overwhelm these unhappy people. But, thank God, it has come before a jury—before you, who are sworn to return, and will return, an impartial verdict; and which verdict will, I trust, be one that will stamp out with ignominy the cruel actors in it."

Rennie asked rhetorically whether the factor here had done his duty. He answered: "No! He had driven the miserable inhabitants out to the barren heaths and wet mosses. He had come with the force of the civil power to dispossess them and make way for sheep and cattle. But had he provided adequate refuge? The evictions in Knoydart, which had lately occupied the attention of the press and all thinking men, were cruel enough; but there a refuge was provided for a portion of the evicted, and ships for their conveyance to a distant land."

The lawyer then shredded the specifics of the charges, observing that the crime of deforcement requires "such violence as to intimidate a person of ordinary firmness of character. Now, there was no violence here, they did not even speak aloud, they merely stood in the door; that might be obstruction, it was certainly not deforcement." He offered more along the same lines. The jury quickly declared the Skye men not guilty, and they withdrew amidst cheers from the Inverness crowd.

The families of these men, Ross adds, were evicted the following Christmas in a cruel and spiteful manner, as invaders drove delicate mothers, half-dressed and carrying newborn infants, out into the drifting snow. Their furniture, blankets and clothing lay for days under the snow while they sheltered in dilapidated out-buildings and barns. These proceedings, later found to be illegal, were widely condemned as unjustifiable and improper, as well as for "the reckless cruelty and inhumanity with which they were carried through."

Lord Macdonald's factor issued a circular insisting that these evictions were "prompted by motives of benevolence, piety, and humanity," and that he ordered them "because [the people] were too far from Church." Decades later, reflecting on this, historian Alexander Mackenzie—who strongly influenced John Prebble—could hardly contain himself: "Oh God! what crimes have been committed in Thy name, and in that of religion! Preserve us from such piety and humanity as were exhibited by Lord Macdonald and his factor on this and other occasions."

18

Back to the Future

WHAT HAPPENED TO ALL THOSE HIGHLANDERS WHO were driven from their homes in Skye and Raasay and Barra and North and South Uist? Impossible to account for all of them, obviously. But we can get a sense of how things unfolded into the present day by tracking the ancestors of Sandy MacDonald, well known in his hometown Halifax as an arts journalist and a musician.

Born in the late 1950s, Sandy traces his roots to the North Uist Clearances. In the spring of 1841, he says, during the sailing season, forty-seven-year-old John MacDonald and his wife, Catherine MacLean, bundled up their seven children and a couple of trunks filled with bare necessities and left their coastal home in Cheese Bay, North Uist, to sail out of the nearby Lochmaddy.

According to the local church records, about three hundred "souls" were leaving North Uist each summer, most heading for Cape Breton Island to start life anew. Many of them had already been driven from their ancestral homes to the coast, where they were forced to make a living by gathering kelp. Now, the market for kelp was drying up, leaving very little to support the inhabitants, all

Gaelic-speaking Presbyterians. Because those poor Scots were all lease-holders, they liked the idea of owning their own land in Canada.

Gazing over the water from Lochmaddy, a visitor flashes into the 1840s and sees three hundred people departing each summer bound for Cape Breton Island in Nova Scotia.

Between 1815 and 1870, some fifty thousand Gaels settled in Cape Breton Island. Some would-be emigrants had died while making the voyage aboard the coffin ships, but the MacDonald family added one member, the baby Donald, before they arrived at Sydney Harbour in June 1841. From Sydney, father John led his family in walking eighteen kilometres to Marion Bridge, where he had secured a lease for 185 acres of virgin forest fronting on the Mira River. With just a broad axe, he cleared the land to get in a garden and build a rudimentary house before the frightful Canadian winter arrived. "Old John and his family went to work," Sandy says, "and carved out an existence on that farm for the next thirty years."

John MacDonald passed the farm to two of his sons, Ewan and Donald. In the 1870s, they petitioned the province of Nova Scotia to purchase the land for 44 cents an acre and made a down payment of $20 (roughly Can$450 today). The government approved the petition in 1876 and the MacDonalds made their final payment in 1903.

The fourth son of Old John—Sandy's great-great-grandfather—was named Alexander, though everyone called him "Little Sandy." He went to sea as a young man, as many did in the 1800s. When he was thirty-four, he came ashore for the last time and purchased 202 acres on the Bengal Road near his father's farm—an area still known as the Backlands of Gabarus. It was not a fertile farming area but Little Sandy managed to wrestle a living out of it.

He and his wife, Kate, raised nine children on the farm, including Alexander C., who would later be nicknamed the "Mira Bully." By most accounts, Alexander C. was a perfect gentleman, but in his younger years he tended to swagger and never backed away from a fight. His daughter Sadie later wrote lovingly about him: "He was a kind and gentle man, unless he felt some injustice was being done to him, his family, or his friends."

Alexander C. was a jack of all trades—a farmer, a gifted carpenter, an upholsterer—and for a time a policeman in Boston. He was a pillar of the community. He also worked in the lumber camps in New Brunswick and at least once boarded a harvest train to western Canada to help bring in the oceans of golden wheat. Though he had only three years of formal schooling, he was an avid reader who perused the Bible front to back many times. His house was still a Gaelic-speaking home, like many in rural Cape Breton. His grandsons recalled visiting and hearing the older folks still speaking the ancient language in a quiet, singsong cadence.

Life was not easy in Cape Breton at the turn of the twentieth century. The island had little fertile farming land. But then people realized that, beneath the surface, the rocky ground contained colossal seams of soft black bituminous coal. In 1903, the Dominion Coal Company, owned by an American syndicate, started producing more than three million tons per year. Eight years later, Cape Breton had sixteen collieries in full operation, and they accounted for fully 40 percent of Canada's total coal production.

That's where the money was. The Mira Bully's two eldest sons, William and Archie, both left the family farm at Little Pond to work nearby in the Old Scotia #4 mine. Archie, who would become Sandy's grandfather, started in the mine at age thirteen. He worked in the coal pits, educating himself while toiling underground to provide for his wife, Edith, and their four sons. Through ambition and talent, Archie rose through the ranks to become the general manager of the Princess Colliery in Sydney Mines, a tough job with more than two thousand miners working under him.

Archie encouraged each of his sons to work underground for a time, to help pay for the higher education he valued so greatly. When Archie moved from the family's rocky farm in Little Pond into Florence, it was the first time any of Sandy's MacDonald ancestors lived in a proper town with running water and an indoor toilet. By then, the family had lived in rural Cape Breton for a century.

Archie's son Bob (Sandy's father) laboured in the pits for a year before going off to Mount Allison University to study education. While there, he became known, not incidentally, as a player of traditional Celtic music. He had grown up in Florence, which Sandy describes as "a hard-scrabble coal mining town with one main street and a couple of small shops. It had a United church at one end of the road and a Catholic church at the other."

Bob MacDonald became a well-respected teacher. He worked in Dartmouth, near Halifax, for most of his career. While at Mount Allison, Bob had met his future wife, Jessie Cameron, and two great clans converged. Jessie traces her roots to the Camerons of Achnacarry near Fort William. She was the daughter of Alex Cameron, who served as a Liberal member of the Nova Scotia legislature until he died of a heart attack in 1960.

By that time, Jessie had married her schoolteacher husband, product of the North Uist clearances, and with him named their first-born Alexander (aka Sandy). Like many of those who trace their Nova Scotia roots to the Highland Clearances, Sandy maintains a keen interest in all things Scottish, and especially Celtic music. He dons his kilt whenever he finds an excuse, sporting the ancient tartan of the MacDonalds of the Isles, and with it he wears a bold tie in the red, green and gold of Clan Cameron.

19

—

Return to Knoydart

ARLY IN NOVEMBER 1853, WHEN OLD JOHN MACDONALD of North Uist had been settled on his farm in Cape Breton for a dozen years, activist Donald Ross collected tents, clothing and supplies and left Glasgow for Knoydart, Glengarry, on the west coast of mainland Scotland—a journey of well over 250 kilometres. He travelled north by road through Fort William and Invergarry and then west through an estate owned by Edward "The Bear" Ellice. At Kinloch Hourn, he hired a boat and sailed westward in rough weather for four-and-a-half hours. At a settlement called Airor, he found the sixteen displaced families he had come to help. Late the previous August, Ross had received a letter from Father Coll Macdonald, a Roman Catholic priest based at Sandaig on the Kyle River coast in Knoydart. The clergyman wrote about a series of ruthless evictions.

I began this book, *Flight of the Highlanders*, with a summary account of how a ship called the *Sillery* ended up carrying 332 newly created refugees to Canada. Father Coll told Donald Ross that, after the *Sillery* sailed on August 9, sixteen families emerged from the rocks and the ridges. These sixty people—most of them frail and elderly but among them a few children—stretched blankets over the walls of their ruined houses and constructed rough shelters from scattered timbers. They were still working in the wreckage when, on August 22, the hired thugs returned and launched a new wave of destruction.

In 1853, when 332 refugees looked back from on board the *Sillery*, they saw the distant mountains of Knoydart for the last time.

"One of the young women lay for some time beside a bush," Father Coll wrote. "She was afterwards brought within the wall of her former house, where she lay for three days so ill that her recovery was very doubtful." Of another ailing woman, fifty-year-old Catherine Mackinnon, he wrote, "It is not unlikely that this cold weather will put an end to her suffering and her life together." Father Coll visited regularly in his little boat and gathered what provisions he could from people nearby, but the sufferers desperately needed shelter and supplies.

Donald Ross wrote to the factor and his law-agent in Edinburgh, seeking permission to send tents, blankets and other supplies to Knoydart. He received no response. Then came another letter from Father Coll, who wrote on October 22, "the stormiest day we have seen this year." The priest described how the factor's men from Inverie were again making their rounds, "destroying the shelters of the outcasts! All these poor creatures are out there exposed to the raging elements. The officers and servants have broken their huts now six times with the first warrant. If this is legal, you know best. Oh do not, I beseech you, lose sight of the poor who are living without shelter in this dreadful winter."

Travelling mostly by coach, Donald Ross reached Knoydart in November 1853. He distributed tents and supplies, then interviewed survivors. Later, he told their stories in *Glengarry Evictions or Scenes at Knoydart in Inverness-shire*. In the opening chapter of this book, I quoted a few excerpts but now summarize a few more.

—John Macdugald, aged about fifty, with a wife and family, was a cottar who earned his living chiefly by fishing. He was in bad health, and when the *Sillery* arrived, he had two sons, stricken with smallpox, in the hospital at Elgin, more than 160 kilometres north. He refused to board the ship and abandon them. The factor and his men turned him out and levelled his house. Next day, Macdugald returned to the family's former abode, used stones and turf to build rough walls, and created a shelter of blankets and old sails.

A few days later, a posse arrived. Macdugald was in Elgin visiting his sons and his wife was off tending a sick relative. Only the two youngest children, Lucy and Jane, were at home. Yelling and screaming, they ran for their lives. The men demolished the shelter and then heaved chairs, stools, tables, spinning wheels and other light articles as far as they could.

When the mother arrived home, she found the shelter wrecked and her little daughters missing. After a desperate, hours-long search lasting well into the night, she found the girls asleep near a rock and some bushes. They had set out to find her and got lost. When Macdugald arrived home, his wife and children were sleeping under a blanket on bare ground. He rebuilt. Again, however, the levellers destroyed his shelter. And now the man himself grew seriously ill. A neighbouring farmer gave him and his family temporary shelter in an out-building, and for this the Good Samaritan received threatening letters.

—Seventy-year-old Charles Macdonald was a widower without family. He was "keeled" for the Colonies, but what would he do there? Clearly, the factor anticipated that Charles would become a pauper and cost the estate four or five pounds a year. Much cheaper to send the old man across the Atlantic. When the factor and his party arrived at Charles's blackhouse, they banged on the door and demanded admission. The factor told the old man to leave.

"As soon as I can," said Charles. Taking up his plaid and staff and adjusting his blue bonnet, he walked out, remarking to the factor that the man who could turn out an inoffensive Highlander of seventy from such a place, and at such a season, would do a great deal more if the laws of the country permitted him. The factor levelled his cabin. Charles took to the rocks and from that day forward never went near his old habitation. He received bits of food from his evicted neighbours and slept alone on the hill in a blanket.

—Donald Ross wrote, also, of forty-year-old Alexander Macdonald, who shared his blackhouse with his wife and four children. His wife was pregnant, but the levellers thrust her out the door and the children after her. Alexander argued and protested to no avail. In a few minutes, his once-comfortable home had become a pile of rubbish, blackened rafters, and heaps of stones. The levellers laughed at him and moved off, leaving him to find what refuge he could.

Like his evicted relations, Alexander burrowed into the rocks and caves until he could erect a temporary shelter amid the wreck of his old habitation. From there he was repeatedly driven away. For three days Alexander Macdonald's wife lay sick beside a bush, where, owing to terror and exposure to cold, she had a miscarriage. She was then removed to the shelter of the walls of her former house, where she lay so ill that her husband feared that she would not live.

—Thirty-five-year-old Duncan Robertson had a wife, thirty-two, and three children. They were very poor. The oldest boy was deformed, weak in mind and body, and required almost constant care from one of his parents. Robertson was warned out like the rest of the tenants and a decree of removal was obtained against him. At levelling time, the factor came up with his men before Robertson's door and ordered the inmates out. Robertson pleaded for mercy because of his sick child.

The factor appeared inexorable. But at last he sent in one of the officers to examine the boy. On re-emerging, the man said the boy was truly an object of pity. The factor said he could not help it, that he must pull down. Some pieces of furniture were then thrown out and the picks were fixed in the walls. Robertson's wife ran out and implored delay, asking the factor, for heaven's sake, to come in and see her sick child. He replied, "I am sure I am no doctor." "I know that," she said, "but God might have given you Christian feelings and bowels of compassion notwithstanding."

"Bring him out here," said the factor; and the poor mother ran to the bed and brought out her sick child in her arms. When the factor saw him, he admitted that he was an object of pity, but warned Robertson that he must quit Knoydart as soon as possible, or his house would be pulled down about his ears. The levellers looked in once a week to see if the boy was alive or dead so that the house might be razed.

Donald Ross wrote that he could detail more cruelties inflicted on the poor wretches who remained—cruelties which would never be tolerated in any other civilized country in the world—but these would suffice. Back in Glasgow, he wrote an article in the *Northern Ensign* and then published his pamphlet. He appealed for supplies and sent what he received to Father Coll for distribution.

The following February, during a harsh winter, Ross went again to Knoydart. Afterwards he published another letter, focusing this time on Catherine Mackinnon, a fifty-year-old woman so sick and feverish she could not walk. In August, the marauders had forced her out of bed and left her lying beside a ditch for seven hours, from 10 a.m. to 5 p.m. Then, fearing she might die, they removed her to a house and provided her with cordials and warm clothing.

Ross called his article *Aunty Kate's Cabin*, pointing ironically to *Uncle Tom's Cabin*, which was exciting widespread outrage throughout Britain at the plight of far-distant African-American slaves. He wrote of how, with Father Coll, he visited poor "Aunty Kate," sheltering under a bush and blankets at Inverie. At first, he could not find her dwelling. But then he spotted "a little mound, like some huge molehill, with some smoke issuing from the end of it."

He heard coughing coming from within. The door consisted of empty sacks hanging from a rope. Father Coll went around to the side, cleared away the snow with his staff, lifted an old divot and called in to the inhabitant. He wrote: "Immediately the poor creature turned around in her bed and putting a little, withered hand out through the hole in the roof, she grasped her friend's hand firmly, telling him that she felt no better, no worse."

Donald Ross peeked inside: "Aunty Kate has a very miserable look, her face is pale, her eyes black . . . her place puts me in mind of where I kept my pet rabbits as a boy." The cabin was divided into sleeping and cooking areas, the latter measuring four feet by four-and-a-half feet, with a height of two feet nine inches. "The entrance to the sleeping apartment is just about the size of a door in an ordinary dog kennel." Such was Aunty Kate's Cabin.

On every visit to Knoydart, Donald Ross travelled through the estate of Edward "The Bear" Ellice (born 1783), a leading "radical" in the Whig Party and an influential member of Parliament. In 1820, Ellice had been instrumental in consolidating the Canadian fur trade under the Hudson's Bay Company (HBC). He became deputy-governor of the HBC and a friend, as it happens, of Arctic explorer John Rae.

Ellice was outraged at what Donald Ross revealed and lent his more powerful voice to the cause of those being dispossessed. He wrote to Scottish diplomat and surgeon Sir John MacNeill, decrying the lack of parochial relief and the absence of any medical man in the parish. He accused the local inspector of the poor of sharing in the destruction of hovels and called for an official inquiry. He described the Knoydart situation as "only part of a system of trying to starve people who, from age or infirmity, are unfit objects for emigration, into submission to being sent out of the country, or, at all events, out of the parish they properly belong to."

Nobody challenged the right of landlords to evict their tenants—certainly not landowner Edward Ellice. But he did pressure the Lord Advocate into ordering an investigation into the conduct of the inspector of the poor. The ensuing report described the paupers as mostly women living in terrible conditions, scantily and miserably clad and lacking any change of clothes. They "are dirty and uncomfortable-looking . . . many are without shoes and stockings." Nor did these people have enough to eat. At least one individual had become deranged.

The solicitor-general took this report to Parliament. He wrote that the condition of the paupers was distressing. But because a conviction against the inspector would be difficult to achieve, he recommended against criminal proceedings. And that was the end of that.

In May 1854, estate owner Josephine Macdonell removed all those she had allowed to remain through the winter for what she called "motives of charity"—this time with a medical officer in attendance. Satisfied that the Knoydart hills were suitably cleared, industrialist James Baird—a Tory member of Parliament—brought in sheep and built a country retreat.

20

Massacre of the Rosses

AS HE PACKED HIS TRAVELLING BAG FOR A SIXTEEN-hour coach journey north out of Glasgow, Donald Ross could hardly contain his outrage. On the last day of March 1854, a laird and a tacksman had violently evicted the hard-working people of Greenyard, less than eleven kilometres from Croick Church. His friends had sent him letters naming the perpetrators: Charles Robertson of Kindeace, a major in the 78th Highlanders, and his perfidious tacksman, Alexander Munro—the same Munro who, a decade before, had expelled the gentle folk of Glencalvie.

Well did Ross know those names. Rattling north along the rough road, he proposed to spend a single night in Inverness. Tomorrow, he would travel seventy kilometres farther north to the Ross-shire county town of Dornoch, near where he had been raised. Born in 1813, Ross had grown up on the Skibo Castle estate, eight kilometres west of town along the road to Bonar Bridge.

In his mid-twenties, after his father died, Donald Ross had taken over as the miller at nearby Clashmore. In 1843, he and his mother were evicted from the mill. Eloquent, courageous and passionately sensitive to injustice, young Ross guided his mother in taking the estate owners to court. They lost the case and had to vacate.

Donald Ross grew up on the estate around Skibo Castle. After fighting the owners over an eviction and losing, he became a leading champion of the dispossessed.

Donald Ross moved south to work for the Glasgow Association in Aid of the Poor, and frequently represented his constituents at court. In 1847, he published *Pictures of Pauperism: The Condition of the Poor Described by Themselves in Fifty Genuine Letters*. In his preface, while criticizing the Poor Laws, Ross described one old widow who lived in a tiny apartment "without food, without proper clothing, without fuel, and without furniture. She was allowed five shillings per month for rent, leaving two shillings a month, or *little more than three farthings a day for food, fuel and clothing*."

In the early 1850s, turning to journalism, Ross had campaigned for the less fortunate and the impoverished through the pages of the *Northern Ensign*. He lambasted local boards of supervision for

the way they administered the Poor Laws and for taking the attitude that an able-bodied man without work, whose family might
be destitute and starving, had simply not looked hard enough to
find a job. This during a depression, when no jobs were to be found.

Now, in 1854, his friends had described this latest clearance as
more ruthless and savage than the one Munro and James Gillanders
had executed in Glencalvie. Then they had acted for Charles's
father, William Robertson, the sixth laird of Kindeace. His wife was
the sister of The Chisholm, scourge of the people of Strathglass. In
1841, at age seventy-six, and while residing comfortably in London,
Robertson had ordered his factor, James Gillanders, to issue writs
of removal on the people of both Greenyard and Glencalvie.

A man much like Patrick Sellar, Gillanders had by then already
driven four hundred people from Strathconon, fifty kilometres west
of Inverness. In the 1840s, he and Munro had conspired to delay a
projected assault on Greenyard to move first against Glencalvie.
Now, in 1854, they had decided to finish the job.

Donald Ross would write a twenty-nine-page pamphlet about
this latest atrocity. Best known by its shortened title, *The Massacre
of the Rosses*, this is probably the most damning of all indictments of
the Highland Clearances. Eloquently written, it repudiates errone-
ous reports that appeared elsewhere. The activist based his pamphlet on some two-dozen interviews with eyewitnesses, most of them
conducted with a medical man at his side.

In 1854, Ross writes, the sixty-four-year-old Major Charles
Robertson had "nothing remarkable in his history, excepting a
strange hatred of human beings as occupiers of his land, and an
inordinate love of sheep and sheep farmers." From his estates on
the south side of the River Carron, his father had removed thirty-
six families from Glencalvie and a dozen from Eidan. That left

only the twenty-four families living in Greenyard, a short distance west of Bonar Bridge along the road to Glencalvie and Croick Church. They paid their rents regularly and were of "very excellent character."

Yet at Robertson's behest, tacksman Alexander Munro went secretly to Tain (thirty kilometres east) and applied for summonses to remove them. On hearing rumours of this, the tenants of Greenyard approached Munro. He flatly denied that he had applied for warrants and declared that "he would have nothing to do with their removal." Not long afterwards, the people were shocked to hear that Munro's warrants had been approved and that a sheriff-officer, William MacPherson, was on his way to Greenyard with warnings to vacate their land. Munro "again appealed to heaven," swearing up and down before them that he knew nothing of these warnings.

On March 7, the well-informed women of Greenyard intercepted MacPherson—who travelled with a policeman, Peter Mackenzie—and refused to let him proceed along the road unless he produced a written mandate from Alexander Munro. MacPherson carried no such document. The women searched him, found the summonses, and burned them. A couple of their menfolk arrived. They led the two visitors to the Inn at Ardgay, six kilometres away, and bought them drinks. Then the two visitors, completely untouched, went on their way back to Tain.

This encounter, Ross writes, "was blazoned about in the local papers as one of onslaught, and of stripping MacPherson naked, etc., and where the females . . . behaved like savages." All of this was complete fabrication. It arose out of a subsequent event, during which three itinerant tax collectors, having quaffed too much ale at a local inn, decided to play a joke on the women of Greenyard. The drunken louts showed up at the entrance of the estate claiming to be sheriffs who had come to "warn out" the tenants. The women sallied forth and demanded to see their warrants, and at last, Ross writes, "the imprudent fellows began to plead for money."

As tensions mounted, the leader of the men—"a long ugly looking fellow with large moustaches"—finally confessed that they were only taxmen playing a joke. The women failed to see the humour and demanded proof. The leader pulled out a gun and threatened the women. A local youth responded by producing a rusty old pistol, which he used to scare away crows, and warning that he intended to protect his mother. The taxman had enough sense to pocket his gun and show his identification papers. He also laid out some money. The women studied the papers and returned them, along with all the money. They ordered the pranksters to clear out and, after much huffing and puffing, the three did so. Back at the inn, the leader wrote a ludicrous fiction about the altercation . . . and several newspapers published it as gospel.

One version turned up in the *Northern Ensign*, alleging that "a preventive officer with two cutter men" had arrived at Greenyard and been mistaken for Tain sheriff-officers: "The signals were at once given, and in course of half-an-hour the poor gauger and his men were surrounded by 300 men and women, who would not be remonstrated with either in English or Gaelic; the poor fellows were taken and denuded of their clothing, all papers and documents were extracted and burnt, amongst which was a purse with a considerable quantity of money. In this state they were carried shoulder-high off the estate and left at the braes of Downie, where the great Culrain riot took place thirty years ago."

As Ross observes, the few dozen women struck none of the men, burned no papers and took no money; and the taxmen "left the district with all the clothes on their backs which they had on coming into it." No matter. The local landlords and their minions found the published fantasy useful. They held a meeting in Tain and resolved to visit Greenyard in force "to uphold the majesty of the law."

The policemen came from Tain, Ardross, Dingwall and even Inverness, the brawniest that could be found in each district. On March 31, 1854, in the wee hours of the morning, forty or fifty of these tough guys gathered at Midfearn, a convenient crossroads. They drank ale, porter and whisky, and then, led by the sheriff, a man named Taylor, they took an oath that they would eat nothing until they had dealt with the women of Greenyard—those brave, innocent women who wished only to live in peace in the homes of their forebears.

The men drank nonstop, gathering their courage for what Ross calls "the savage onslaught on the poor females of that district." The brigade boarded carriages and, having rattled along the rough roads, arrived at daybreak on the outskirts of Greenyard. There they paused to refresh themselves still further. Then they marched. Naturally, the people had got wind of their approach. They confronted the invaders in the road that led to the settlement—sixty or seventy women, a few boys and girls, and a dozen men in the rear. The sheriff told them to clear the way so that he could serve summonses.

Within seconds, having elicited no instant obedience, the sheriff ordered the police to move forward and clear the way. The hand-picked toughs, unleashed at last, sprang forward among the unarmed women, young and old, swinging their batons and clubbing them to the ground. "The police struck with all their force," Donald Ross reported, "not only when knocking down, but after the females were on the ground. They beat and kicked them while lying weltering in their own blood. Such was the brutality with which this tragedy was carried through that more than twenty females were carried off the field in blankets and litters, and the appearance they presented, with their heads cut and bruised, their limbs mangled and their clothes clotted with blood, was such as would horrify any savage."

A woman of forty-seven, the mother of seven children, was clubbed to death on the spot, and women were kicked in the face with hobnailed boots, some later dying from their injuries. One David Munro gave the police the most serious resistance they encountered. Attacked by three constables, he was struck on the head by one, and then the other two beat him unconscious. Having satisfied their oath, the police ran wild through the settlement, burning down houses. They took prisoners back to the Tain jail and charged them with rioting and disorderly behaviour.

At this point, Donald Ross slows his narrative. Having himself arrived at Greenyard on April 14, two weeks after the vicious assault, he devotes ten pages to detailing what happened to twenty different women. Here, summarized for length, are seven of his examples. This was not an era when a writer could use the word "rape." But that drunken brutes raped many of the women of Greenyard, some of whom they carried off to jail, he makes clear enough.

—Elizabeth Ross, aged twenty-two, daughter of Alexander Ross, tenant, was struck violently on the head with a baton, knocked to the ground, and kicked on the breast and shoulder. She suffered a deep cut, three-and-a-quarter inches long, on the crown of her head. The blow was so fierce it shattered her skull and destroyed parts of her frontal and parietal bones, causing concussion and compression of the brain. She had a second deep cut on her head and severe bruises on her arms and shoulders. Her breasts and shoulders bore the marks of policemen's boots. Her clothing was completely red with her blood. Pieces of the skin of her head had been stripped off by the batons of the police and her long hair, clotted with blood, could later be seen lying in quantities spread over the ploughed land. Elizabeth was a tall, pretty young woman. She was well known in the district as a quiet, respectable girl who was dutiful and kind to her parents. She suffered from such intense pain in the head that she could not think straight. From the treatment she received at the hands of the police, Ross wrote, she would never recover.

—Margaret Ross, sister of Elizabeth, was also beaten violently on the head. Her cap was cut, and the parietal bone shattered, leaving an ugly cut two-and-three-eighths inches long. One blow fractured the occipital bone, causing both concussion and compression of the brain. She was struck violently after she fell and lost a great deal of blood. This young woman had been handcuffed and carried off to the jail in Tain. Her head was not bandaged and her face, arms, breasts and shoulders were all red with her blood. She was kept at the jail for twenty-four hours. She now suffered from vomiting, a tearing frontal headache, cold and sudden perspiration, and "alienation of the mental faculties."

—A second Margaret Ross, aged eighteen, daughter of Thomas Ross, tenant from nearby Amatnatua, was most shamefully and brutally used by the police. Margaret was a very nice young girl, healthy and active, and a general favourite in the district. On hearing that the police were on their way to Greenyard, she raced from her father's house and, being swift of foot, soon reached Greenyard and fell in with the other females who went out to meet the police. When the police rushed in upon the defenceless women, striking them with their batons, Margaret had nothing to defend herself with but her bare arms.

She was trying to assist a woman who lay weltering in her blood when she was attacked by the police, one of whom struck her three violent blows with his baton across the breasts. She turned and ran across a field, pursued by the police. But her strength failing her, she plunged into a thicket whither the police followed her, but could not use their batons, owing to the bushes.

One of them, however, kicked her in the head with his shoe, and another kicked her feet. Margaret crept out from beneath the bushes and tried to escape again. But the police pursued her, and one of them struck her three or four times with his baton across the shoulders, which brought her prostrate to the ground, where she lay gasping for breath. The police now proceeded to put handcuffs upon her; and one of them placed his knee upon her breast, while adjusting and holding up her hands, while another put them in irons.

Donald Ross found it "impossible to exaggerate the savage brutality of the police." Margaret bore marks across her breasts and shoulders. Her flesh was mangled and one shoulder-blade shattered. When [Donald Ross] visited this girl in her father's house, he found her lying on a couch and very weak. Her face was pale, and she frequently vomited blood of a blackish colour. Ross could see that Margaret's internal organs had been ruptured, and that however long she would live, she would never recover from her injuries.

—Janet Ross, or Mackenzie, wife of John Mackenzie, tenant, had gone after her sisters to Greenyard to induce them to come home. The first thing she saw was two policemen beating her sister Elizabeth—one of them pummelling her with a baton, the other kicking her on the back and shoulders while she lay weltering in her blood. Mrs. Mackenzie ran forward to protect her sister, but the police turned and attacked her. They cut her head and thrashed her arms and shoulders. One of the police struck her across the shin bone, above the ankles, and then rolled her over into the ploughed land. "And there she was with her face in the earth," Ross wrote, "the blood gushing from the wounds in her head and shoulders, her strength entirely gone, and no one to assist her, and nothing heard around but the moans, and groans, and cries of the bruised and the wounded." Today we would call this what it was.

—Margaret McGregor, or Ross, aged forty-seven years, was the wife of William Ross, tenant, Greenyard. This poor woman met with savage treatment at the hands of the police. She wanted to reason with the sheriff on the impropriety of his conduct, because Mr. Munro, the tacksman, had denied all knowledge of the warrants of removal. The answer she got was a blow on the shoulder, and then another on the left ear with a baton. That blow was so violent that it cut up the gristle of the ear, breaking the skull and shattering the temporal and sphenoid bones. Result: concussion and compression of the brain. The blow was so forceful that it knocked the poor woman to the ground and caused blood to flow copiously from both ears.

Even after she was on the ground, the police struck her with their batons, and with their feet; and then left her with her head in a pool of blood. Donald Ross could see not the smallest hope of recovery. She was the mother of seven helpless children, and when he saw the poor little things going backwards and forwards, "toddling" around her sick bed, looking with sorrow at her death-like visage, he felt his heart break. The few sentences which the poor woman managed to speak went clearly to show that she had been barbarously treated. Ross's firm conviction was that she was as cruelly murdered as if a policeman had deliberately shot her on the links at Tain.

—Christina Ross, aged fifty years, wife of John Ross, tenant, Greenyard, and the mother of eight children, was also most shamefully and inhumanly treated. Her husband was one of the tenants who was summoned to remove. He had paid his yearly rent for twenty-six years and was not one farthing in arrears. Mrs. Ross was most anxious to see if the sheriff had any written authority from Mr. Munro for serving them with summonses. She wanted to show him a letter Munro had written denying that he ever authorized or would accept responsibility for these removals. Thinking the sheriff would listen to her, she went out and was the first to meet him. She tried to speak, but within seconds she had three policemen beating on her head. Their batons cut through her mutch (close-fitting cap), and left her face, breast and shoulders red with blood. She got a severe kick on the back of the head and had other serious bruises and cuts elsewhere on her body. After she had lain on the field for nearly half an hour, the police came around, took her prisoner, and carried her off to jail. The result, Ross wrote, was that "reason has been thrown completely off her seat, and the victim is now insane."

—Naomi Ross, aged twenty-four years, daughter of Hugh Ross, tenant, had her scalp battered in. She also had three or four most ugly cuts on the front and side of her head. After the poor girl was knocked down, a monster of a policeman kicked her. Nothing in savage life could exceed the brutality of the police in this case; for, although this girl was covered with blood, and the ground around her red with it, they showed her no mercy. On the contrary, she was violently kicked on the breast and in the most delicate part of her person. She was carried off the field and has never left her bed since. "It is my firm belief," Ross wrote, "that she will never recover from the injuries she received. Her neighbours, and many respectable people in the district, declare that a more innocent, quiet, inoffensive, or a more respectable young girl could not be found within the range of their acquaintance. Had poor Naomi been wandering on the banks of the Danube, and had been ill used there, I could understand it; but, in Christian Scotland, to be butchered alive . . . who can think of it without a blush of shame coming over his cheek."

In *Massacre of the Rosses*, the author provided not just seven, as above, but twenty personal accounts of the savage attacks on the women of Greenyard. As for the men, some were off working in the fields some distance away, while others were engaged in the Crimean War, serving at Sebastopol with the 93rd Regiment. But those few men who were in the vicinity, the police brutally assaulted. One sixty-eight-year-old man, an onlooker named Donald Ross, was beaten to the ground and kicked. Later, he said that although he had fought in nine battles on the continent, he had never seen wounded soldiers or prisoners of war abused as badly as the defenceless, inoffensive women of Greenyard.

The police preferred to attack in twos or threes. A young lad, George Ross, fought three of them. They thrashed him with their batons and left him on the field with his head, face, and arms covered in blood. Yet another Donald Ross narrowly escaped with his life. He fought off two policemen and knocked both to the ground.

These two got to their feet, called in two allies, and the four of them went at Donald pell-mell, breaking at least one ash baton into splinters over his head and shoulders. When he, too, fell to the ground, his assailants beat him about the head, stopping only when they thought he was dead. Similarly, a David Munro from Culrain fought off three policemen, but they brought him down by beating his legs. Fighting on, he sent one attacker sprawling onto his back. Others rushed up and beat the man until he, too, lay unconscious.

None of the tenants of Greenyard had so much as dreamed of instigating violence. They had gathered to question the right of the sheriff to serve summonses without the sanction of Major Robertson or Alexander Munro. They had not prepared for physical confrontation and when the thugs arrived "were as defenceless and as unprepared as if they were in a church." The fields ran red with blood. "Such was the awful nature of the scene," Donald Ross writes, "that Mr. Munro's brother-in-law harrowed the ground under cloud of night, to hide the blood."

When it was over, Sheriff Taylor and his officers went to the house of the tacksman, Alexander Munro, and drank whisky with him. The police arrested and handcuffed four women, all badly injured, and took them into custody as ringleaders in what they called the rioting and mobbing. Eventually one woman, Ann Ross, was sentenced to twelve months in prison, and one man got eighteen months at hard labour. The story was reported in some newspapers, though it proved so appalling that others refused to print it.

Donald Ross wrote an open letter to the Lord Advocate, chief law officer in Scotland, demanding an inquiry into "the slaughter at Greenyard." Sheriff Taylor and his allies had prepared a rebuttal. It is obviously riddled with lies and utterly lacking in credibility. The Lord Advocate called no inquiry. And one year later,

Robertson and Munro completed their clearance. According to the *Northern Ensign*, policemen from Tain went to Greenyard and removed the last few holdouts.

In a now familiar process, they heaved furniture into the fields. They extinguished the fires in the houses and evicted the remaining tenants "like a band of felons." They carried one bedridden woman outside in her bed, where she lay "exposed to the piercing cold in intense frost and snow storm" until rescue arrived from across the river. The *Ensign* judged that, "what had been left unfinished by . . . the revolting tragedy of last spring has been accomplished."

PART FIVE

WESTERN TRAVAILS

Lord Selkirk's Grant

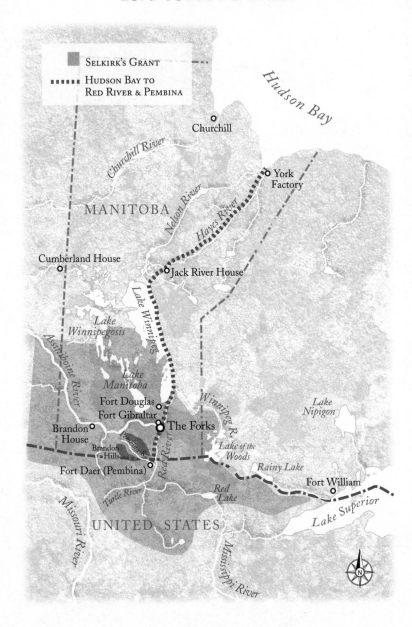

21

From Culbokie to the Pacific

T HAT WAS THE NADIR OF THE HIGHLAND CLEARANCES: the massacre of the Rosses. Evictions did not cease, exactly, but that 1854 horror show would prove to be rock bottom. Those Highlanders who had left Scotland during the early phase of the Clearances, starting in the late 1700s, had escaped the worst of the violence—at least in their homeland. Many of them were prosperous, educated people who could see which way the wind blew. What they could not anticipate was how things would play out on the far side of the Atlantic.

Often they sailed to the warmer colonies—to Virginia or one of the Carolinas. As a result, many would become refugees not immediately but in a two-stage process. This was the case, for example, with the mother of Simon Fraser, who would become a celebrated explorer. She and her children were among ten thousand Loyalists who flooded into present-day Ontario, settling along the St. Lawrence River from Montreal to beyond Kingston, as well as in the Niagara region and in the southwest corner of the province.

Another thirty thousand Loyalists—6o to 75 percent of Scottish origin—fled to Atlantic Canada. In Quebec, smaller numbers settled in the Gaspé and the Eastern Townships southeast of Montreal. Contemporary historian Peter McLeod writes that the Loyalists "were basically war refugees like people from Bosnia or Rwanda today."

In 1773, the same year the *Hector* sailed, Isabella Fraser and her husband, Simon Fraser Sr., travelled 120 kilometres south from Culbokie to Fort William. There they boarded a superior ship, the *Pearl*, that would, they imagined, take them to a wonderful new life in the New World. British government laws enacted post-Culloden were threatening their Gaelic culture and they looked forward to living a life free of menace and intimidation.

They were leaving behind no mean existence. Isabella had been born a Grant and her father had been the laird of Daldregan. Both she and her husband, whose forebears were tacksmen to the Frasers of Lovat, had received a classical education. They emigrated at the urging of Fraser clansmen who in the 1760s had settled in the Albany area. They brought with them a library of rare books and papers—a wealth of ancient Gaelic literature—and sailed with roughly 280 Roman Catholic Gaels (some sources say 425).

The *Pearl* sailed early in the year and reached New York in just six weeks—five weeks faster than the *Hector* reached Pictou. The new arrivals spent a year in Albany living among extended family. Then, having explored their options, they bought a farm sixty kilometres northeast of Albany, near Hoosick, New York.

The farm consisted of 160 acres, 100 of which had been cleared, together with a farmhouse and several outbuildings. Before long, the family had cleared another 5 acres, while taking care of twenty-four sheep, twenty cattle (including six oxen) and three horses, as well as chickens. Isabella went to work spinning, weaving, churning butter, washing clothes, making soap and candles, and educating her children.

Unfortunately, the farm was situated in a jurisdiction claimed by both New York State and pre-revolutionary New Hampshire (which then had different boundaries). The upshot was that the Frasers were stripped of their title to 60 of the 160 acres they had bought, much of it from the cleared area. Not only that, but they found themselves surrounded by evangelical Protestants. Tensions mounted after April 1775, when just outside Boston, British troops and local militiamen fired the first shots in the Revolutionary War.

Two of Isabella's older brothers-in-law had fought at Quebec in 1759 as officers with the Fraser Highlanders. In July 1777, with the war well begun, her husband and oldest son, William, joined the British Army. Because of his education and family connections, Simon Fraser Sr. was commissioned as a captain. On August 16, 1777, when his namesake youngest son was one year old, he was among seven hundred Loyalist troops who were surprised and routed by a rebel force of two thousand at Wolloomsac near Bennington, a few miles from his homestead. Americans call this encounter the Battle of Bennington.

Simon Fraser Sr., the once-proud Highlander, was wounded and taken prisoner on the battlefield. Transported to Albany and jailed, he was beaten and starved and died in jail early in 1779. Isabella became a widow with small children. In *Simon Fraser: In Search of Modern British Columbia*, author Stephen Hume writes that her neighbours "looted the farm and stripped it of its livestock and utensils, even its furniture. They destroyed her books and her rare old Gaelic poetry manuscripts."

Hume quotes a pamphlet in which a British officer described the flight of "old grey-haired men and women, husbands and wives with large families of little children, women with infants at their breasts, poor widows whose husbands had lost their lives in the service of King and country, with a half-dozen starved bantlings tugging at their skirts." These people were taking leave of their tearful friends, who were unable to leave or preferred to "trust to the mercy of their persecutors."

The eyewitness continues: "The rebels, like so many furies or rather devils, entered the town and a scene ensued the very repetition of which is shocking to the ears of humanity. The loyalists were seized, hove into dungeons, prisons and provosts. Some were tied up and whipped, others were tarred and feathered, some were dragged to horse ponds and drenched till near dead, others were carried about the town in carts with labels on their backs and breasts with the word 'Tory' in capitals written thereon. All of the loyalists were turned out of their houses and obliged to sleep in the streets and fields . . . a universal plunder of the friends of government took place."

Not surprisingly, thousands choked the roads leading north. Against this backdrop, Isabella Fraser hung on at the farm, worried about travelling with young children. Finally, one morning in the spring of 1784, when she was fifty years old and in poor health, Fraser led most of her nine children out the door of her farmhouse in upstate New York. The youngest, Simon, was eight years old. The oldest, William, had long since joined the British army.

Having received a generous gift of money from her Montreal-based brother-in-law, John Fraser—once an army captain, now a judge in a court of common pleas—the widow Fraser embarked on stage two of her difficult emigration from the Scottish Highlands. She quit the family farm and, with her children in tow, journeyed north to Montreal, travelling 350 kilometres by horse-drawn cart and ferry. This educated Highland woman would end her days an ailing widow in Saint Andrews, just north of Cornwall, at the western end of Glengarry Settlement.

This painting, *Tory Refugees on the Way to Canada* by Howard Pyle, shows that Loyalist Isabella Fraser was far from alone.

Because it had been settled by the military, Glengarry was far more prosperous than most early settlements in Upper Canada. By the late eighteenth century, it had become a magnet for more immigrants. Tens of thousands of Highlanders took the two-stage flight from Scotland, travelling first to Britain's southern colonies and then, during the Revolutionary War, fleeing north. It would be easy to multiply anecdotes, snippets and fragments, but more instructive, I think, to track the story of young Simon Fraser. Having travelled north with his mother, he remained with her in Glengarry County until 1790, when he turned fourteen. Then he moved to Montreal, a frontier city of about 8,500 inhabitants, and launched into what would become a spectacular career.

The youth resided with his Uncle John, a judge, while attending a rough-country version of secondary school. His relatives were involved in the burgeoning, Highlander-run fur trade, which was hastening the growth of Montreal. Two of his mother's brothers, Patrick and Donald Grant, were partners in the North West Company (NWC), which was competing with the Hudson's Bay Company by sending voyageurs deep into the North Country. There they would trade with First Nations people who supplied the furs, so saving those hunters and trappers an arduous canoe trip to one of the HBC forts that ringed the coast of Hudson Bay.

This approach demanded a keen understanding of the river system in the northwest. Imagine the excitement, then, of a fourteen-year-old schoolboy when in 1790, Alexander Mackenzie, a born-and-raised Highlander just twenty-five years old, returned to Montreal having mapped a river (now called the Mackenzie) that descended to the Arctic coast of the continent. Mackenzie's father, a widower-tacksman named Kenneth Mackenzie, had orchestrated the emigration of his extended family from the Isle of Lewis.

In 1774, at age ten, Alexander had followed his father to New York, accompanied on the *Peace and Plenty* by two maiden aunts and a hundred other emigrants. Two years later, during the American Revolution, his father joined a Loyalist regiment and young Mackenzie fled north with his family—first to upstate New York and then to Montreal, where he attended school before entering the fur trade. With all this young Simon Fraser could identify.

In 1793, after travelling mainly by canoe from Montreal, Mackenzie would become the first explorer to reach the west coast of North America, doing so a dozen years before the Lewis and

Clark Expedition. By then, Simon Fraser had turned sixteen and signed on to apprentice as a clerk with the North West Company. He knew where his future lay and he spent the next dozen years working in the Company's Athabasca department.

In 1805, now a young partner, Fraser took on the task of building inland trading posts in what, though he called it "New Caledonia," would become British Columbia. At present-day McLeod Lake, he established the first permanent European settlement west of the Rocky Mountains. He directed the creation of Fort St. James, Fort Fraser, and Fort George (now Prince George). From this last, in 1808, despite warnings that the west-flowing river was impassable, he set out to lead two dozen men in four canoes down what is now called the Fraser River.

They called the river impassable, but here we have *Simon Fraser Descending the Fraser River, 1808* by Charles W. Jeffreys.

Almost incredibly, he made his way through rapids and gorges and "a succession of falls and cascades" and, with the assistance of friendly First Nations, managed to reach the Pacific Ocean at present-day Vancouver. There he encountered hostility, which made his return journey even more difficult. After quelling a fear-driven near-mutiny, Fraser made it back to Fort George, the entire journey having taken almost two-and-a-half months (May 28 to August 6).

Fraser spent most of the next few years as the partner in charge of the Mackenzie River District. He remained with the North West Company until 1818, when he settled on a 240-acre farm near family in St. Andrews West. Within two years, he had married Catherine Macdonell. Seventeen years after that, he took an active role in quelling the 1837 Rebellion as captain of the first regiment of the Stormont Militia. In 1862, when at eighty-six he died, he left behind five sons and three daughters. He had ranged widely in the west, exploring from the Rockies to the Pacific Coast, but Simon Fraser never escaped the shadow of the Highland Clearances.

22

Creating Red River Colony

AFTER PUTTING THE PRINCE EDWARD ISLAND COLONY on a solid footing—listening to settlers, assigning lands, appointing leaders—Thomas Douglas, the 5th Earl of Selkirk, decided to write a book advocating emigration to what is now Canada as a solution to domestic problems in Scotland. He proposed to establish a series of distinctive "national settlements" that would protect language and culture, guarding immigrants "from the contagion of American manners." Each would be "inhabited by Colonists of a different nation, keeping up their original peculiarities and all differing in language from their neighbors in the United States."

Backed by the Colonial Office, Selkirk chose what looked like a promising location on Lake St. Clair, near the border to the United States in the southwest corner of Upper Canada. He visited the site, which he named Baldoon. He hired a manager and, with the first Highlanders on their way from Scotland, watched construction begin.

Back in Britain, Selkirk began writing a book championing Scottish emigration. In 1805, as he finished it, he heard that

Baldoon was faring poorly. By sheer bad luck, he had visited the site during one of the driest seasons in decades. Soon after he left, heavy rains had transformed low-lying areas into swampland, which gave rise to poor crops, illness and even deaths from malaria. So he focused in his book on his successful Prince Edward Island colony, and his considered arguments began altering attitudes about Highland emigration.

The situation in Baldoon went from bad to worse. Fifteen families had arrived in September 1804—a total of 102 people—only to discover that they were living adjacent to a mosquito-infested swamp. When Selkirk visited, those lands had been high and dry and rich in loamy soil. In choosing the site, he had been thinking strategically. He wanted to set a barrier against American influence. "The Scottish Highland emigrants," he wrote, "are of all descriptions of people, the most proper for the purpose, since independently in their character and in other respects the very circumstance of their using a different language would tend to keep them apart from the Americans.

"The emigrants, who in a few years must unavoidably leave Scotland, would be sufficient to form a colony of such force as would render Upper Canada safe from any attack it is likely to be exposed to and to be an effectual check on the disaffected French of the Lower Province."

Within two months of reaching Baldoon, sixteen settlers had died, including five heads of family. But against all odds, the remaining Highlanders made progress. They moved a short distance to another part of the land grant, built houses and planted crops. Eventually, the settlement would thrive. But in 1809, it looked like a failure.

Chastened by that, and discerning that the clique controlling

Upper Canada wanted no rivals, Selkirk began speculating about settling an area farther west.

Several years before, in *Voyages through the Continent of North America* by Alexander Mackenzie, Lord Selkirk had read that fertile lands existed in the Red River district controlled by the HBC. Having recently married Jean Wedderburn, an intelligent, courageous woman fifteen years younger, Selkirk now found a powerful ally in her brother. With Andrew Wedderburn, Selkirk began buying shares in the Hudson's Bay Company. He had realized that to colonize the west, he would need to work in concert with fur traders. But he underestimated the challenges and failed to appreciate that by bringing settlers into the northwest, he would directly threaten an economy, a way of life and, indeed, a distinct people who had evolved out of the fur trade.

By late 1810, together with his brother-in-law, Selkirk owned enough shares to control the HBC. But the fur trade was in competitive crisis as a result of the overharvesting of beaver. To strengthen the HBC, Andrew Wedderburn had started recruiting Highlanders from the western islands of Scotland, offering them land in exchange for three years of service. When the North West Company approached the HBC with a plan to reduce increasing tensions by partitioning the fur trade, Selkirk rejected the proposal. He intended to leverage the HBC's 1670 charter, which granted a monopoly over all the lands draining into Hudson Bay.

Selkirk dusted off an old proposal to develop the fertile Red River area as a settlement for retired fur traders. He would not stop there. He proposed to create a substantial colony, the first in a string that would extend across the west. In March 1811, he cut a deal with the Hudson's Bay Company. In exchange for financing and founding a settlement at Red River, Selkirk would gain control of 116,000 square miles (300,000 square kilometres) of land—an area five times the size of Scotland.

Some denounced this Red River Settlement as madness. The place was too deep in the wilderness. But Selkirk saw Red River as resolving three major challenges. It would lay the foundations of a faithful British colony west of Upper Canada. It would address the deteriorating situation in Scotland caused by the Highland Clearances. And it would provide a buffer against the expansion of the American colonies. He saw Red River Settlement as becoming his greatest legacy, the product of all that he had learned from his Belfast and Baldoon.

But Selkirk had a blind spot. He failed to see that helping the refugee Highlanders would mean displacing another people—the Bois-Brûlés (Burnt-Wood People), or Métis. Their economy relied on hunting and the fur trade. Selkirk meant to build a world around farming. Conflict was inevitable.

Thomas Douglas, also known as Lord Selkirk, saw Red River Settlement as resolving three major challenges. But he did have a blind spot.

The partners in the North West Company had no such blind spot. They saw immediately that Selkirk's settlement would strain the region's resources, interfere with their Athabasca fur-trade route and decimate their profits. In Britain, they mobilized too late to block the deal. But they did not regard the battle as lost. During the next decade, Red River would become the centre of an epic struggle in which past met future.

By the early 1800s, almost five thousand voyageurs worked in the Quebec-based fur trade. They paddled the rivers and lakes between Montreal and the North Country. Most of them were French Canadians and many had married Indigenous women *à la façon du pays* and fathered children. It was those offspring, born into the fur trade, who called themselves the Bois-Brûlés. As Selkirk's plan took shape, their resistance would grow and spawn the politically conscious Métis nation.

Here we discover a great irony. Refugees arriving from the Highlands and Islands, driven out of their own homeland, were destined to get caught in a crossfire. The Highlanders, displaced from their ancestral homes, were unwittingly caught up in displacing a people as innocent as themselves of schemes and machinations—but equally committed to fighting for the way of life into which they had been born.

In 1811, Selkirk appointed the ill-prepared Miles Macdonell first governor of Assiniboia, which comprised all territory within fifty miles (eighty kilometres) of the junction of the Red and Assiniboine rivers. Born into a distinguished Roman Catholic family in Inverness in 1767, Macdonell had sailed at age six on the same ship, the *Pearl*, as the parents of Simon Fraser. Having retreated north during the American Revolution to Glengarry County, Macdonell had impressed Selkirk as a well-mannered gentleman who "could get work done when nobody else could."

Macdonell set out for Stornoway on the Isle of Lewis to collect about a hundred recruits gathered from far and wide. The transport ships did not reach their destination until July 17. The recruits had arrived weeks earlier, and when they weren't drinking, fighting or grumbling, they had time to fret over a dark, destructive article that appeared in the *Inverness Journal*.

Written by an anonymous Highlander—in fact, Simon McGillivray of the North West Company—it warned recruits that they faced a hazardous voyage, an extreme climate, and a hostile reception: "Even if they escape the scalping knife, they will be subject to constant alarm and terror. Their habitations, their crops, their cattle will be destroyed and they will find it impossible to exist in the country." Small wonder that some men bailed at the last moment, leaping overboard and swimming ashore.

Customs officials, probably bribed by the NWC, delayed departure on technicalities. They refused to let the livestock on board, alleging that the old ship could not carry enough water. Finally, on July 26, 1811, the *Edward and Ann* sailed for Hudson Bay. The voyage, hampered by headwinds and storms, lasted an interminable sixty-one days. The ship reached York Factory on September 24, so late in the season that nobody could then set out for Red River, 1,124 kilometres away.

At York Factory, the superintendent of the HBC's Northern Department, a veteran fur trader named William Auld, demonstrated his determined opposition to the colony. He sent the settlers forty kilometres up the Nelson River to spend six or seven cold, dark winter months in freezing log huts. Food grew scarce and Miles Macdonell struggled to control the men. A riot led to the jailing of two men (later sent back to London); an armed insurrection culminated in the departure of nine more men; and an outbreak of scurvy cost one man his life. The river ice lingered and

Macdonell couldn't break camp until June 22, 1812—nine months after arriving.

He started up the Hayes River with an advance party of twenty-one workmen, determined, as he wrote Selkirk, to "take possession of the tract and hoist the Standard." They reached their destination, the junction of the Red and Assiniboine rivers, on August 30, 1812. Historian Vera Kelsey describes them as arriving "footsore, weather-beaten, mosquito and black-fly bitten"—and to no enthusiastic welcome. There, at the Forks in present-day Winnipeg, they set to work building Fort Douglas, headquarters of the Red River Colony.

Now the challenges came thick and fast. Macdonell had to secure a steady supply of food for the settlers who soon followed and to establish friendly relations with people living in the vicinity—local representatives of the rival fur-trading companies, as well as First Nations and Bois-Brûlés. These last spent a lot of time in this area hunting buffalo, from which they derived pemmican, the staple food of the fur trade. It was a concentrated, portable, high-protein mixture of pounded meat, fat or grease, fruits and berries. Any trader heading out onto the rivers carried pemmican.

Having arrived too late in the season to do more than begin building a settlement, Macdonell sent most of his men 115 kilometres south to build the smaller Fort Daer at Pembina, which was part of the Selkirk territory, but is today just across the border in the United States. He continued clearing and preparing the site for Fort Douglas, slated to be a landmark edifice at fifty-five feet by twenty-one feet. In October, when the snows began to fly, he, too, proceeded south.

Miles Macdonell had brought builders and carpenters. Late in October, the first contingent of settlers—men, women and children, some of them sick—arrived at Pembina. Seventy people, hailing originally from Ireland and the Scottish Hebrides, had sailed from Sligo on June 24 aboard the *Robert Taylor*. Their promised houses had yet to be built. Macdonell brought some of the women and children into the emerging Fort Daer and billeted some families among friendly First Nations.

Arrival of the Selkirk Settlers, 1812. Some of the earliest arrivals resided with friendly First Nations people. Image courtesy of Red River North Heritage.

At Pembina, the Bois-Brûlés, too, welcomed the newcomers. According to Métis historian Richard D. Garneau, Charles Peltier led the immigrants to land cleared and ready for cultivation. He provided horses and carts to build Fort Daer—so named after Selkirk's late older brother, Lord Daer—and then lent his cart and canoe to an immigrant family.

Baptiste Roy took care of the immigrants' seed grain. François Delorme and his son supervised the building of family houses. Jean-Baptiste Lagimodière, a French "freeman," or freelance voyageur, led a hunting party of fifteen Bois-Brûlés, among them Bostonnais Pangman, to secure food for the Scots. A hunter named Isham, probably the son of well-known HBC man James Isham, supervised the breaking of soil and became chief interpreter, while his son worked as a hunter for the newcomers. Initially, then, relations were friendly, even convivial.

The ensuing winter brought hardship, hunger and misery. Historian Samuel H. Wilcocke quoted from an on-location letter: "Take a view of the state of one family, and it will show you what the sufferings are of these people: an old Highlander, his wife, and five children, the youngest eight or nine years of age, poor, and consequently badly provided with clothing to encounter the rigors of the climate, where the hottest summer never thaws the ground to any considerable depth—see this family, sitting on the damp ground, freezing for want of sufficient covering, pinched and famishing for want of food; and the poor woman had to take the well-worn rug from her own miserable pallet, to sell for a little oat-meal to give her dying children, and in vain, for two of them did not survive this scene of misery."

During a buffalo hunt, the newcomers took on the difficult task of hauling meat back to camp. This they did, a Nor'Wester (an employee of the North West Company) reported, "destitute of all necessities, such as snow-shoes, caps, mittens, leather or blanket coats, socks, kettles, fire-steel or flint." Not only that, but "some of these wretches, for want of the means of making a fire, have buried themselves in banks of snow to prevent their being frozen to death, and have often been forced to eat the raw meat off their sledges."

On June 22, 1814, one year after sailing out of Stromness with a contingent of Kildonan settlers, Archibald McDonald reached Red River Settlement. Together with a few hunter-guides, he had led forty-one of the fittest colonists on a thirteen-day snowshoe trek from Churchill to York Factory, and then brought them forward, covering a total distance of more than a thousand kilometres. One of the leaders of the new arrivals was a young woman from Helmsdale on the east coast of Sutherland.

Catherine (Kate) McPherson was twenty-six when, with her eighteen-year-old brother, John, she had sailed out of Stromness on the *Prince of Wales* on June 28, 1813. These were relatively early days in the Clearances, before most of the burnings and violence erupted. Kate came from one of the ninety-six families from the Kildonan River Valley in Sutherland that had been offered a choice. Their lands were to be given over to sheep, no choice there.

But they themselves could either relocate to the rocky, windswept cliffs of northeast Scotland, where they could fish and collect kelp, or else they could emigrate. Most of her family stayed in Scotland for now, promising to follow later, should they receive positive reports from Kate and brother John.

Lord Selkirk himself had come north to dispatch these colonists—most of them paying passengers from Kildonan, with a few from Ireland and Orkney. He had received more than seven hundred applications for this sailing but the HBC ship could carry a hundred passengers at most, and the North West Company had cleverly leased all other available vessels. Crossing the Atlantic was seldom easy in these small wooden ships, and this voyage, like most, ran into rough, heaving seas. This worsened the usual miseries deriving from overcrowding, lack of privacy and dank, dark, stinking living quarters.

In Helmsdale, they call this statue *The Emigrants*. In Winnipeg, an exact copy is called *Selkirk Settlers*. The sculptor of the original is Gerald Laing.

Typhus broke out and spread until sixty passengers were infected. The disease would claim the lives of several people, one of them the only medical man on board, Dr. Peter Laserre. At that point, Kate McPherson showed her mettle. She it was who, at the risk of her own life, took the lead in nursing the feverish and the sick. The settlers had paid passage to York Factory, where they had been promised accommodation, but the captain insisted, despite furious resistance, that they debark on the desolate coast at Sloop Cove near the old Fort Churchill.

Probably he feared the further spread of typhus, though some suggest he, too, had accepted a North West Company bribe. Either way, he impeded progress. The refugees landed on August 19, 1813, too late in the season to journey south. The HBC men already present, frightened by the typhus, pitched tents for the new arrivals and retreated before they settled into them. To avoid contact, the HBC commander sent the newcomers almost thirty kilometres inland to Herriot Creek. A couple of locals showed them how to construct rough shelters using spruce logs and moss, and they went to work.

Many of them had been relatively comfortable in Scotland. But now, as Donald Gunn writes in his *History of Manitoba*, "Logs had to serve for chairs; the mud flooring had to supply the want of beds, sofas, tables. We can easily fancy that these habitations were of the most simple construction, and very ill-adapted to defend the inmates from winter frosts, so often accompanied by heavy gales of wind, while Fahrenheit's thermometer ranged for months from 35 degrees to 50 degrees below zero.... [the people] had to drag on flat sleds the scanty rations dealt out to them from the company stores, and to receive the same and return with it to their families, they had every week to perform a journey of thirty miles on snow-shoes."

Several more refugees died from fever, and three from "consumption," or tuberculosis. According to a 1975 article by Laurie Tegelberg, one forty-five-year-old woman was left with a family of four, and another with three little children, one of them just two years old.

Come spring, with supplies running low, Archibald McDonald undertook to lead an advance party of the fittest colonists in donning snowshoes and hauling sleds through the rough country to York Factory—a difficult journey of more than two hundred kilometres. The sick, the older settlers and the children would follow when the ice broke up and they could travel by boat.

On April 5, thirty-one men and twenty women set out, together with Indigenous guides and hunters. As Anne M. Henderson writes in *Manitoba Pageant* magazine, they travelled in single file, drawing their supplies on sleds. They "camped at nightfall, moved on at daybreak, a gunshot rousing them at 3:00 a.m. to have breakfast and hit the trail." A piper marched along at mid-point in the march, while "other stalwarts bringing up the rear gathered in the stragglers and helped the weary to keep up." Three collapsed along the way, according to historian George Bryce, "and were carried by the stronger men." W.J. Healy added that, "in the march to York Factory, the courage of Kate McPherson strengthened the waverers in the line."

At one point, McDonald allowed a halt, after learning (to his dismay) that one of the trekkers was four months pregnant. Jean McKay, travelling with her husband, Angus, would give birth at Fort Douglas. Now, three weeks after leaving Churchill, the advance party reached York Factory. After a few days rest, they set out on May 23 and proceeded up the fast-flowing Hayes River in York boats, sturdy craft that the Hudson's Bay Company used to carry furs and trade goods along the rivers of Rupert's Land. This traditional fur-trading route invariably demanded that travellers track or drag the boat by a rope, often walking along a high back rendered soft and slippery by rains. At times men had to jump into the water and heave their boats over large stones.

On June 22, 1814, the first wave of Kildonan settlers—Kate and John McPherson among them—arrived at the Forks, where Fort Douglas was under construction. Estimates differ, but historian George Bryce suggests that by year end, the total number of settlers was 180 or 200. The latest arrivals went to work with a will, clearing small farms to run in long, narrow strips back from the Red River. Only now, on arriving, did they learn of the provocative Pemmican Proclamation, which prohibited the Nor'Westers from transporting food they needed to survive while working far afield. Only now, one year to the week since they sailed out of Stromness, did they realize that their trials had scarcely begun.

23

The Two Razings

RELATIONS BETWEEN THE NOR'WESTERS AND THE arriving refugees had begun to deteriorate early in 1813. Acting on orders relayed from Montreal, the Bois-Brûlés refused to deliver a pre-paid supply of meat to the settlers. Miles Macdonell wrote to outlying HBC traders asking them to stockpile pemmican. The following month, the newcomers went north from Pembina to build houses and plant crops around Fort Douglas.

In July, Macdonell wrote to Selkirk that, because the seed had grown old, the crops planted late last season were not doing well. He travelled north to York Factory to meet the ninety-four Kildonan settlers due to arrive on the *Prince of Wales*. But on reaching the fort, he learned that typhus had broken out during the voyage and that they had been forced to debark at Churchill, 320 kilometres north. Miles Macdonell could only turn and retrace his steps.

Arriving back at Fort Douglas in October 1813, he learned that the crops had failed. The settlers would have to overwinter again in what had become the unfriendly environs of Pembina. The Kildonan Highlanders would arrive in the New Year, and Lord Selkirk himself had also promised to come. How to feed all these people? The Nor'Westers, too, anticipated a food shortage. They had begun buying up as much pemmican as they could. From Fort Douglas, Macdonell watched as hunters streamed into the North West Company's Fort Gibraltar with venison, bear meat, fish, waterfowl, cereal, pemmican and even maple sugar.

On January 8, 1814, as another cold, hungry winter took hold, the worried Macdonell issued his reckless "Pemmican Proclamation." Noting that the settlers required food, and that more people would arrive next autumn, this proclamation forbade the export of provisions from the HBC territory of Assiniboia for one full year. No fur trader from any company, nor "any individual, or unconnected trader or persons whatever, shall take out any provisions, either flesh, dried meat, grain, or vegetable." Macdonell would buy these goods at the customary rates.

The Nor'Westers and the Bois-Brûlés received this proclamation as a declaration of war—and they weren't far wrong. But Macdonell, full of bravado, wrote that he believed he had "sufficient force to crush all the N.Westers in this river should they be so hardy as to resist openly authority. We are so well-armed and I have a parcel of fine active stout fellows that will execute any order they receive." When the Nor'Westers showed signs of ignoring the proclamation, Miles Macdonell signalled his resolve by launching a series of blockades and confiscations.

In May 1814, one month before the arrival of the first Kildonan settlers, a formidable Highlander named Duncan Cameron took charge of the Red River Department for the North West Company. Born in 1764 in Glenmoriston, sixty-five kilometres southwest of Inverness, he was a wily, eloquent, convivial Scot who would later represent Glengarry County in the Upper Canadian House of Assembly. A veteran fur trader, Cameron, like Macdonell, had emigrated to New York with his parents on the *Pearl* in 1773. As a youth, he had fought with a Loyalist regiment in the Revolutionary War before entering the fur trade in Montreal. The man himself arrived at Fort Gibraltar in August 1814 in grand style, wearing a crimson uniform and a sword.

On orders relayed from Duncan Cameron, Bois-Brûlés hunters employed by the North West Company had already begun deliberately "running the buffalo" some distance before killing them, and then hauling the meat home. As a result, agricultural settlers, who lacked horses and had to stalk the herd on foot, "were deprived of the means of subsistence." The colonists were growing hungry. They needed food. On July 14, 1814, Macdonell published a second proclamation, this one forbidding the hunting of buffalo on horseback. He stipulated a penalty of three months imprisonment for a first offence, and for the second, three more months and the forfeiture of the horse.

Macdonell failed to appreciate that the Bois-Brûlés hunters—young, fit, armed, excellent shots—constituted a potentially powerful fighting force. From Lord Selkirk, he received letters critical of his performance. No stranger to depression, Macdonell felt ready to resign. He wrote to Selkirk asking that "your Lordship be not prevented by any delicacy to send a suitable person to take my place, as I find myself unequal to the task of reconciling so many different interests."

Late in July, he set out for York Factory to greet the rest of the Kildonan settlers, due to arrive by boat. He got there on August 22 and seemed distracted. But he pulled himself together and got the remaining Kildonan settlers back to Red River on October 20. In his absence, the North West Company had repudiated a truce he had arranged with a senior NWC partner passing through the area.

Macdonell reiterated that Selkirk owned this territory and ordered the Nor'Westers to quit Fort Gibraltar. They rejected his assertion of ownership and refused to leave.

Short of ordering an attack, Macdonell could do nothing. Faced with food shortages, he again had to dispatch colonists south to Pembina for the winter. He sent notes to all the nearby NWC posts in the name of Lord Selkirk, ordering them to clear out within six months. Then he raised a company of volunteer militia from among the settlers and armed them with muskets.

With the Saulteaux First Nation showing considerable sympathy for the newly arrived settlers, Duncan Cameron realized that the Nor'Westers needed the support of the other identifiable people in the area, namely the Bois-Brûlés of mixed heritage—Indigenous and French or Scottish. From among the Bois-Brûlés clerks of the North West Company, Cameron chose four who might be able to "channel the energy and provoke the anger of the Metis on behalf of the NWC." Before long, one of these four "captains of the Metis," the handsome, charismatic Cuthbert Grant, emerged as especially daring and resourceful. Later, as the conflict escalated, Cameron would make him "Captain-General of all the Half-Breeds."

Cameron, given to parading around in a kilt, invited some of the most influential settlers to dine with him at Fort Gibraltar, and then—a brilliant stroke—conversed with them in their native Gaelic. He warned of Indian attacks, apparently now in the planning, even though most First Nations remained sympathetic to the colony. He expressed sorrow at the difficult circumstances in which the settlers were now living and painted a halcyon picture of life to the east in Upper Canada.

Some of the settlers switched allegiance to the Nor'Westers. To one of them, Cameron wrote: "I am glad that the eyes of some of you are getting open at last . . . and that you now see your past follies in obeying the unlawful orders of a plunderer, and I may say, of a highway robber, for what took place here last spring can be called nothing else but manifest robbery."

VISIT TO AN ENCAMPMENT OF INDIANS.

While residing at the Red River Colony in the early 1820s, artist John West made frequent excursions among the First Nations.

One settler, George Campbell, received a letter from Cameron telling him that, to prevent mischief, he and his fellows should steal the colony's cannons. One night, Campbell and his pals carried off a couple of them, then fired a shot as a signal. Together with Cuthbert Grant and William Shaw, Cameron emerged from a nearby wood with a few armed men. This party escorted the cannons and their takers to Fort Gibraltar, then toasted the theft with whisky.

On May 19, 1815, a senior HBC man, Peter Fidler, arrived from Brandon House, 212 kilometres west. He had just come upon five of the colony's valuable horses, lying dead and filled with arrows. The Nor'Westers blamed the First Nations. Tensions escalated as Elizabeth MacKay, the half-Cree daughter of a Scottish HBC factor, ran off from Fort Douglas to follow Cuthbert Grant. The Nor'Westers tore down the security fence around the fort and took pot shots at the main building. Duncan Cameron offered one influential Highlander, Alexander McLean, 200 British pounds to leave the settlement with his family.

Early in June 1815, Cameron mustered his forces and supplied them with horses, arms, ammunition and clothing. He told them that, if the colonists increased in number, "they will make you slaves, put hoes and spades in your hands, and oblige you to till the ground for them." He would give the settlers one final warning. If they refused to leave, he said, "you are then to destroy and exterminate them by every means in your power, and you shall be rewarded with all the plunder and property which you may find in the colony."

To the colonists, Cameron detailed his final offer. The North West Company would transport by canoe, free of charge, to Montreal or elsewhere in the east, all those who wished to leave. The company would supply each departing colonist with a year's provisions and two hundred acres of fertile land. On June 11, the Métis and other Nor'Westers stationed themselves in a grove of trees not far from Macdonell's house, the largest building in the settlement. They took a few potshots and narrowly missed both the surgeon and the storekeeper. The colonists manned the bastions and fired back. One of them, John Warren, suffered serious injury when the old cannon he was firing blew up. He later died.

This exchange lasted half an hour. The Nor'Westers demanded the surrender of Miles Macdonell. Some of the colonists urged the governor to give himself up. He refused, but on June 15, the Nor'Westers renewed their attack. They took prisoners and trampled crops. Next day, two North West Company partners arrived from Fort William—those celebrated explorers, Highlanders both, Alexander Mackenzie and Simon Fraser. They took charge and sent word to Miles Macdonell that if he personally surrendered, the colony would be left in peace. Macdonell secured verbal assurances that the colony could keep 200 bags of pemmican and that the NWC would provide an additional 175 bags of pemmican or the equivalent during the winter.

On June 22, 1815, Miles Macdonell left Fort Douglas as a prisoner, bound for Fort William, accompanied by Mackenzie and Fraser. On the way, Fraser learned that Macdonell had emigrated from the Highlands on the *Pearl*—the same ship as his own parents—and had settled into St. Andrews West, like members of his own family. Fraser was so disturbed by this conflict between Métis fur traders and Highland settlers that, on arriving in Montreal, he sought to retire. His partners implored him to put in one more year and finally he agreed.

Macdonell was brought east to stand trial for alleged crimes, among them the "illegal" confiscation of pemmican—though he would be freed and never tried. Meanwhile, more than two-thirds of the settlers, having accepted Duncan Cameron's offer of safe passage, set out to voyage more than two thousand kilometres via Lake Superior and Georgian Bay to Holland Landing and Newmarket, sixty kilometres north of Toronto.

Those forty or forty-five settlers who did not wish to go east agreed to leave the settlement in peace. Under the freely offered protection of local Saulteaux, they climbed into canoes and made their way five hundred kilometres north to Jack River—later renamed Norway House.

During this process, a few Highlander families were separated. Kildonan settler Kate McPherson had fallen in love with one Alexander Sutherland, who had arrived earlier that year. She retreated with him to Jack River. Her brother John, now twenty, accepted Cameron's offer and went east.

The Nor'Westers burned Red River Settlement to the ground.

No, that was not the end of it. The conflict between Lord Selkirk and the Nor'Westers, having embroiled the Highlander refugees and the Bois-Brûlés, would intensify still further. This is not the place to rehearse every twist and turn of the bitter struggle. The most competent man Selkirk ever hired, a veteran trader named Colin Robertson, arrived at Red River, saw what had happened, and canoed to Jack River. He retrieved the Highlander refugees who had retreated there and, with twenty additional men, returned to Red River and set about rebuilding Fort Douglas.

But then, early in November 1815, Selkirk's newly appointed governor Robert Semple arrived with yet another party of Kildonan settlers. Semple had been a merchant, a travel writer and a former British Army captain. He would prove to be the worst of Selkirk's appointments. Writer Vera Kelsey judged him utterly unsuitable: "A pompous ass personally, he knew nothing of farming, military service or government. He was not impressed by the buckskinned Nor-Westers at Fort Gibraltar. To a man of action like Robertson, a man of words like Semple was a disaster."

In March 1816, with Semple's blessing and twenty men, Colin Robertson seized and searched Fort Gibraltar, finding correspondence that threatened war. Two months later, on June 11, ignoring Robertson's advice, Semple demolished Fort Gibraltar and burned it to the ground. He also razed the NWC Fort in Pembina. Robertson, knowing these actions to be insanely provocative, said goodbye and set out paddling down the Red River towards York Factory, signalling his contempt for Semple's stupidity by flying not the usual red ensign but an empty pemmican sack on a stick.

To the Métis, the destruction of Fort Gibraltar was an outrage. At Portage la Prairie, eighty-five kilometres west of Red River, 120 prepared for war. On June 19, 1816, at five o'clock in the afternoon, Semple watched through his spy-glass as between fifty and seventy heavily armed Métis swept across the plain four or five kilometres from Fort Douglas. When they came upon five settlers weeding potatoes, they took them prisoner. Semple reacted by calling for volunteers. With almost thirty men, among them both HBC workers and Highlanders, Semple rode out from Fort Douglas to inquire as to what this army intended.

A few decades later, HBC factor James Hargrave would note that these men carried guns, "but they were in an unserviceable state, some being destitute of locks and all more or less useless." That Semple believed a vain exhibition of useless weapons would "intimidate nearly three times their number of men to whom the saddle and gun were instruments of their daily occupation is almost incomprehensible."

On the Frog Plain, near a copse of trees known as Seven Oaks, a collision occurred. Historians have been arguing about what exactly happened for two centuries. Basically, when the two sides drew close, the mounted Métis formed a half circle around the settlers. At a nod from Cuthbert Grant, one of them dismounted, stepped forward and demanded of Semple: "What do you want?"

Semple retorted: "What do YOU want?"

"We want our fort."

"Well, go to your fort then."

"You destroyed out fort, you *maudit Anglais*! Why did you destroy our fort?"

The man lifted his rifle and Semple grabbed the barrel. Somebody fired a first shot. Everybody started shooting. For the

Métis hunters, these farmers and fur traders were fish in a barrel. Within minutes, most of them lay dead on the ground, Robert Semple among them.

Historians differ on precise numbers. Best estimate: of those who followed Semple onto the plain, twenty died and six survived, including two who escaped by swimming across the river. Of the identified dead, eight came from the Highlands, seven from Ireland, and three from Orkney. On the other side, one Métis died, a sixteen-year-old, and another was wounded.

So what do we call this tragic event? Through the nineteenth and twentieth centuries, Caucasian historians usually referred to Seven Oaks as a massacre. Today most call it a battle—the Battle of Seven Oaks. Métis historians refer instead to the Victory of Frog Plain (la Victoire de la Grenouillère).

At Fort Douglas, the colonists wept for their dead. The First Nations who arrived too late to make a difference, Saulteaux and Cree, lamented the deaths, according to settler John Bourke, "hardly less than the colonists themselves." Prior to Seven Oaks, Semple had foolishly rejected their offer of assistance. Now the First Nations "assisted in bringing some of the dead bodies of those who had been murdered to Fort Douglas and burying them."

The next day, Cuthbert Grant arrived and dictated the terms of surrender. Accompanied by seventeen or eighteen well-armed men, he gave the settlers three days to clear out. Families who had left the Scottish Highlands filled with hope piled everything they owned into large canoes. They set off down the Red River to cross Lake Winnipeg and take refuge at Jack River. Once again, the Métis razed the settlement.

24

Highlanders Rise Again

S O THAT WAS THE END, RIGHT? WRONG. THE EARL OF Selkirk had been delayed from visiting the colony because he had raised a British regiment to fight Americans in the War of 1812—a war in which an American invasion of Upper Canada destroyed his Baldoon Settlement. That war was still raging when, in autumn 1814, Selkirk received a letter from fur trader Colin Robertson, warning him from Montreal that North West Company partners were mounting serious opposition to Red River Colony. Robertson had proceeded west with twenty men to those ends already recorded.

Lord Selkirk reached New York in late October 1815. There, to his outrage, he learned that the NWC had destroyed Red River Colony, removed 140 settlers to Upper Canada, and driven the rest into the wilderness. He went north to Montreal and, while the Nor'Westers denied all responsibility, interviewed several Red River settlers who had recently arrived in that city.

Selkirk gathered information early in 1816. He got himself appointed a justice of the peace for the Indian territory and wrote a scathing indictment of NWC trading methods, which he published in London later that year. In March, while still in Montreal, Selkirk received astonishing news. From Red River, Colin Robertson had sent a messenger to report that he had revived the settlement. Travelling in winter with two companions, the Métis voyageur Jean-Baptiste Lagimodière had trekked 2,300 kilometres to convey this information.

At Red River, Robertson had chanced upon a camp of friendly Saulteaux led by Chief Peguis, who "found much fault with the N.W.Co. and seemed anxious that I should attempt to re-establish the Colony." At the settlement site, Robertson visited the only building still standing, the blacksmith's shop inhabited by John McLeod and used as a store. He also met several Métis who, he reported, "told me frankly that they had been paid by the North West Company to drive away the Colonists."

On his own initiative, and having seen also that the fields were greening, Robertson set out northward down the Red River. With a few men, he spent most of a month paddling the length of Lake Winnipeg to Jack River (Norway House), where thirty-five holdout settlers had taken refuge. He convinced them to return and rebuild at Red River. Historian Chester Martin writes of the returnees: "To their surprise, the plots of ground which they had sown along the banks had suffered less than they had expected." They harvested four hundred bushels of wheat, two hundred of barley and five hundred of oats.

Back in Montreal, Selkirk and the North West Company partners—who had also heard of the Red River revival—perceived that next summer would be decisive. Selkirk managed to raise an army of 180 HBC employees and 150 discharged soldiers from the disbanded De Meuron and De Watteville regiments. But the NWC's annual spring brigade to Fort William left Montreal first.

The partners sent an advance party with orders to destroy the revived settlement and blame the action on the Indians.

Selkirk and his soldiers left soon afterwards, but with twelve boatloads of arms and supplies, they travelled more slowly. On July 25, 1816, at Sault Ste. Marie, Lord Selkirk received horrific news. The Métis had again razed Red River Colony. This time, at Seven Oaks, they had killed Robert Semple and more than a dozen settlers. They had then carried off prisoners to Fort William.

Some of Selkirk's men, fearing an assassination attempt, urged him to return immediately to Montreal. Sick with fury, Selkirk flatly refused. He insisted on proceeding westward another 1,100 kilometres to Fort William. As a legally appointed magistrate backed by a regiment of ex-soldiers, Selkirk set out, as biographer John Morgan Gray would write, "to confront the most formidable set of men the Canadas possessed on their own doorstep." In mid-August, on reaching Fort William, Selkirk took care to ensure that those behind the walls got a chance to see the size of his army. As a result, he entered the fort without a struggle.

Selkirk released the three miserably confined prisoners the Nor'Westers had brought from Seven Oaks. After conducting preliminary hearings, he arrested nine of the NWC's most senior men and sent them off to Montreal as prisoners. These North West Company men, virtually all ex-Highlanders, had long since become the richest, most powerful men in that city. On arriving in their home town, they quickly secured their release on bail.

Yet their ignominious return marked a turning point in the protracted war between fur traders and settlers. The North West Company would never regain its former eminence. Within five years, it would be absorbed into the Hudson's Bay Company. The end game would take years to play out. Inevitably, the whole business wound up in the courts, where for wealthy men in the colonies, connections made a difference.

But first, from Fort William, Selkirk proceeded west to Red River, where he spent several weeks. Showing extraordinary resilience and determination—in two words, Highland spirit—the settlers who had retreated north to Jack River in the wake of the second destruction came back yet once more to rebuild Red River Colony.

With the recovery well launched, Selkirk returned east. At Sandwich (present-day Windsor), Upper Canada, he answered warrants he had previously avoided and got released on bail. But then, after months of legal wrangling, he saw the Nor'Westers implicated in Seven Oaks slip away unpunished. With his health failing, Selkirk returned to England and answered the Colonial Office over a ludicrously ill-informed letter that had given rise to false charges against him. In June 1819, while said to be "far advanced in a deep consumption," he retreated to southern France with his wife and two sons.

When he died there the next year, the *Montreal Gazette* acknowledged that while his personal endowments and qualifications commanded respect, "perhaps some people would deduct something from his worth on account of his rage for colonization." Some would—certainly in that fur-trading town. Today, most might be inclined to agree with historian Lucille H. Campey, who writes that no nineteenth-century figure understood emigration better than Selkirk: "His liberal views placed him well ahead of his time, and in many respects he would have been far better suited to our own era. He believed that emigration enabled poor people to achieve a better life and that, by moving to British North America, they actually strengthened British interests overseas."

Today, the city that evolved out of Red River Settlement is the capital of Manitoba. Home to more than 800,000 people in its metropolitan area, Winnipeg is Canada's seventh largest city, and a

regional centre of commerce, industry, culture, finance and government. The Métis people, with their unique culture, traditions and
language (Michif), have developed communities along the rivers
and lakes of the old fur-trade routes, most notably in Manitoba,
Saskatchewan and Alberta. Many of the Métis, who number around
400,000, live in Canada's urban centres. As a people, they continue
to fight for their rights and to defend their existence as a distinct
Aboriginal nation.

But what of the refugee Highlanders? Do we have any idea
what happened, for example, to Catherine (Kate) McPherson and
her brother, John, who together reached Red River Colony but
went their separate ways in 1815? On July 7 of that year, all unawares,
their brother, William, had written from Sutherland explaining that
more family members were "not going out this year" because their
mother was not well. Also, he could "not sell our beasts unless we
would sell them for half price." He added, "we sold the best of them
before we paid your own passage."

The Protestant Church, and Mission School, at the Red River Colony. Engraving by John
West in the early 1820s.

William noted that in the Highlands, the family was "getting good and bad reports concerning the place [Red River], but whatever account you will give—that is what we will believe." He asked if there was a kiln or mill: "we hear there is no mill nor stones in the place to put up a mill." He wanted to know what tools they should bring if they emigrated. In the end, William and the rest of the McPherson family would follow Catherine's brother to the Talbot Settlement in Upper Canada.

Catherine and her husband, Alexander Sutherland, considered moving there but decided to stay in Red River. Catherine gave birth to a son, John, in 1821, and the family stayed put even through a plague of grasshoppers. In 1826, a flash flood drove the colonists from their homes. One of them, Alexander Ross, wrote that he went to lock a store door a few yards away, and "before I could get back the water was knee-deep—and in the space of an hour the water had made a clean sweep of all moveables."

But even that did not persuade Kate McPherson to move. On the banks of the Red River, she spent her early married life in a log house built by her husband, Alexander Sutherland. In 1870, their only son, John Sutherland, became sheriff of Manitoba, and was then appointed to the Senate by the government of Sir John A. Macdonald.

Kate McPherson, aka Mrs. Sutherland, lived until autumn 1873. Her husband had died that summer. In *Women of Red River*, her granddaughter, by then Mrs. W.R. Black, reported: "After his death, my grandmother [Kate M.] became frailer in body, but her spirit was strong. She was in her eighty-seventh year, but she never needed glasses to read her Bible. I have her Testament yet. . . . That testament, with the ribbon in it, she brought with her from her home in the Highlands when she came across the Atlantic."

And Catherine's brother, John McPherson? Having left Red River in 1815, he was among a group of Selkirk Settlers who, early in 1817, turned up at the Talbot Settlement in Upper Canada. He received a farm in Dunwich County on Talbot Road West. Two years after settling, John McPherson wrote to his sister: "The goodness of the country I cannot express and I encourage you to come here."

Catherine and her husband seriously considered joining him, because letters from John, quoted in *Manitoba Pageant*, answered questions about the soil, travel routes and the church. John reported abundant harvests and rising property values and noted: "The kirk is 9 miles on our side and a man that preaches Gaelic and English stationed on the other."

When the flash flood of 1826 did major damage at Red River, John McPherson again urged his sister, "come—and locate near us." He reported that "your beloved mother lived only two weeks after arriving at my house and died of a fever." But "your brother, Donald, is biding with me on my farm ever since he arrived; and Sandy lives five miles from me—and your sister is married to an Englishman and lives sixty miles from us." Catherine McPherson must have been sorely tempted.

In the 1840s, as quoted in a local history prepared by Colin A. McGugan, her other brothers were still issuing invitations. Alexander (Sandy) wrote in 1841 of the "rich fertile soil, chiefly heavy timbered land and well calculated for raising stock and crop, our chief productions are wheat, rye, Indian corn, pease, oats, barley and potatoes. Our average crop per acres is about thirty bushels, rye about the same, Indian corn 50 bus. to the acre.

"If you were to leave that place you certainly cannot come to a better country or a healthier country, there is plenty of land to be got here very easy, our climate is so moderate in winter we do not stable our cattle, our snow seldom exceeds more than one foot and our summers are not excessively hot, we are never subject to great droughts or excessive rains."

In 1844, brother Donald McPherson added his voice, saying "there are a great many emigrants coming out from Britain this year and last season, which will have a tendency to raise the price of land and make it scarce near to good markets." Despite the encouragement, Catherine McPherson remained at Red River with her husband and son and never saw any of her siblings again. She died peacefully in her bed a few months after her husband.

Early in the twentieth century, author William James Healy wrote in *Women of Red River* that, in the presence of Kate McPherson's granddaughter, he interviewed a Miss Bannerman. "We Bannermans have always had a special affection for you Sutherlands," she said, "because of the way Kate McPherson nursed my uncle John before he died in the winter camp on the Churchill."

That woman's uncle, John Bannerman, was the son of George Bannerman, the man who played the bagpipes to encourage the marchers between Churchill and York Factory. John, the father of Mary Florence Bannerman, became the grandfather of John George Bannerman Diefenbaker in 1895. Born in Neustadt, Ontario, Diefenbaker became a lawyer, got into politics and, in 1975, became Canada's thirteenth prime minister.

The following year, during an official visit to Scotland, Diefenbaker made a side-trip to Kildonan. Later, he observed: "All that remains there today is the occasional ruin. The ruin of my great grandfather's cottage is still to be seen and is not more than two or three feet high."

During his time in office, which ended in 1963, Diefenbaker

opposed allowing apartheid South Africa into the British Common-
wealth and extended the right to vote to First Nations and Inuit
peoples. He appointed the first female minister to his cabinet,
and the first Aboriginal member of the Senate. Diefenbaker also
installed a Canadian Bill of Rights that paved the way for the
Canadian Charter of Rights and Freedoms of 1982.

IN MEMORY OF GEORGE BANNERMAN OF KILDONAN,

GREAT-GRANDFATHER OF THE RIGHT HONOURABLE

JOHN G. DIEFENBAKER, P.C., Q.C., M.P.,

PRIME MINISTER OF CANADA 1957-1963, AND OF ALL THE

SELKIRK SETTLERS FROM KILDONAN WHO, IN 1812

AND 1813 MIGRATED TO THE RED RIVER SETTLEMENT

TO WHAT IS NOW THE PROVINCE OF MANITOBA.

JULY, 1968.

In 1968, Canadian
Prime Minister John
Diefenbaker placed
a commemorative
plaque on the church
at Kildonan. It is still
there.

In July 1968, during a second visit to the Highlands, Diefenbaker unveiled two plaques. The first, affixed to a stone cairn outside the hamlet of Rogart, was dedicated to Sir John A. Macdonald, Canada's first prime minister. It was installed at the site of his great-grandfather's croft, destroyed during a Clearance. The second, located twenty minutes north, was erected in memory of George Bannerman, Diefenbaker's great-grandfather, "and of all the Selkirk settlers from Kildonan, who in 1812 and 1813 migrated to the Red River Settlement."

PART SIX

UPPER CANADIAN PIONEERS

Upper Canada, 1784-1820

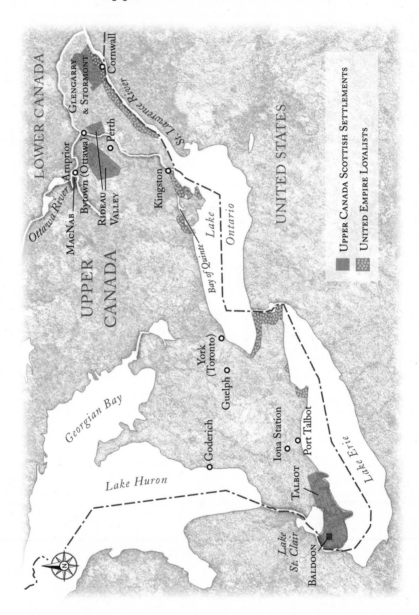

25

The Talbot Fiefdom

WHILE THE RED RIVER REFUGEES MET TUMULT AND violence, those of the Talbot Settlement encountered a mere dollop of political tyranny leavened by many happy endings. The man who created the settlement, Colonel Thomas Talbot, was born in 1771, emerging into the Anglo-Irish aristocracy at Malahide Castle near Dublin. At age twenty-one, after serving with the British military in Montreal, the well-connected Talbot became private secretary to John Graves Simcoe, the first lieutenant governor of Upper Canada (later Ontario). Over the next four years, while acting for Simcoe, Talbot got to know the southwest corner of the province around Lake Erie. He then resumed military duties in Holland, Gibraltar and England.

On Christmas Day 1800, at twenty-nine, he surprised everyone who knew him by selling his commission and emigrating to Upper Canada. Simcoe had begun granting entire townships to leading individuals, who would then allocate lots to settlers. Talbot began farming on the north shore of Lake Erie and pulled enough strings in England that in 1803, he received a field officer's grant of five thousand acres.

He requested Yarmouth Township but received Dunwich and Aldborough, fifty kilometres south of London, and made his own home in Dunwich at Port Talbot, near the mouth of Talbot Creek. According to *The Early History of Dunwich Township*, edited by Colin A. McGugan for the West Elgin Genealogical and Historical Society, Talbot and four hired men sailed along the north coast of Lake Erie in a small boat and landed at Port Talbot in the rain. In his journal, Talbot noted: "Sunday, 22nd May 1803 took possession of Dunwich."

In the early 1800s, Colonel Thomas Talbot built a gristmill to attract settlers. He then built roads, thus setting the bar for other township developers.

The settlement Talbot launched that day would thrive and set the bar for development in Upper Canada. Like other township developers, Talbot agreed to give heads of family fifty acres each of his original five thousand. Each time he did so, he would receive an additional two hundred acres from land adjoining the townships. In 1806, Talbot built a gristmill as a way of attracting settlers. And the following year, he began settling tenants outside his five-thousand-acre allotment. Later, he would explain that within his immediate surroundings, "I do not like to have settlers, as I find too near Neighbours a great nuisance."

The government went along with this and granted him two hundred acres per family wherever he put them. Talbot also began claiming and allocating land without registering transfers, so that he kept the only record. During the five years ending in 1808, according to the *Dictionary of Canadian Biography*, Talbot had settled only twenty families. To overcome the relative isolation of his holdings, Talbot needed roads, and so got himself appointed a district road commissioner.

By 1810, he was placing settlers along his proposed route east to Niagara, so extending his influence. Incomers had to clear land and erect a dwelling within three years, and eventually clear ten acres. Soon Talbot was building roads in every direction, allocating settlers lands along them. Some provincial officials objected, having already earmarked those lands. During the War of 1812, which moved complaints onto the back burner, Talbot supervised all the militia regiments in the London District.

In 1815, for the first time, Talbot had to submit records of his allocations. He listed 350 families and two years later, 804. He wished to recruit Englishmen. "My advice," he later wrote to a friend, "is that you should, as much as possible, avoid placing Highland Scotch settlers . . . as of all descriptions they make the worst settlers on new roads—English are the best." After the War of 1812–1814 American settlers were no longer welcome, since during the war many had turned on their neighbours and sided with the Americans.

But precious few English folk were being driven from their homes by rack-renting or worse, so Talbot had to make do with Highlanders. When the first Scots arrived between 1816 and 1818, Talbot clustered them together in Aldborough and Dunwich townships. Some came directly from the Argyll Highlands, among them one family of Galbraiths, whose descendants would include

John Kenneth Galbraith, and another of McGugans, to whom I am related. Others arrived from New York State and the turbulent Red River Colony, like John McPherson, originally from Kildonan.

The first three Highland families to settle in Aldborough arrived in 1816 via Caledonia, New York. Archibald Gillies, Alexander Forbes and Neil Haggard researched the area before approaching Colonel Talbot to request allotments. They lived in log houses with bark roofs, filling the chinks and holes in the walls with pieces of clay. With antiquated firearms, they hunted wild turkeys by trapping them in pens using trails of grain as bait. Although they brought a few oxen and cattle with them, few families had animals until later in the 1820s. Once or twice a year, men would travel south to Buffalo to obtain flour and other necessities. They relied for light on open fireplaces and in the autumn made candles to get them through the dark winter.

Duncan McKillop and his wife left Argyllshire in 1816. After landing in Quebec, they made their way to Port Talbot, where they knew three former neighbours. The McKillops, like the McNabbs, McKellars and McDougalls, had been farmers and fishers. With only one cow to support his family, Duncan worked as a hired hand in the winter. His wife found a job that paid one dollar per week. At the end of the winter, the couple had managed to save enough money to purchase a second cow. The next season, their fifty-acre lot yielded enough corn, potatoes and oats to sustain them, but several harvests passed before they got a good supply of wheat.

The settlement suffered poor harvests and deadly diseases in its early years. The Scots who came to Aldborough had, for the most part, brought little more than blankets, clothing and a few utensils, and lived in poor conditions for many years. Unable to sell anything but their labour, these pioneers nevertheless succeeded because they kept their spirits high and looked after one another. Highlanders came out of a culture of communal cooperation.

During long winter evenings, two or three families would gather in a neighbour's house to socialize. Surrounded by the warmth of the fire, as John Kenneth Galbraith later related, they "would recount incidents of their earlier days in the heathery hills of 'auld Scotia.'" Pious Presbyterians, these families often debated religion with zeal and enthusiasm. Most spoke Gaelic as their first language.

Following the War of 1812–1814, when American raiders burned down the mill at Port Talbot, emigrants from Argyll who might once have gone south chose now to come to Canada. Back in Argyll, most large estates were owned by members of the Clan Campbell, the Duke of Argyll chief among them. They divided estates into large farms or townships and leased them to four farmers, who worked the land collectively. These farmers sublet plots of land to tenants, who helped to harvest oats, barley and potatoes, and kept cattle, sheep and horses. Exorbitant rent increases encouraged them to emigrate.

From 1816 onwards, these Highlanders usually ended their long journey from Scotland at Port Glasgow, thirty kilometres west of Port Talbot. They would come ashore at Sixteen Mile Creek, where a wooded knoll extended out into the lake. Colin McGugan writes that the promontory was called Nellie's Hill because one Nellie Campbell carried a barrel of salt to its top. Later, alluding to the first landing site of immigrants who arrived on the *Mayflower*, people would call it the Plymouth Rock of Aldborough.

In 1817 and 1818, around the time John McPherson arrived, more than fifty Argyll families reached Port Glasgow and the Talbot Settlement. The next two years brought two more ships with thirty-six families. In 1819, Donald McGugan settled his family on 50 acres in Aldborough, but then traded and bought lots, and so ended up with 150 acres in Dunwich. From Colonel Talbot he received deeds for the lots in 1824.

Talbot issued these deeds only after settlers had cleared ten acres of land, plus one half of the road allowance in front of their lot, and had also built a house measuring at least sixteen by twenty feet. Talbot's records often contained discrepancies. Sometimes he neglected to register deeds, as the settlers were responsible for the registration fees and simply did not have the money. Even so, like most others who arrived here, the McGugans flourished and, around 1853, Donald's son John built a fine hotel at Coyne's Corners, a busy crossroads.

Family connections played a crucial role in developing this settlement. In June 1842, for example, Donald McGugan received a letter from his sister, who signed her name Mary McCougan. She sent it with Hector McNeill, who was leaving next day "for America" and promised to bring it. She lamented his long silence and brought him up to date about her children—one at sea, planning to emigrate; another a dairymaid, a third in the low country, and two "just now at home with ourselves."

Then she arrives at her main purpose: "my oldest daughter Christy and her husband and 2 fine boys her sons sailed from Liverpool on the 30th May on board the *Victorya* and I trust my dear Brother you will be kind to them and pay them some attention as she has an excellent man and a good worker—but there is know work to be got in this country and its not easy to bring up a family when there is know employment. . . . I have every dependence on you and my two sisters and my worthy brother-in-law . . . that you will find him and her deserving of your kindness."

The earliest settlers faced the most hardships. They had to

bring in food until they cleared enough land to harvest crops, and then they had to build their log houses. Their forested lands often contained swamps and only the best lots drained naturally via creeks. Stores were few and money was scarce. New arrivals could buy grain from those who preceded them but then had to grind it using a hand mill.

Those already settled did their best to help. From the Highlands, they had brought a culture of building bees and logging bees. This area was far healthier than Selkirk's Baldoon, which lay farther west, but fever and cholera did strike occasionally. In two weeks in September 1819, Colin McGugan writes, fourteen adults died in Aldborough. Still, the colonists erected schools and churches, and kept the Gaelic language alive in the area at least until the end of the nineteenth century. A second wave of emigrants arrived from Argyll in the 1840s and '50s—among them the daughter of Mary McCougan.

Areas of the Talbot Settlement became distinctively Scottish, English or American, as newcomers sought to remain with people of their own background. In 1818, some Highland Scots initially accepted poor land in fifty-acre lots in Dunwich and Aldborough. Later, when they heard of other settlers acquiring two hundred acres each, some of them voiced their displeasure—and resented Talbot. They relayed their bitterness from father to son, mother to daughter.

The provincial government began watching more closely and demanding payment of land-grant and survey fees. Talbot wanted to continue collecting those fees and retain control of record-keeping. He would pencil in names on maps and, if he decided he didn't like someone, simply erase their names and tell them to move. The provincial government brought in new regulations, highlighting fee payment. Talbot responded by going to England. From the colonial secretary, he secured support for his way of doing things and incidentally gained control of another 65,000 acres.

Most settlers went along with his system, though in some cases they did not receive land patents for two or three decades. As early as 1828, the Talbot settlement included parts of twenty-nine townships and extended 210 kilometres from east to west. An 1836 accounting indicated that despite long occupation, only 37 percent of 3,008 lots had been reported as settled and only 25 percent as patented. Talbot was collecting money from settlers and neglecting to register their deeds.

Though he wielded considerable power, Talbot rarely got involved in politics. In 1832, he gave a speech denouncing would-be reformers to several hundred people in the town of St. Thomas. Four settlers publicly accused him of abuse of power. And in 1838, when he was sixty-seven, the lieutenant governor asked Talbot to turn the settlement over to the province. In the *Dictionary of Canadian Biography*, we read: "He had clearly acted unjustly in the case of John Nixon, whose land he had forfeited owing to his strong distaste for Nixon's reform politics, and political antipathy may have played a significant part in two of the other cases."

Talbot was closely linked with the Family Compact, the clique that ran the province, and the political pressure he exerted on those he settled is considered one of the causes of the Upper Canada Rebellion of 1837. Even so, titles to more than five million acres in twenty-nine townships passed through the hands of Thomas Talbot.

As to what lay ahead, certainly the aristocratic Talbot would have deplored the fact that his settlement gave rise to the most progressive major economist of the twentieth century. John Kenneth, or Ken, as he preferred to be called, Galbraith was born in 1908 at Iona Station, ten kilometres north of Port Talbot. His great-grandfather, Neil Galbraith, had arrived in Dunwich with his wife in 1819.

The world-famous economist John Kenneth Galbraith (1908–2006) had a paternal ancestor who arrived at the Talbot Settlement in 1819.

Young Ken grew up Scottish Protestant on a fifty-acre family farm where his father raised cattle. In a wry memoir called *The Scotch*, he would later paint a vivid picture of "the uncompromising Calvinism of our upbringing"—a portrait that showed the enduring power of Highland Protestant culture. The local school "was a plain rectangular structure of white brick," Galbraith wrote, "and consisted of one small room together with a very small entry where we hung our coats on hooks and stowed our lunch boxes on a shelf above." Here Galbraith learned to read and write—mostly, he suggests, despite his teachers.

As for the Baptist church he attended, "it contained nothing, literally nothing, but square oaken pews and a plain wooden pulpit. Church doctrine forbade a choir, organ—in fact music of any kind. The singing of Psalms was allowed." Galbraith found the austerity hard to bear and the sermons worse. Yet he would become so clearly a product of his early environment—independent, duty-driven, overachieving—that in retrospect he serves as a poster boy for Scottish Canadian Protestantism, minus the religious faith.

After completing high school in the nearby town of Dutton, Galbraith attended the Ontario Agricultural College (now the University of Guelph). Here he discovered and honed a talent for storytelling, co-founded a campus newspaper and wrote a weekly column for two small-town papers. He won a fellowship to study economics at the University of California, hit his intellectual stride and moved on to Harvard. Ultimately, Galbraith would publish 1,100 articles and four dozen books, which together would sell seven million copies in thirty-odd languages. One of the most popular was his memoir about growing up "in a patch of Ontario that was more Scottish than much of Scotland."

26

The MacNab Debacle

IN THE SPRING OF 1826, WHEN THOMAS TALBOT WAS expanding his fiefdom in the southwest corner of Upper Canada, six hundred kilometres to the northeast, a young family man called on the clan chieftain who had brought him from Scotland to a pioneering settlement roughly eighty kilometres west of Ottawa. Alexander Miller asked permission to leave the "township" for a time to find work so he could feed his wife and small children. To his astonishment and dismay, he received a peremptory, "No, you may not."

Young Miller did not know which way to turn. Surely the chief would relent? For six long weeks, he worked without remuneration on clearing township roads. But then, with his cupboard almost bare and his children crying for food, he left the township without permission. In *The Last Laird of MacNab*, author Alexander Fraser tells us that Miller found paid employment with William and John Thompson in Nepean, just south of Ottawa. He was toiling dutifully when a sheriff turned up, showed him a writ ordered by the chief and hauled him off to jail in Perth, ninety-five kilometres south of his home.

At a time when those running Upper Canada, the Family Compact, had decreed that a person could be arrested for a debt of forty shillings, the chief—Archibald McNab, aka The MacNab— was claiming that Miller owed him eighty pounds. "Poor Miller lay in jail for two days without eating any food," Fraser writes, "and would have starved to death had it not been for the kindness and humanity of Mr. James Young, then the benevolent keeper of the country prison."

Never mind that, according to the contract he had signed in Scotland, young Miller owed the chief no money at all until he had been settled in Upper Canada for seven years. And that he had arrived just two years before. No matter. For six weeks Miller remained in jail before those back home got wind of where he was. Immediately, five men from the settlement journeyed south to Perth along the rough wooded tracks, and there posted bail on behalf of six settlers.

Archibald McNab took the names of these six "black sheep" and saw to it that, when the matter came to trial, each of them was ordered to pay him fifty pounds. For several months, the six avoided being served. Whenever a stranger appeared in the Flat Rapid area of the 1,500-acre settlement, people would blow horns and fire guns in the air as a signal for the men to hide.

Alexander Miller left the settlement and for many years taught school at Beckwith, about sixty-five kilometres southwest. "He was the first martyr to the Laird of MacNab's despotism," Fraser writes, "and he was thus victimized as an example to the rest." Another settler who had stood with Miller, one James McLaurin, was driven out shortly afterwards. And over the next decade, the vindictive McNab would hound and persecute the other "black sheep" who had dared to stand against him, until finally the battle, chieftain versus settlers, would build to a crescendo.

———

IF SOMEONE had set out to discredit Upper Canada's system of encouraging immigration and settlement, they could not have found a greater champion than Archibald McNab. The system involved appointing a wealthy gentleman agent to bring immigrant-farmers across the Atlantic and rewarded him for settling them on a massive land grant in a designated area. Despite missteps, setbacks and abuses, the system worked tolerably well with such figures as Lord Selkirk, Thomas Talbot and John Galt.

But this Archibald McNab was a different animal. Born in Glen Dochart, Scotland, in 1781, McNab knew early that, because his uncle lacked a legitimate heir, he himself would one day become clan leader—The MacNab. Raised by Presbyterians, he rebelled. By 1806, he was running wild in London, where he earned a reputation, according to the *Dictionary of Canadian Biography* (*DCB*), "as a drunkard, braggart, and whore-master."

In 1816, he inherited the Macnab estates. They were mortgaged to the hilt, bringing a debt of £35,000 on an annual rental income of £1,000. Using this trick and that, McNab staved off collapse for several years. Finally, creditors foreclosed on his property. Threatened with debtor's prison, McNab abandoned his wife and children. With the help of friends, he fled first to England and then to Upper Canada, arriving in 1822. That winter, through articles in the *Kingston Chronicle*, he announced that he had found the lost sword of Bonnie Prince Charlie in Glengarry County, and that he hoped to present it to King George IV.

But that same winter, having discovered the Upper Canadian system of encouraging settlement, he forgot all about the sword and went to York (Toronto) with a better idea. Strutting around in his Highland finery, the tall, imposing McNab lobbied for a land grant on the Ottawa River with a view to bringing in settlers from Auld Scotia. Dubious at first, the government was so anxious to encourage settlement that in November 1823, it relented and put McNab in charge of 1,200 acres initially, with another 3,800 to follow if he delivered. In 1824, with the land surveyed, McNab moved into a newly built log house where the Madawaska River flows into the Ottawa. He called it Kennell Lodge.

In 1810, Henry Raeburn painted him as *The MacNab*. He spelled his name Archibald McNab. Bottom line: he was a piece of work.

McNab, as noted above, liked to stride around in a kilt. According to a clerk of works on the Rideau Canal, he "dressed always in *full Highland costume*, the *piper* going before." And historian Henry Scadding, in his 1873 book *Toronto of Old*, described how during visits to York, McNab would lead his kinsfolk in marching "with dignified steps along the whole length of King Street, and down or up to the Kingston Road." Scadding noted that "the Chief always wore a modified highland costume, which well set off his stalwart, upright form: the blue bonnet and feather, and richly embossed dirk, always rendered him conspicuous, as well as the tartan of brilliant hues depending from his shoulder after obliquely swathing his capacious chest; a bright scarlet vest with massive silver buttons, and dress coat always thrown back, added to the picturesqueness of the figure."

In social situations, as Alan Cameron and Julian Gwyn remark in the *DCB*, "few, if any, ever saw his sordid side." But the settlers he lured to the township of McNab? They saw little else. McNab began exploiting them even before they boarded a ship in Scotland. Through an all-too-trusting friend, a Dr. Hamilton, he had them sign an onerous bond setting out the terms under which those who booked free passage would repay him year after year into eternity. How many sailed at his expense? In 1839, McNab would claim that twenty-nine families had done so. Yet of the 142 families by then installed on the estate, only twelve affirmed his assertion.

The first group of settlers, eighty-four men, women and children, sailed from Greenock on the *Niagara*, leaving on April 19, 1825, and reaching Montreal on May 27—not a bad voyage. The chief met them, piper in tow, and slowly revealed that, although they had been promised speedy transport to the settlement, in fact the continuation would be, shall we say, difficult. The newcomers proceeded seventy kilometres west to Pointe Fortune on a series of batteaux, or large barges.

From there, they shuttled their luggage forward, mostly on ox carts. They travelled two hundred kilometres on foot, trekking through unbroken forest—"a pathless wilderness," Alexander Fraser writes, "where the bear and the wolf roamed uncontrolled." They reached their destination near Arnprior in late June, after an overland journey of twenty-eight days.

On arrival, contrary to the terms he had agreed to as a government agent, McNab acted as if he owned the settlement. He had the newcomers—mostly Gaelic speakers, few of them literate—sign a second agreement, this one binding them under a feudal arrangement to pay him, his heirs and successors in perpetuity "one bushel of wheat or Indian corn, or oats of like value, for every cleared acre" on their lots. This seemed little enough, except that the lots were entirely wooded and, even when partly cleared, would initially produce nothing like what the Highlanders were accustomed to seeing back home.

The people held firm in their belief that a clan chief would never set out deliberately to exploit his people. They believed McNab when he claimed that he personally owned the settlement lands. They signed and set to the back-breaking work of felling trees and building rough log cabins in the forest. McNab's agent in Scotland, that well-meaning but naive Dr. Hamilton, had promised that the chief would provide them with sufficient food for one year. But McNab gave them nothing. He said they had misunderstood.

For the next two years, after receiving permission, male settlers would hire themselves out to work miles from home whenever they could, and then carried provisions home on their backs. Alexander Fraser writes: "For days the wives and children of the settlers were kept alive by potatoes alone, with a little salt as a relish, and when a bag of flour was got by one neighbour, it was immediately divided among the whole."

The settler Alexander Miller, formerly a schoolteacher and better educated than most, had run afoul of the chief when he sold the timber on his land to a lumberman named John Brill. Such was his original sin. Vowing to deal with Miller in good time, McNab hurried off to confront Brill, and discovered him to be "an athlete of gigantic proportions." He drew himself up and warned the man to cease buying timber from settlers or he would be held accountable. In Fraser's recreation, Brill says, "And who are you?"

The chief, who was merely administering government land, replied: "I, sir, am McNab of McNab, and this township and all that is in it belongs to me. And you, fellow? Who are you?"

"I am Jack Brill of the Brilliants, sir." He picked up an ox goad, a heavy wooden stick used to prod oxen or cattle. "And if you don't clear out in five minutes, I'll rope's end you to your heart's content."

The chief may not have been clear on what "rope's ending" meant but understood well enough to beat a retreat. And he soon took revenge on Alexander Miller by having him jailed. Not only that, but he had enough influence with certain government figures to force Brill to pay him duty on any timber he cut.

Archibald McNab had transformed himself into a feudal lord. The settlers, his serfs, had undertaken to clear the land. That meant felling trees and turning them into timber. But money from the sale of that timber flowed directly to McNab. Oh, and anyone who challenged the chief, even inadvertently, might find himself in jail in far-away Perth.

That was the message. People didn't have to like it. McNab spent months trying to serve writs on the six "black sheep" who had stood bail for Miller and eventually forced four of them to pay him fifty pounds each. In the settlement, resistance smouldered. The township became divided, as those in opposition, led by Miller's backers, faced off against those who clung to the old ways, and to the clan system, and stood uneasily behind the tyrannical chief.

In Scotland, McNab's last loyal friend, Dr. Hamilton, got wind of what was happening across the sea. In January 1827, when McNab asked him to send out more settlers, Hamilton refused. He washed his hands of the whole business. Having contracted with the government to settle the township, McNab travelled to Montreal, met some newly arrived immigrants, and enticed them to come to "his" township.

Two settlers, Alexander and Daniel Ross, had improved their assigned lot with a view to erecting mills on it. Then they learned that their land had never belonged to McNab, but rather formed part of a Clergy Reserve—a tract of land set aside, in both Upper and Lower Canada, for the support of "Protestant Clergy" by the Constitutional Act of 1791.

Why would the Rosses pay The McNab a duty to build on lands he had never owned? They refused. McNab took to his paperwork. He assigned the two a different lot, asserted personal ownership of the lot they had improved, and evicted the Ross brothers. They moved across the Ottawa River to Bristol in Lower Canada, but sent an anonymous scathing letter to Sir John Colborne, the lieutenant governor of Upper Canada, laying out the truth of what McNab was doing and denouncing the government's inaction.

Because they did not sign this communication, Colborne refused to accept it as credible and instead forwarded it to his friend, the laird of McNab. Surprised by its audacity, the chief resolved to find out who had written it and to punish the miscreant severely. He suspected a man who shared his surname, Alexander McNab, who had emigrated as a teacher and so received two hundred acres instead of fifty. As the best educated man in the township, Fraser writes, he had "shown symptoms of insubordination some time previously."

The MacNab summoned his kinsman to Kennell Lodge on March 13, 1829: "Degraded Clansman, You are accused to me by Sir John Colborne of libel, sedition, and high treason. You will forthwith compear before me . . . and if you show a contrite and repentant spirit, and confess your faults against me, your legitimate Chief, and your crime against His Majesty King George, I will intercede for your pardon. Your offended Chief, McNab."

The young man appeared, astonished and upset at being charged with a crime he had never so much as contemplated.

"Well, my man," the Chief said, "I must send you to jail, and I assure you that your neck is in danger."

Instead of begging for mercy, the spirited young man stoutly denied having committed any crime. The Chief drew up a warrant, swore in two constables, and sent Alexander McNab to Perth, there to be jailed without bail. When, after six weeks, the assizes arrived in Perth, young McNab was quickly acquitted. Those who attended the trial included Alexander Ross, author of the offending letter, ready to confess if the verdict went the other way. The young teacher returned home victorious.

A turning point came in 1834, when a settler named George Buchanan married the sister of John Powell, formerly a member of the legislature. Through Powell, Buchanan learned that McNab owned just a small corner of the township and managed the bulk of it on behalf of the government. When McNab sought to collect his annual subsidy, the Buchanans refused to pay, arguing that the chief had lied to them when he claimed ownership, and so had tricked them into signing the original bond.

McNab invoked the common-law courts, but the Buchanans appealed to a superior court for an investigation. In the autumn of 1835, the arbitrators decided against the chief. McNab appealed still higher. The Buchanans sought a compromise and, after the chief refused, they went into bankruptcy. Still, their initial victory had awakened many of the settlers to the falsity of the chief's position.

Earlier in the year, during a January town meeting that elected local officials—town clerks, assessors, collectors, pathmasters—a deputy-sheriff arrived from Perth with a posse of bailiffs. The MacNab had summoned them to wreak vengeance on two of the men, John and Peter McIntyre, who had stood bail for Alexander Miller nine years before. In an action evocative of the Highland Clearances, the lawmen seized John McIntyre's cattle and started driving them off.

Alexander Fraser writes, "Mrs. McIntyre, with the spirit and courage of her grandfather, who had fought at Culloden, regardless of law or of the consequences, rushed with a wooden pitchfork on the bailiffs and belabored them soundly, till she was disarmed and carried off a prisoner to Kennell." The sheriffs drove off all the cattle belonging to both men.

The MacNab had ordered this public, high-profile action to strike fear into the hearts of the settlers. In the short term, the move succeeded. People feared that what had happened to the McIntyres might happen to them. Fraser dips into the collective thinking: "The Laird was all-powerful. He was supported and assisted by the government. He held the social position of a great gentleman and was undoubtedly a Highland Chieftain. To oppose him was useless, and not to submit and obey was worse than madness."

Despite the freezing cold, Mrs. McIntyre had been bundled off to Kennell, the Laird's mansion, without so much as a cloak. The MacNab released her next day but by then she was so sick that she took to her bed for weeks. The McIntyre cattle were sold and barely covered the family's alleged debts. Miller and Alexander McNab had been driven from the township and the Buchanans into bankruptcy. Now the McIntyres had been ruined. Who would dare to stand against The MacNab?

On and on it went, with Archibald McNab emerging as a caricature of the Highland chief gone bad. But then capital-H

History intervened with the Upper Canada Rebellion of 1837. On December 5, William Lyon Mackenzie led a ragtag army down Yonge Street towards York (present-day Toronto). He was turned back, but suddenly the whole province was taking arms on one side or another. On December 15, The MacNab made a typically grand gesture in a short missive to the new Lieutenant Governor, Sir Francis Bond Head: "The only Highland Chieftain in America," he wrote, "offers himself, his clan, and the McNab Highlanders, to march forward in the defence of the country. We are ready to march at any moment. Command my services at once, and we will not leave the field till we have routed the hell-born rebels."

Head immediately appointed The MacNab colonel in charge of forces from the townships of McNab, Fitzroy and Pakenham. On Christmas Day, McNab mustered the men and made a rousing speech to dozens. But when he asked for volunteers only two men stepped forward. "What?" he cried. "No more? Then I must proceed to ballot and force you."

From the rear, someone shouted, where was his authority for this ballot? The Chief drew himself up and told those assembled that he would soon summon them again for that purpose. Dismissed, the men found their way to a meeting of their own. And then to another. And then to a third. On January 22, 1838, with the help of a gentleman named Allan Stewart—the leading Gaelic scholar in the county, perhaps in the province—more than one hundred heads of families put their name to a petition addressed to Sir Francis Bond Head.

After a preamble, it said, "we the undersigned, one and all of us, consider ourselves true and loyal subjects, and are willing to serve Her Majesty in any part of British North America, where Your Excellency may think proper to call us, under any other commander than McNab." It noted that "a number of us have suffered severely from McNab through the course of the Civil Law and are therefore afraid to come under him in the Martial Law, being harsh in his disposition and also inexperienced."

The petition called on "Your Excellency to look into our circumstances as misled people by McNab, who made us give bonds for Quit-Rents, which we, not knowing what the poor lands in this part of the country could produce, gave without hesitation." The petitioners asked to be set on "the same parallel with other loyal subjects in the province," and freed from those quit-rent agreements that would have them paying McNab in perpetuity.

The Rebellion had fizzled out and its leader, William Lyon Mackenzie, had decamped to the United States. The government responded quickly, assuring the settlers that martial law had not been proclaimed and was not likely to be. Head was recalled early in 1838. McNab resumed his depredations. But Head's replacement, Lord Durham, arrived in May. He did not stay long but wrote a report and returned to England. When the smoke cleared, Sir George Arthur had become the new lieutenant governor of Upper Canada.

In June 1840, the settlers, seeing now that they had a way forward, produced a wider-ranging petition. They declared that "for the last fifteen years your petitioners, as settlers under the Laird of McNab, have been persecuted, harassed with law-suits, threatened with deprivations of their lands, and subjected to threats by the McNab of being driven from their present locations by the government for disobedience to the Chief." They added that "said chief has impoverished many families" and completely ruined some of them. They had resisted and would "continue constitutionally to resist any attempts to impose the feudal system of the Dark Ages upon your petitioners or their descendants."

The petitioners asserted that McNab had "never expended a single shilling of his own money" to improve the township. And they asked that a special commissioner be appointed to investigate, and to carry out the original order in council, which made a free grant of the lands of the township to those settlers who came out at their own expense. Sir George Arthur was sufficiently disturbed that he appointed a special commissioner to investigate the complaints of the settlers.

That commissioner, Francis Allan, was a staunch Conservative and naturally inclined to favour the chief. But he was also diligent and fair-minded. And when after a month he had finished investigating, he produced a report so scathing that it amounted to an indictment. It ran for pages. Allan declared that he had "not found a single instance" where truth contradicted the settlers. The roads were in miserable condition. The settlers had been forced to neglect them while working instead on roads built to benefit Archibald McNab.

McNab had never "laid out one shilling for the repair of roads." Many settlers had been harassed with the law, he wrote, and "many more kept in constant alarm by threats of being sued by the MacNab." Allan cited the case of John Campbell, a blacksmith, who arrived at his own expense and refused to pay rent or grant a mortgage on the lot. "The Laird therefore, upon what authority I know not, seized his tools and kept them for a great number of years."

Through legal chicanery, the chief drove one Duncan McNab off his assigned lot, "thus utterly ruining a poor man with a young family." Independent of "the wanton oppression and outrages of humanity which the settlers allege against him, McNab has conducted the affairs of the township in the worst possible manner for the interests of the settlers or the country." To access a gristmill, many of the settlers had to travel fifteen or sixteen miles (about twenty-five kilometres) over roads that Francis Allan could only deem disgraceful. McNab's system of rent and mortgage, "added to an arbitrary bearing and persecuting spirit, seems to have checked all enterprise and paralyzed the industry of the settlers."

In sum, The MacNab "could not have followed a course more calculated to produce discontent and disaffection amongst a people. The devotion of Scotch Highlanders to the Chief is too well known to permit it to be believed that an alienation such as has taken place between McNab and his people could have happened unless their feelings were most grossly outraged."

This was not a report from which even the wily Archibald McNab could recover. He fought back with equivocations and barefaced lies. But then came a series of articles published in the *Examiner* in what was now Toronto. Together with Allan's report, Alexander Fraser wrote, these articles "struck the Chief's moral standing as the battle axe of a puissant knight would fell his mailed antagonist, crashing through shield and helmet and prostrating the foe."

McNab brought a libel suit to no avail. In August 1842, the government acted on Francis Allan's report. McNab had to give up all remaining lands and his patent for the timber. The settlers' labour and illegal rents were deducted from what McNab would otherwise have been owed.

In the *Dictionary of Canadian Biography*, Allan Cameron and Julian Gwyn conclude that, while The MacNab could be charming and stately in a drawing room, "he proved himself a consummate liar and felon who by various means, at times sophisticated and subtle, robbed both the crown and the poor." His greed "gave the settlers the means to uncover the real nature of his settlement scheme and to break his grip on McNab Township and drive him from his last home there, on the shores of White Lake."

In 1844, The MacNab moved to Hamilton, where he was supported by his relation Sir Allan Napier MacNab. He stayed there until September 1851 and then, having accepted his deserted wife's gift of a modest estate in Orkney, he returned to Scotland and took up with the daughter of a Leeds ironmonger, with whom he had a daughter. They moved to France and ended up in Brittany, where McNab died in 1860.

As for those who remained in the Ottawa Valley, Alexander Fraser wrote that the Highland spirit of their ancestors "animated the settlers in McNab to struggle even against hope, to battle for their rights, and amid poverty, persecution, and imprisonment, win one of the greatest moral victories ever recorded in the historic annals of Canada, or of any other country."

27

John Galt's Legacy

I
N THE SUMMER OF 1827, A LARGE GROUP OF DESTITUTE
Highlanders arrived unannounced in Upper Canada, having
been promised that a consortium of Scottish businessmen run
by author John Galt would provide them with free land. Two years
before, forty families, or roughly two hundred people, had left
Cromarty (north of Inverness) on a ship called the *Planet*, bound
for South America. These Highlanders intended to settle on land
owned by the Colombian Agricultural Society of London. The
company had described its holdings in the Topo Valley, north of
Caracas near La Guaira in Venezuela, as ideal for growing cotton,
coffee and indigo.

On arriving, the settlers found the supposedly green valley to be
a barren wilderness—agriculturally hopeless. Then the society went
bankrupt and washed its hands of them, leaving them to starve in a
world where nobody spoke Gaelic or English.

In *The Scottish Pioneers of Upper Canada, 1784–1855*, Lucille H.
Campey quotes a letter from one of the abandoned, which was
published in the *Glasgow Herald*: "I hope all Scotchmen will take
pity on us. . . . Our number is about 150 souls, without means or

friends to help us in our great distress. I hope all our countrymen will have the feeling of Christians by sending us speedy relief as we are in a country where no kind of employment is to be had."

British officials in South America finally responded, sending the unfortunate settlers first to New York and then onwards to Upper Canada, with promises that there, the Canada Company would settle them on free land. When in 1827, these indigent Highlanders arrived at York, the man in charge of field operations, John Galt, faced a conundrum.

Well known in Britain as an author, an inventive businessman and a friend of Lord Byron, the forty-eight-year-old Galt had created the Canada Company as a business venture. He had gained the backing of Britain's wealthiest financiers by convincing them that the company would make excellent profits by acquiring land in Upper Canada and then selling it to immigrants. What was he to do with these penniless Highlanders?

John Galt was born in Irvine, Ayrshire, in 1779. He was the son of a naval captain and a no-nonsense, down-to-earth mother. At age ten, as a gangly youth of considerable height, he moved with his family to Greenock, that port town west of Glasgow. As a child, when he wasn't gazing out to sea, Galt spent his time reading and listening to the tales and ballads of old women who lived behind his grandmother's house.

His mother scoffed at his bookishness and sought to turn him towards active, practical pursuits. She also bequeathed him what he called his "hereditary predilection for oddities." At sixteen, Galt went to work as a clerk, first in the Greenock custom house, then with a local firm. He also began publishing stories and poems in local newspapers, and with two fellow intellectuals, created a literary society. In 1804, the young men hosted an event with James

Hogg, the celebrated "Ettrick Shepherd" and friend of Walter Scott, who declared their conversation "much above what I had ever been accustomed to hear."

That same year, John Galt moved to London and set up a brokerage with a fellow Scot. He shuttled between business and letters, and in 1807, in the *Philosophical Magazine*, he published an essay, "Statistical Account of Upper Canada." This was informed by an emigrant-friend, the leading Roman Catholic priest Alexander MacDonell, and echoed Lord Selkirk in arguing that emigration to the New World might provide the solution to overcrowding in Europe.

Two years later, one of his commercial ventures suffered a reversal and Galt withdrew from business to study law at Lincoln's Inn. At age thirty, after recovering from an illness, he went travelling around the Mediterranean. With Napoleon's blockades hampering British business, he was seeking a profitable trade route through the Ottoman Empire. During a voyage to Sardinia, he met George Gordon, Lord Byron, later famous as the most flamboyant of romantic poets. For several months, he travelled with Byron. While visiting Athens, he helped Thomas Bruce, the 7th Earl of Elgin, pack the controversial "Elgin marbles" and ship them to England.

Galt returned to London in 1811 and married Elizabeth Tilloch, the only child of Alexander Tilloch, publisher of the *Philosophical Magazine*. While involving himself sporadically in business ventures, he applied himself to writing as a profession. From 1812 onwards, he produced plays, travel memoirs, novels, textbooks and biographies at an impressive rate. In 1820, he scored a hit with a book called *The Ayrshire Legatees*, and he followed that with his acclaimed *Annals of the Parish*, which treats the social and industrial changes engulfing Ayrshire.

He got seriously involved in Scottish emigration to Canada early in the 1820s, when he agreed to act for Upper Canadian Loyalists seeking redress for damages suffered during the War of 1812. Galt had gained a reputation as a lobbyist during a debate over the building of a canal, but now parliamentarians turned a deaf ear to his arguments for paying these reparations.

During this period, while communicating with MacDonell, Galt conceived the idea of using the colony's own resources to acquire funds to pay the Loyalists. Why not sell off the lands reserved for the crown and the clergy by the Constitutional Act of 1791, and use the revenues to reimburse his clients? When this idea went nowhere, Galt tried a variation. In 1824, he organized leading London merchants and bankers into a one-million joint-stock consortium, the Canada Company, designed to buy those reserved lands and sell them to immigrants at a profit.

In spring 1825, Galt visited Upper Canada to launch the endeavour. Inevitably, he came up against the recalcitrant ruling oligarchy, the Family Compact, which was dominated by the Reverend John Strachan, another Scottish immigrant, and Attorney General John Beverley Robinson. In 1826, to get around their resistance, Galt led the Canada Company in purchasing not the reserved lands but more than one million acres of wilderness (the so-called Huron Tract) to the west of York (Toronto), and another million acres of Crown lands scattered around the colony.

That year, too, charged with running the Company's field operations, Galt moved with his family to Upper Canada and established an office at York. In March 1827, he sent his right-hand man—fellow Scot William "Tiger" Dunlop, officially the "Warden of the Forests"—into the Huron Tract to locate a site for a township he would call Guelph. This was a nod to King

George IV, a Hanoverian descended from a branch of the House of Welf, or Gwelf.

Dunlop chose and marked a giant maple tree. On April 23, John Galt travelled west from York with Dunlop and three other men: George Pryer, his lead surveyor, and two woodsmen. A storm came on and the five got lost in the forest. Eventually, they found the correct path. After a cold, wet march of about thirty kilometres, they located the giant maple that marked the centre of the proposed town.

This bronze bust of John Galt is situated a short walk from the spot where Galt felled a giant maple tree to found Guelph. Sculptor: John Miecznikowski, 1979.

Galt struck the first blow with an axe. Dunlop and Pryor each took a turn, and then the two local men finished felling the tree. "To me at least," Galt wrote later, "the moment was impressive—the [echoing] silence of the woods . . . was as the sigh of the solemn genius of the wilderness departing forever." Dunlop produced a flask of whisky "and we drank prosperity to the City of Guelph."

Meanwhile, some distance to the southwest, Thomas Talbot was installing settlers across 65,000 acres of land—a sizable area, but one representing a small fraction of the territory now controlled by the Canada Company. And in the eastern reaches of Upper Canada, starting in the 1780s, Cornwall and Perth had attracted hundreds of Scottish settlers, many of them Loyalist ex-soldiers. Those two centres had emerged organically as part of an evolving network of rivers and roads.

But now, in the forested heart of the colony, the town of Guelph came into being thanks largely to the vision and industry of one man. Inspired by the thriving settlements he had seen in upstate New York, John Galt sought to develop Guelph as a magnet for colonists. He also ventured still farther west to Lake Huron, on whose shores he established Goderich—a marvel of town planning.

In 1825, Upper Canada had a population of 158,000. Over the next four years, Galt and his allies attracted more than 50,000 settlers to the colony, most of them Highlanders fleeing the Clearances, and willing and able to subsist in the harsh conditions they confronted. By autumn 1828, Galt had built a twelve-foot-wide road from Guelph to Goderich. Such initiatives, reminiscent of Lord Selkirk, established conditions that enabled immigrants to flourish. The population of Upper Canada would reach 397,000 in 1837, when political upheaval put an end to the dramatic increase.

Yet all was not right with the world—not for John Galt. He was on a collision course with Reverend Strachan and his Family Compact allies. Galt had shown too much religious tolerance and far too much sympathy for the local First Nations, whose land claims he had represented in London in 1825. Worse, he had insulted the self-important lieutenant governor, Sir Peregrine Maitland, by hosting an extravagant ball and failing to invite Lady Maitland to be his official hostess.

All this he might have survived. But John Galt went too far when he responded with decency and generosity to that large party of destitute Highlanders, refugees in contemporary parlance, who turned up after their rude awakening in La Guaira, Venezuela. Galt declined to give them free land but he did allow them to settle on lots without requiring a down payment. He then assisted them in building houses in the "Scotch Block" on Elora Road, six kilometres north of Guelph.

Galt reasoned that these immigrants should obviously be designated wards of the state and so covered the costs of settling them by withholding £1,000 of the £10,000 that the Canada Company owed the government of Upper Canada. As a way of encouraging settlement, the decision worked wonderfully. The next year, emigrants from Paisley, near Glasgow, founded the Paisley Block ten kilometres northeast of Guelph. By 1830, the township had more than two hundred houses.

John Galt had launched a process that would change the demographic future of Ontario. From the early 1830s onwards, Gaelic-speaking Highlanders from Perth and Inverness flowed into Puslinch Township, just south of Guelph. More settlers arrived from Roxburghshire in the Scottish Borders. By 1846, that Block was six kilometres long and, according to *Smith's Canadian Gazetteer*, boasted "good farms which are generally well cultivated." In 1850, emigrants from South Uist arrived. They had sailed to Hamilton and then, to the sound of bagpipes, walked thirty kilometres north to Puslinch.

The proud Highlanders who had arrived from La Guaira would eventually repay every penny they borrowed. No matter. To their everlasting shame, Maitland and his government cronies declined to designate the destitute refugees as wards of the state. They refused to honour British government promises made in New York or to accept any responsibility whatsoever. Instead, they started a whispering campaign against John Galt, accusing him of mishandling funds.

In far-distant London, Canada Company investors began to worry about their money. They decided to send an emissary— ostensibly an accountant, really a spy to investigate and report back. Predictably, given that Galt was far more a visionary than a bookkeeper, this ambitious bean counter, Thomas Smith, turned up enough irregularities to justify his appointment. With purloined Canada Company documents, he decamped to England.

John Galt realized that he needed to return as well, to reassure the investors. But on reaching New York early in 1829, he learned that he had been recalled. By the time Galt reached London on May 20, newspapers had already reported this downturn. Several of his personal creditors called their loans. And in July 1829, unable to quickly turn his Upper Canadian holdings into cash, John Galt was forced to declare bankruptcy and take refuge in King's Bench Prison.

This institution, located in the London borough of Southwark, was the least onerous of debtors' prisons. Located behind a fifty-foot brick wall, it had two hundred rooms and a large courtyard with a market. In *John Galt: The Life of a Writer*, Ian A. Gordon notes that "inmates were free to roam those surrounding streets which fell within the traditional 'rules' or 'liberties.'" Galt, mortified by his situation, sent and received letters and even book advances through Herbert's Coffee House, which was within the area of confinement. According to a fellow prisoner, he spent most of his time writing "in dour silence and with imperturbable stoicism."

Galt remained confined at King's Bench for five months, earning money by writing. Before he paid his debts and emerged, Galt wrote all or most of his *Life of Lord Byron* and two notable novels that drew on his Canadian experience: *Lawrie Todd* and *Bogle Corbet*. The latter work, published in 1831, follows an immigrant from the Outer Hebrides to Upper Canada and is still read as a portrait of pioneer life. The novel has a political edge and champions "reciprocal civility" and a cooperative attitude to settlement, as opposed to the rampantly individualistic approach Galt saw developing south of the border. Canadian academic Elizabeth Waterston called *Bogle Corbet* the "first major work to define Canadianism by reference to an American alternative."

By 1832, almost incredibly, Galt had regained business credibility. He took to leading a second colonial venture, the British American Land Company, through which he proposed to develop the Eastern Townships outside Montreal. Galt was contemplating a permanent move to Canada when ill health forced him to resign.

His sons did emigrate. All three became highly successful, and one of them, Alexander Tilloch Galt, who began his career as a fifteen-year-old clerk with the British American Land Company, eventually became a father of Confederation. In 1834, John Galt and his wife moved from London to Greenock, where he had spent most of his youth, and five years later he died in that port town. Galt's greatest legacy may well be the way he encouraged Scottish emigration.

In 1812, most people living in Upper Canada had arrived from the American colonies. These included 35,000 early Loyalists and 25,000 later settlers. Only 20,000 had come directly from the British Isles. Between 1826 and 1830, assisted by William "Tiger" Dunlop, John Galt's initiatives played a huge role in attracting more than 50,000 settlers to Upper Canada—most of them from Scotland.

In the decades after Galt's initiative, farmers began to experience a shortage of cleared farmland in the southern areas of Upper Canada and began edging north into Muskoka, Haliburton and Renfrew. For those who did not wish to move, a system of tenancy developed, as several rich land-holders gained control of large areas. Between 1855 and 1866, tenant farmers increased in number by ninety percent.

Often these tenants dreamed of owning their own farms and so spent as little as possible on maintenance, equipment and improvements. They used oxen instead of more expensive horses and did most work by hand rather than machinery. Farm wives struggled to cook over an open hearth, much as their forebears had done in Scotland. Visitors to Upper Canada Village, halfway between Kingston and Montreal, can see how the pioneers lived and make their own comparisons.

Today, the province of Ontario has a population of just over twelve million. Thanks partly to the wizardry of John Galt, more than two million of those claim Scottish ancestry.

28

Three William Frasers

S TAYING WITH ONTARIO AND THE TWENTY-FIRST CEN-
tury, if you stand out front of the Royal Ontario Museum in
downtown Toronto and look east across Queen's Park boule-
vard, you will see an elegant, three-storey building that, like so much
else in Canada, owes its existence to the Highland Clearances. In
this case, the architect who designed the classical building, William
Fraser, was descended from an eighteenth-century weaver, also
named William Fraser, who was evicted with his family from his
ancestral home northwest of Inverness—not to make way for sheep,
but for cattle.

These stories are invariably convoluted. That particular clearance launched a slow-motion exodus to Canada, not atypical,
that would extend across generations and through three William
Frasers. The first was born in 1787 in Tarradale, a crofting area
twenty kilometres west of Inverness near Beauly. Like his father,
who had served in one of the Highland regiments that arose after
the Battle of Culloden, William trained and worked as a weaver.
When his first wife died in childbirth, he married again, one Mary
Bisset.

Around 1820, when the Frasers were cleared, the crofting township of Tarradale would have looked a lot like the Gearrannan Blackhouse Village on the Isle of Lewis.

By 1820, the demand for beef was skyrocketing, thanks to demand from the army, the navy and the lowlands. Two new bridges over nearby rivers encouraged the development of a huge tryst, or cattle market, at Tarradale. Drovers were driving huge herds of cattle through this location from farther north and east, one thousand or more at a time. They needed pens and corrals.

William's landlord saw a chance to increase the profitability of his estate. He ordered his tenants to clear out. Having grown up through the increasingly violent Sutherland Clearances, William knew what resistance could bring. He did not resist. Forced out of his home, he moved with his wife and six children (three from his first marriage) into Inverness, hoping to find work weaving sails. The family crowded into Merkinch, a rough district by the docks where at least everybody spoke Gaelic.

Three of their sons went to sea and were never heard from again. But in 1824, while struggling to get by, William and Mary had another son and named him—wait for it—William. When the boy was five, William the father caught a fever and died, leaving his family fatherless and destitute. The boy, remembering in tranquillity, wrote: "My father died when I was very young. My recollection of this is that he was a godly man, and I recollect the last words he ever spoke to me were, "Poor Willie, what will become of you."

Against all odds, Mary Bisset Fraser kept the family going. She looked to the Scottish kirk, which ran sessional schools to educate the poor. Her son, the second William, excelled at school. He was nineteen when in 1843, during the Great Disruption, 450 evangelical ministers broke away from the established church to create the Free Church of Scotland, mainly in support of the right of parishioners to choose their own ministers.

Two years later, when the breakaway clergymen established the Free Church Training College in Glasgow, the second William, now twenty-one, became one of the first students to enrol for teacher training. He worked his way through college doing manual labour. After graduation, he taught for a few years, excelling, before he took ministerial training at the newly created Free Church Normal Seminary. In 1861, at age thirty-seven, William Fraser was ordained a Free Church minister. As such, he was able to provide a pension to his mother, Mary Bisset, and he did so until she died in 1872.

Meanwhile, in 1864, at Greenock just west of Glasgow, this second William Fraser had married Violet Ferguson, the daughter of a ship's chandler, or dealer in provisions. Together, they had seven sons and two daughters, all born in Lochgilphead, Argyll.

William the minister had learned the paramount value of education and communicated this to his children. One of his sons, Rev. Dr. Donald Fraser, became a leading Free Church missionary in Malawi, Africa. Another son, Ebenezer (Ebie) Fraser, studied engineering with Lord Kelvin at University of Glasgow. He worked with the Caledonia Railway and the Great India Peninsula Railway and, during the First World War, commanded a group of army engineers in building a 540-kilometre railway in Iraq from Basra to Baghdad.

But the minister's son who concerns us is the third William Fraser, this one born in 1867—the year of Canadian Confederation. He trained as an architect at University of Glasgow and University of London, then worked with a Glasgow firm until 1896, when he won a competition and designed the Burns National Memorial in Mauchline. In 1898, this third William Fraser married Maud Marion Timpson, whose father was a master mariner who sailed first for the textile-famous Clarks of Paisley, then for the Vanderbilt family of New York. William and Maud Marion Fraser settled in Dunoon and had three children.

In 1907, during an economic downturn, and like many a Highlander before and after, this third William Fraser seized an opportunity to come to Canada. He joined a firm of Canadian architects (G.M. Miller) and moved to Toronto. After designing several schools and office buildings, Fraser found himself working with Lillian Massey Treble (1854–1915), the sister of Vincent Massey, who in 1950 would become Canada's first Canadian-born governor general. She wished to create a building for female students at the University of Toronto. In 1912, the third William completed the Household Science Building—the edifice you can see opposite the Royal Ontario Museum.

Sheena Fraser McGoogan at the Clan Fraser Memorial on the Culloden Battlefield.

Five years later, when during the First World War an infamous explosion decimated Halifax, William Fraser was one of the architects sent by the Canadian government to rebuild the city. After a couple of years designing buildings in the Hydrostone area, he fell ill with cancer, returned to Toronto, and surrounded by wife and children, passed away. In June 1922, an effusive obituary in the *Globe and Mail* mentioned the Burns Memorial at Mauchline and the School of Household Sciences in Toronto as memorials to his outstanding skill and workmanship.

After the death of the third William Fraser, his widow moved to Montreal to be near family. One of her (their) grandchildren married the present author and became Sheena Fraser McGoogan. She is the one who got me interested in Scotland and, more specifically, the flight of the Highlanders.

Epilogue

WHILE RESEARCHING THIS BOOK, I HAVE COME across counter-narratives and polemics concerning what happened at Red River Settlement and Seven Oaks. Anyone who goes online will probably encounter these fanciful scenarios, often angry, that have no basis in fact. To those who remain uncertain or who crave relentless documentation, I recommend *The Seven Oaks Reader* by Myrna Kostash, who lays out the evidence and invites readers to draw their own conclusions. In my view, the Highlander refugees—brave, much-maligned figures, both there and elsewhere in the country—were the making of Canada.

On another front, some Scottish historians will no doubt complain that in this book I ignore the Lowland Clearances. For them I recall the words of I.F. Grant, creator of the Highland Folk Museum at Newtonmore. In her book *Highland Folk Ways*, she writes: "Contemporary Scots history was written by Lowlanders who say as little as they can about the Gaelic Lordship." To that, I would add: "And who prefer to minimize and downplay the Highland Clearances."

In closing, I will invoke a Clearance-related moment from my recent rambles around the Highlands and Islands with Sheena Fraser McGoogan. One afternoon we made our way onto a beach in the Outer Hebrides on the tiny island of Eriskay, which is linked to South Uist by a two-lane causeway and to the Isle of Barra by ferry. Known as the Prince's Shore, this beach is where, on July 23, 1745, that hubristic twit Bonnie Prince Charlie first set foot on Scottish soil. Driven by an astonishing sense of entitlement, the prince had sailed from France, where he had been born and raised, to claim the kingship of Scotland, which he believed to be rightfully his.

When Bonnie Prince Charlie arrived in Scotland in 1745, he came ashore on this beach on the tiny island of Eriskay. Local students built a cairn to mark the spot.

After landing on this beach and dismissing the advice of more than one Scottish chieftain—"Go back to France, you daft bastard!"—the prince set about enlisting troops. He raised just enough of them to launch an ill-conceived assault on Scotland's far more powerful neighbour to the south. That Big Mistake led to the catastrophic Battle of Culloden, complete with atrocities, and so to the Highland Clearances—in short, to more than a century of hardship and suffering. Doubtless the Industrial Revolution would have arrived here eventually. But the process of change, the transformation, would have been so much more cooperative, so much less brutal, violent and racist.

If I were a Time Lord, I would confront the Bonnie Prince as he set foot on this beach. Back to France I would send him, dead or alive. No Big Mistake, no Culloden, no Clearances. A different narrative. In the real world, the students of Eriskay School built a cairn here in 1995, overlooking the location of the prince's arrival. We hiked along the beach to that spot, Sheena and I, and stood looking out, imagining what might have been. That was where I felt it in my bones, standing by that cairn: stop one man at the right moment and you change history.

To end this book, I went looking for a quotation from James Boswell and found nothing that worked. I thought of John Banville writing in *The Sea* that "the past beats inside me like a second heart." Why didn't Boswell say that? Then I remembered an old favourite nugget from F. Scott Fitzgerald, who had no connection whatsoever with clearances or refugees. But he did anticipate Banville in a way that strikes me as apposite. At the end of *The Great Gatsby*, Fitzgerald suggests that no matter how we fight and flail, we can never escape history. "So we beat on," he writes, "boats against the current, borne back ceaselessly into the past."

ACKNOWLEDGEMENTS

—

MY RIGHTLY CELEBRATED EDITOR PATRICK CREAN DESERVES pride of place in these acknowledgements. His observations and suggestions, even those I initially found dubious, enabled me to develop this book to its full potential. What more can a writer ask? Answer: the outstanding professionals at HarperCollins Canada, who have contributed hugely to creating and supporting eight of my previous books. Led by Iris Tupholme and Leo MacDonald, the team includes Alan Jones, Michael Guy-Haddock, Cory Beatty, Noelle Zitzer, Stephanie Conklin, Angelika Glover, Allegra Robinson, Stephanie Fysh, Mike Millar and those who, like Mike Mason and Terry Toews, work on the front lines. All of you are much appreciated. And I will always owe Beverley Slopen, my literary agent and savviest friend, for steering me to HCC and for continuing guidance and counsel.

I am heavily indebted to the folks at Adventure Canada who have taken me and Sheena voyaging in the Arctic and circumnavigating Ireland and Scotland. I thank the Swan family—Matthew, Cedar, Matthew James, Alanna, Jason, Devon, Brian—and our fellow voyagers, many of whom have become friends and have taught me so much. I started naming names and realized when I hit thirty that I was being ridiculous. You know who you are!

Special thanks to Stephen Patrick Clare and *Celtic Life International* for publishing my articles about travelling in Scotland. Terrific layouts! And to John Geiger and the Royal Canadian Geographical Society for sending me on a whirlwind speaking tour: Dumfries, Galashiels, Ayr, Helensburgh, Perth, whew! Thanks to the Royal Scottish Geographical Society for extending such a warm welcome. In Orkney, we owe our friends Tom and Rhonda Muir big time and Andrew Appleby and the John Rae Society for bringing me to speak at their annual festival . . . and for providing excellent shelter.

I owe a shout-out to my colleagues in the MFA Program in Creative Nonfiction at University of King's College in Halifax for their ongoing support and for keeping me engaged and inspired. I thank the National Library of Scotland in Edinburgh for admitting me on short notice and for not expelling me when, having laid hands on a rare pamphlet, I took out my cell phone and went click, click, click for a good half hour. Also, I want to say hey to the Toronto Public Library and especially to the Beaches Branch, where folks never question my daily comings and goings in the name of research.

Above all, I wish to thank my life partner and fellow traveller, Sheena Fraser McGoogan, for keeping us both on the road and for so much else. Without Sheena and the family we share— Carlin, Keriann, Sylwia, Travis, James, Veronica—this book would not exist. Finally, I want to say thank you to my mother, Phyllis McGoogan, that brave Nova Scotia girl who joined the war effort, met and married a dashing Montrealer, and brought me into the world. Party on!

SELECTED SOURCES

—

Several works proved useful in more than one part of this book. I have listed them at the first significant use. More than once, in search of a fact or a confirmation, I consulted the admirable *Dictionary of Canadian Biography*.

PART ONE: THE GAELIC WORLD

Chambers, Robert and Robert Forbes. *Jacobite Memoirs of the Rebellion of 1745*. San Bernadino, California: Ulan Press, 2012 reprint of a work compiled in 1834.

Grant, I.F. *Highland Folk Ways*. London: Routledge & Kegan Paul, 1961.

Keegan, John. *The Face of Battle: A Study of Agincourt, Waterloo and the Somme*. London: Bodley Head, 2014.

Marsden, John. *Somerled and the Emergence of Gaelic Scotland*. East Linton: Tuckwell, 2000.

McDonald, R. Andrew. *The Kingdom of the Isles: Scotland's Western Seaboard c. 1100–c. 1336*. Edinburgh: Tuckwell, 1997.

Moffat, Alistair. *The Sea Kingdoms: The History of Celtic Britain & Ireland*. Edinburgh: Berlinn, 2001.

Prebble, John. *Culloden*. Harmondsworth, Middlesex: Martin, Secker & Warburg, 1961.

Riding, Jacqueline. *Jacobites: A New History of the '45 Rebellion*. London: Bloomsbury, 2016.

Sage, Donald. *Memorabilia Domestica; or Parish Life in the North of Scotland*. Edinburgh: Albyn Press, 1975.

Sinclair, Colin. *Thatched Houses: A Contribution to the Social History of the Old Highlands*. Edinburgh: Oliver & Boyd, 1953.

Thompson, Francis. *Crofting Years*. Glasgow: Bell & Bain, 1984.

Tranter, Nigel. *Lord of the Isles*. London: Hodder & Stoughton, 1983.

PART TWO: OMENS OF RESISTANCE

Devine, T.M. *Clanship to Crofters' War: The Social Transformation of the Scottish Highlands*. Manchester: Manchester University Press, 1994.

———. *To the Ends of the Earth: Scotland's Global Diaspora*. London: Allan Lane, 2011.

Loch, James. *An Account of the Improvements on the Estates of the Marquess of Stafford in the Counties of Stafford and Salop, and on the Estate of Sutherland: with remarks*. Appendix, p. 133. London: Longman, Hurst, Rees, Orme, and Brown, 1820.

MacKinnon, Charles. *Scottish Highlanders*. New York: Barnes & Noble, 1995.

Macleod, Donald. *Gloomy Memories: The Highland Clearances of Strathnaver*. Bettyhill: Strathnaver Museum, 1996.

MacLeod, Norman. *Reminiscences of a Highland Parish*. London: S.W. Partridge, 1877.

Richards, Eric. *The Highland Clearances: People, Landlords and Rural Turmoil*. Edinburgh: Berlinn, 2013.

———. *The Highland Estate Factor in the Age of the Clearances*. Isle of Lewis: Islands Book Trust, 2016.

Richardson, Dorothy. *The Curse on Patrick Sellar: An Incident in Sutherland in 1814*. Stockbridge: Longstock, 1999.

Transactions of the Gaelic Society of Inverness, Vol. 16: 1989–90.
Inverness: Wentworth Press, 2009.

PART THREE: ATLANTIC ARRIVALS

Bumsted, J.M. *Lord Selkirk: A Life.* Winnipeg: University of
Manitoba, 2008.

Campey, Lucille H. *After the Hector: The Scottish Pioneers of Nova
Scotia and Cape Breton, 1773–1852.* Toronto: Natural Heritage
Books, 2004.

———. *The Silver Chief: Lord Selkirk and the Scottish Pioneers of
Belfast, Baldoon and Red River.* Toronto: Natural Heritage
Books, 2003.

———. *With Axe and Bible: The Scottish Pioneers of New
Brunswick, 1784–1874.* Toronto: Natural Heritage Books,
2007.

Harper, Marjory. *Adventurers & Exiles: The Great Scottish Exodus.*
London: Profile Books, 2003.

Hunter, James. *A Dance Called America: The Scottish Highlands, the
United States and Canada.* Edinburgh: Mainstream, 1994.

MacKay, Donald. *Scotland Farewell: The People of the Hector.*
Toronto: McGraw-Hill Ryerson, 1980.

Melnyk, George. "Six Waves of Refugees." *Alberta Views,*
September 2016.

Patterson, Rev. George. *A History of the Country of Pictou.*
Montreal, 1877, reprinted Belleville, Ont.: Mika Studio, 1972.

Raphael, Ray. *A People's History of the American Revolution: How
Common People Shaped the Fight for Independence.* New York:
New Press, 2001.

Selkirk, Thomas Douglas. *Lord Selkirk's Diary, 1803–1804.*
Introduction by Patrick C.T. White. Toronto: Champlain
Society, 1958.

Selkirk, Thomas Douglas. *Observations on the Present State of the Highlands of Scotland, with a View of Emigration.* Toronto: Clarke Irwin, 1969.

PART FOUR: BARBAROUS CLEARANCES

Craig, David. *On the Crofters' Trail: In Search of the Clearance Highlanders.* London: Jonathan Cape, 1990.

Devine, T.M. *Clanship to Crofters' War: The Social Transformation of the Scottish Highlands.* Manchester: Manchester University Press, 1994.

———. *The Scottish Clearances: A History of the Dispossessed.* London: Penguin/Allen Lane, 2018.

Hunter, James. *Last of the Free: A History of the Highlands and Islands of Scotland.* Edinburgh: Mainstream, 1999.

———. *Set Adrift Upon the World: The Sutherland Clearances.* Edinburgh: Berlinn, 2015.

Immigration Report of 1851: *From the British Parliamentary Papers, 1852 XXXIII (1474).*

Mackenzie, Alexander. *The History of the Highland Clearances.* Inverness: A&W Mackenzie, 1883.

———. *Stories of the Highland Clearances: The Brutal Betrayal of the Scots.* Newtongrange: LangSyne, 2012.

MacLennan, Ian. *Rape of the Glens. The Spectator,* 18 October 1963, page 26.

Prebble, John. *The Highland Clearances.* London: Penguin, 1963.

Rixson, Denis. *Knoydart: A History.* Edinburgh: Berlinn, 1999 and 2011.

Ross, Donald. *Glengarry Evictions or Scenes at Knoydart in Inverness-shire; Pictures of Pauperism: The Condition of the Poor Described by Themselves in Fifty Genuine Letters; Real Scottish*

Grievances; *The Russians of Rosshire, or Massacre of the Rosses in Strathcarron*. Glasgow: G. Gallie, 1854.

Stewart, James A. Jr. "The Jaws of Sheep," *Proceedings of the Harvard Celtic Colloquium*, Volume XVIII, 1998.

www.isleofbarra.com/desertedvillage.com.

PART FIVE: WESTERN TRAVAILS

Calloway, Colin G. *White People, Indians, and Highlanders: Tribal Peoples and Colonial Encounters in Scotland and America*. Oxford: OUP, 2008.

Campbell, Marjorie Wilkins. *The North West Company*. Toronto: Macmillan, 1957.

Douglas, Hugh. *Flora MacDonald: The Most Loyal Rebel*. Gloucestershire: Sutton Publishing, 1993–99.

Gray, John Morgan. *Lord Selkirk of Red River*. Toronto: Macmillan, 1963.

Gunn, Donald. *History of Manitoba: From the Earliest Settlement to 1835*. Ottawa: Maclean, Roger, 1880.

Healy, W.J. *Women of Red River*. Winnipeg: Women's Canadian Club, 1923.

Henderson, Anne M. "The Lord Selkirk Settlement at Red River," *Manitoba Pageant*, Volume 13, Autumn 1967.

Hume, Stephen. *Simon Fraser: In Search of Modern British Columbia*. Madeira Park, BC: Harbour Publishing, 2008.

Kostash, Myrna. *The Seven Oaks Reader*. Edmonton: NeWest Press, 2016.

La Rocque, Barbara Wall. *Wolfe Island: A Legacy in Stone*. Toronto: Natural Heritage Books, Dundurn, 2009.

McLean, Marianne. *The People of Glengarry: Highlanders in Transition, 1745–1820*. Montreal: McGill-Queens, 1991.

PART SIX: UPPER CANADIAN PIONEERS

Campey, Lucille H. *An Unstoppable Force: The Scottish Exodus to Canada*. Toronto: Natural Heritage Books, 2008.

———. *The Scottish Pioneers of Upper Canada, 1784–1855: Glengarry and Beyond*. Toronto: Natural Heritage Books, 2005.

Campsie, Alison. "Six Abandoned Communities of Scotland." *The Scotsman*, July 26, 2017.

Coyne, James M. *The Talbot Papers*. Ottawa, Royal Society of Canada, 1908.

Fraser, Alexander. *The Last Laird of MacNab: An Episode in the Settlement of MacNab Township, Upper Canada*. Renfrew, Ontario: Renfrew University Women's Club, 1899–1974.

Galt, John. *Bogle Corbet: Or, the Emigrants*. Toronto: McClelland & Stewart, 1977. Originally London: Colburn and Bentley, 1831.

Gordon, Ian A. *John Galt: The Life of a Writer*. Toronto: University of Toronto Press, 1972.

Hamil, Fred Coyne. *Lake Erie Baron: The Story of Colonel Thomas Talbot*. Toronto: Macmillan, 1955.

McGugan, Colin A. *The Early History of Dunwich Township, 1790–1903*. Dutton, On.: West Elgin Genealogical and Historical Society, 2004.

Timothy, H.B. *The Galts: A Canadian Odyssey, John Galt 1779–1839*. Toronto: M&S, 1977.

ILLUSTRATION CREDITS

———

Original maps by Dawn Huck: pages 2, 112, 230, 274.

Photos by the author: pages 37, 139, 181, 189, 314.

Photos by Sheena Fraser McGoogan: pages 8, 11, 18, 19 (2), 21, 24, 27, 64 (2), 65, 90, 93, 95, 106, 114, 120, 127, 128, 142, 157, 162, 171, 176, 187, 193, 249, 271 (2), 311, and 316.

The MacNab by Henry Raeburn, 1810, is from the National Portrait Gallery (NPGD38119): page 288.

All other images come courtesy of Wikimedia Commons, which makes available material in the public domain. Additional details are as follows:

Page 45: *An Incident in the Rebellion of 1745* by David Morier, 1746. Royal Collection Trust.

Page 46: *The Highland Chace or the Pursuit of the Rebels*, 1746. National Library of Scotland (75241604).

Page 50: *Highland Soldiers* by Francis Grose, 1801. *Military Antiquities Respecting a History of the English Army, Vol.* 1, page 166.

Page 55: *Highland Brigade Camp Looking South* by Francis Grose, 1801. Library of Congress (2002695359).

Page 69: *John Lockhart-Ross (1721–1790)* by James Stanier Clarke, 1801. *Naval Chronicle.*

Page 74: *James Boswell*, engraving by Samuel Freeman, 1856. *A Biographical Dictionary of Eminent Scotsmen, Vol.* 1.

Page 77: *Colonel Alastair Ranaldson Macdonell of Glengarry* by Sir Henry Raeburn, 1812. Scottish National Gallery (NG420).

Page 91: *Elizabeth, Duchess-Countess of Sutherland* by George Romney, 1782. Cincinnati Art Museum.

Page 98: *Harriet Beecher Stowe, circa 1870s–80s*. The National Archives and Records Administration (535784).

Page 132: *A First Settlement*, engraving by William Henry Bartlett, 1840. Library and Archives Canada (C-002401).

Page 145: *John Paul Jones seizing the silver plate of Lady Selkirk* by Henry Davenport Northrop, 1901. Library of Congress.

Page 150: *Mrs Flora MacDonald*. National Library of Scotland (Blaikie SNPG).

Page 174: *Cluny Castle* by Cosmolinzeegordon, 2014.

Page 208: *From Skye to Knoydart* by grumpylumixuser, 2008.

Page 216: *Skibo Castle* by Graeme Smith on Geograph, 2013.

Page 235: *Tory Refugees on the Way to Canada* by Howard Pyle. Appeared in *Harper's Monthly* in December 1901.

Page 237: *Simon Fraser Descending the Fraser River, 1808* by Charles W. Jeffreys, 1927.

Page 242: *Lord Selkirk's Centennial, 1912*. Ransom Engraving Co., Ontario Council of University Libraries.

Page 246: *Arrival of the Selkirk Settlers, 1812*. Red River North Heritage.

Pages 257 and 267: *Visit to an Encampment of Indians* and *The Protestant Church, and Mission School, at the Red River Colony* from *The Substance of a Journal During a Residence at the Red River Colony, British North America: And Frequent Excursions Among the North-West American Indians in the Years* 1820, 1821, 1822, 1823 by John West, 1827.

Page 276: *Thomas Talbot*, 1881. From *The Last Forty Years: Canada Since the Union of* 1841, *Volume* 2 by John Charles Dent. British Library (HMNTS 9555.f.7).

Page 283: *John Kenneth Galbraith*, guest speaker in Amsterdam at Top Management Forum, by Hans van Dijk, February 22, 1982. Dutch National Archives (931 9937).

Page 304: *John Galt Bust* by John Miecznikowski, 1979, outside Ontario City Hall in Guelph by Alethe, 2008.

INDEX

NOTE: Locations of maps and illustrations are given in italics.